T0345340

"From *The Ring* to *The Host* and beyond, Asian horror has become a regional brand with global reach. Yet, this culturally and commercially significant phenomenon has been conspicuously neglected — until now. *Horror to the Extreme* is the book we've all been waiting for. Focusing heavily on Japanese and Korean films, but extending to Hong Kong and Southeast Asia, it follows the contours of the hit genre and examines it from a variety of angles, making this an ideal book for newcomers and connoisseurs alike."

— Chris Berry, Goldsmiths, University of London

Horror to the Extreme
Changing Boundaries in Asian Cinema

This book compares production and consumption of Asian horror cinemas in different national contexts and their multidirectional dialogues with Hollywood and neighboring Asian cultures. Individual essays highlight common themes including technology, digital media, adolescent audience sensibilities, transnational co-productions, pan-Asian marketing techniques, and variations on good vs. evil evident in many Asian horror films. Contributors include Kevin Heffernan, Adam Knee, Chi-Yun Shin, Chika Kinoshita, Robert Cagle, Emilie Yeh Yueh-yu, Neda Ng Hei-tung, Hyun-suk Seo, Kyung Hyun Kim, and Robert Hyland.

Jinhee Choi is a lecturer of film studies at the University of Kent.

Mitsuyo Wada-Marciano is an assistant professor of film studies at Carleton University.

Horror to the Extreme

Hong Kong University Press thanks Xu Bing for writing the Press's name in his Square Word Calligraphy for the covers of its books. For further information, see p. iv.

TransAsia: Screen Cultures

Edited by Koichi IWABUCHI and Chris BERRY

What is Asia? What does it mean to be Asian? Who thinks they are Asian? How is "Asian-ness" produced? In Asia's transnational public space, many kinds of cross-border connections proliferate, from corporate activities to citizen-to-citizen linkages, all shaped by media — from television series to action films, video piracy, and a variety of subcultures facilitated by internet sites and other computer-based cultures. Films are packaged at international film festivals and marketed by DVD companies as "Asian," while the descendents of migrants increasingly identify themselves as "Asian," then turn to "Asian" screen cultures to find themselves and their roots. As reliance on national frameworks becomes obsolete in many traditional disciplines, this series spotlights groundbreaking research on trans-border, screen-based cultures in Asia.

Other titles in the series:

The Chinese Exotic: Modern Diasporic Femininity, by Olivia Khoo

East Asian Pop Culture: Analysing the Korean Wave, edited by Chua Beng Huat and Koichi Iwabuchi

TV Drama in China, edited by Ying Zhu, Michael Keane, and Ruoyun Bai

Cultural Studies and Cultural Industries in Northeast Asia: What a Difference a Region Makes, edited by Chris Berry, Nicola Liscutin, and Jonathan D. Mackintosh

Horror to the Extreme
Changing Boundaries in Asian Cinema

Edited by

Jinhee Choi and Mitsuyo Wada-Marciano

香港大學出版社
HONG KONG UNIVERSITY PRESS

Hong Kong University Press
14/F Hing Wai Centre
7 Tin Wan Praya Road
Aberdeen
Hong Kong

© Hong Kong University Press 2009

Hardback   ISBN 978-962-209-972-2
Paperback   ISBN 978-962-209-973-9

British Library Cataloguing-in-Publication Data
A catalogue record for this book is available from the British Library.

Secure On-line Ordering
http://www.hkupress.org

Printed and bound by Kings Time Printing Press Ltd., Hong Kong, China.

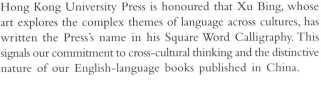 Hong Kong University Press is honoured that Xu Bing, whose
art explores the complex themes of language across cultures, has
written the Press's name in his Square Word Calligraphy. This
signals our commitment to cross-cultural thinking and the distinctive
nature of our English-language books published in China.

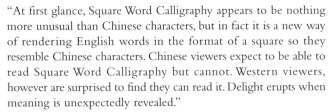 "At first glance, Square Word Calligraphy appears to be nothing
more unusual than Chinese characters, but in fact it is a new way
of rendering English words in the format of a square so they
 resemble Chinese characters. Chinese viewers expect to be able to
read Square Word Calligraphy but cannot. Western viewers,
however are surprised to find they can read it. Delight erupts when
meaning is unexpectedly revealed."
                              — Britta Erickson, *The Art of Xu Bing*

Contents

Contributors

Robert L. CAGLE is the cinema studies specialist at the University of Illinois at Urbana-Champaign Library and an assistant professor in the University of Illinois at Urbana-Champaign Unit for Cinema Studies. He writes about film and popular culture.

Jinhee CHOI is a lecturer of film studies at the University of Kent, U.K. She previously taught at Carleton University, Canada, and was a postdoctoral associate at Yale University. She is the co-editor of *Philosophy of Film and Motion Pictures* (2005) with Noël Carroll. Her articles on the philosophy and aesthetics of film have appeared in the *Journal of Aesthetics and Art Criticism*, the *British Journal of Aesthetics*, *Post Script*, *Asian Cinema*, *Film Studies*, *Jump Cut*, and *Film-Philosophy*. Choi has completed a book on contemporary South Korean cinema, titled *The South Korean Film Renaissance: Local Hitmakers, Global Provocateurs* (forthcoming).

Kevin HEFFERNAN is an associate professor of cinema-television in the Meadows School of the Arts at Southern Methodist University, where he teaches courses in film history, screenwriting, and film production. He is the author of *Ghouls, Gimmicks, and Gold: Horror Films and the American Movie Business, 1952–1968*, and his essays on horror movies, Asian cinema, exploitation film, and the American underground have appeared in a number of journals and critical anthologies. He is currently working on two books, tentatively titled *A Wind from the East: Trends in East Asian Popular Film after 1997* and *Nuts 'n' Gum: Dumb White Guy Culture and Politics in Contemporary America.*

Robert HYLAND is currently teaching English, drama and media studies at Ming Dao University in Taiwan, while concurrently finishing a doctoral degree in film studies at the University of Kent at Canterbury. He has written for the journal *Asian Cinema* and has presented papers on Japanese film at conferences in Korea and China.

Kyung Hyun KIM is an associate professor of East Asian languages and literatures at the University of California, Irvine. He also holds a joint appointment in the Department of Film and Media Studies. His essays and reviews have appeared in *Cinema Journal, Film Quarterly, positions: east asia culture critique,* and *Film Comment.* He is also one of the co-producers of *Never Forever* (a feature film directed by Gina Kim and starring Vera Farmiga and Ha Jung Woo) and the author of *The Remasculinization of Korean Cinema* (2004). He has just completed a new book manuscript, tentatively titled *Virtual Cinema: Korean Cinema of the Global Era.*

Chika KINOSHITA is an assistant professor of film studies at the University of Western Ontario, Canada. She is completing a book on Mizoguchi Kenji, mise-en-scène, gender, and power.

Adam KNEE is an associate professor in the Wee Kim Wee School of Communication and Information at Singapore's Nanyang Technological University. He has also held teaching posts in the U.S., Australia, Taiwan, and Thailand, where he was a Fulbright lecturer/researcher at Chulalongkorn University, Bangkok. He has published several essays on Asian cinema, and his writing on horror has appeared in the anthologies *Horror International* (2005) and *The Dread of Difference: Gender and the Horror Film* (1996).

Neda Hei-tung NG received her MPhil degree from Hong Kong Baptist University. Her thesis deals with the representation of mothers in J-horror. She has published refereed articles in *Film Appreciation Journal* (Taiwan) and *Film Art* (Beijing).

Hyun-suk SEO is an experimental filmmaker and film theorist. His recent visual projects include a companion video piece to his essay in this anthology. *Derivation* is a video re-assemblage of recycled moments taken from recent

Korean horror films. Edited together, the recurrent clichés of false startlers, quick head-turns, screams, and sudden awakenings form repetitive musical patterns and create secondary horror infused with purely sensory attractions. In theoretical studies, Seo takes the psychoanalytic framework to examine various questions in documentary, experimental film, and early cinema. His forthcoming book in Korean deals with two goblin-like animation superheroes created by Morikawa Nobuhide. He teaches at Yonsei Graduate School of Communication and Arts in Seoul.

Chi-Yun SHIN is a senior lecturer of film studies at Sheffield Hallam University, U.K., where she teaches contemporary East Asian cinemas, alternative cinemas, and contemporary British cinema. She has co-edited *New Korean Cinema* (2005) with Julian Stringer and her articles on black British cinema and East Asian cinema have appeared in the journals *Paragraph* and *Jump Cut,* and the anthology *Seoul Searching* (2007). Currently, she is editing an anthology on Asian film noir provisionally titled *Eastern Connection.*

Mitsuyo WADA-MARCIANO is an assistant professor of film studies at Carleton University. Her research interests are Japanese cinema, especially in relation with Japanese modernity in the 1920s and 1930s, new media's impact on Japanese cinema, and East Asian cinemas in global culture. She is the author of *Nippon Modern: Japanese Cinema of the 1920s and 1930s* (2008), and its Japanese translation is published by Nagoya University Press in 2009. Her articles and reviews are published in *Film Quarterly, Camera Obscura, Canadian Journal of Film Studies, The Journal of Asian Studies, Post Script,* and *Asian Cinema.* She is currently working on a project concerning digital technology's impact on contemporary Japanese cinema and visual culture.

Emilie Yueh-yu YEH is a professor in the Department of Cinema-TV and director of the Centre for Media and Communication Research at Hong Kong Baptist University. Her publications include *Taiwan Film Directors: A Treasure Island* (2005, co-author), *Chinese-Language Film: Historiography, Poetics, Politics* (2005, co-editor), *East Asian Screen Industries* (2008, co-author), and over 30 journal articles and book chapters.

Introduction

Jinhee Choi and Mitsuyo Wada-Marciano

One may be taken aback by the moral and visceral extremes manifest in recent Asian horror cinema. In *Audition* (*Odishon*, Miike Takashi, 1999), the female protagonist Asami amputates one of the male protagonist's feet and tortures him with acupuncture needles. In *Oldboy* (Park Chan-wook, 2003), the character Dae-su cuts off his own tongue, both as penance for the indiscrete remarks he made in high school that led to someone's death and in an attempt to prevent his daughter from learning of their incestuous relationship. In *Dumplings* (*Gaau ji*, Fruit Chan, 2004), the character Ching relishes dumplings made out of fetuses and hopes that these delicacies will rejuvenate her fading beauty. Setting aside the moral ramifications of such manifest extremities, we can identify the current boom enjoyed by Asian horror and extreme cinema and discern a complex nexus of local, regional and global relationships in play. The popularity of Japanese horror cinema (J-horror), initially a product of low-budget independent filmmaking, has propelled horror film cycles in other Asian countries such as South Korea, Hong Kong and Thailand. Furthermore, the warm reception of the Hollywood remakes of Japanese horror films such as *Ringu* (Nakata Hideo, 1998) and *Ju-on* (Shimizu Takashi, 2000) have also helped Asian horror cinema earn global saliency.

Horror to the Extreme examines the global processes embedded in a regional formation of screen culture, and inquires how "Asian-ness" and national specificities are differently configured at various stages of production cycles. This volume begins with the shared view that the category "Asian cinema" has been used to refer to both filmmakers' conflicting aims and aspirations and audiences' multifaceted experiences, which makes this volume an ideal site to search out new ways of approaching Asian popular cultures in the age of cultural globalization. There is a long history of "Asia" as a tableau for projections of imagined topography and as a hub source for cultural production. Yet, we are skeptical of the idea that "Asia" is a fixed territory, and argue instead that it has been constructed out of various historical, political, and economic necessities. The notion of Asian cinema provides both a converging point as well as the point of departure, as one moves one's attention from production to distribution and consumption. Asian cinema does not merely function as a supra-category that encompasses the numerous national cinemas, but more importantly registers the changing mediascape and the increasing interdependence of local cinemas within the Asian region. The spatial proximity and cultural kinship among Asian countries can expedite the interactions among them, but more importantly the political and economic changes in East Asia for the last two decades provide fertile ground for a regionalization, in which each nation-state involved perhaps shares the same bed with the others but with different dreams.

The primary concern of this volume is not to determine the directionality of cultural exchanges between West and East — Americanization or Japanization — or to locate the origin of such exchanges. Rather, it traces out the interactions and mutual transformations that take place at various levels and scales of cultural production and consumption. We stay away from the spatial analogies employed in much literature on globalization, despite the inevitable spatial connotations associated with the local, the regional, and the global. Instead, we approach them relationally as the grids through which one can examine complex nexus within the operations of globalization. A regionalization of film culture embodies many of the characteristics attributed to the business practices of globalization such as the concentration of capital with the fragmentation and spatial extension of production. Toby Miller and others locate the power of Hollywood dominance in its command of a "new international division of cultural labor," which provides Hollywood control over production, distribution, and exhibition worldwide.[1] In a similar manner, perhaps smaller in scale in terms of the budget and targeted audiences, Asian film industries seek to draw on film personnel and crews across nation-states. For instance, Peter Chan, who is one of the leading producers in the region, promotes numerous co-production projects including *The Eye* (*Gin gwai*, Danny and Oxide Pang, 2002), the horror trilogy *Three* (*Saam gaang*, Peter Chan, Kim Ji-woon, Nanzee Nimibutr, 2002), and *Three Extremes* (*Saam gang yi*, Fruit Chan, Park Chan-wook, Miike Takashi, 2004) as an attempt to reach audiences beyond one nation-state.

The presence of, and enthusiasm for, Asian cinema in Hollywood is palpable both at the box office and among industry personnel. *The Grudge* (2004), Hollywood's remake of the Japanese original, *Ju-on* (2003), set the U.S. record for the biggest opening weekend for a horror film.[2] The U.S. audiences recently saw the latest Hollywood's re-telling of Asian horror, *The Eye* (David Moreau, Xavier Palud, 2008). Hollywood studios were lined up for the remake rights to such film as the Cannes second-prize winner *Oldboy* and *The Cure* (Kurosawa Kiyoshi, 1997). The visibility of Asian horror in Hollywood may be viewed as a case of a reverse form of media globalization, which is usually thought of as the worldwide dissemination of Western culture. However, such a claim preserves the dichotomy between the center and the periphery, and the implicit hierarchy among different "stages" a local or national cinema aspires to ascend. As the geographer Erik Swyngedouw observes, the scales of social relations and norms — local, national, regional, and global — do not operate hierarchically but simultaneously.[3] Social relations and norms, as Swyngedouw further notes, are fluid, contested, and perpetually transgressed rather than fixed. The transnational aspects of world cinema within the age of late capitalism not only reside in the production, distribution, and consumption of its products across national borders, but are also found in its capacity to appropriate and transform cultures and products of other national origins. As Aihwa Ong reminds us, "transnationality" connotes both "moving through space or across lines" and "changing the nature of something."[4] An approach that is attentive to the complex relationships among the local, the regional, and the global will thus yield a finer, more subtle understanding of mutual transformation of screen culture taking place in the Asian region.

Cultural exchanges exemplified by the current horror boom across Asia-Pacific are not completely a novel phenomenon. The 1970s saw increasing co-production between Hong Kong and South Korea. The Korean production company, Shin Film, which was founded by one of the country's leading film directors, Shin Sang-ok, teamed up with Hong Kong's Shaw Brothers to produce historical epics. Furthermore, traffic in cinema between Hollywood and Asia has also been two-way. Kurosawa Akira successfully exported "westerns" back to the United States via his samurai films. Martial arts and kung-fu films of the 1970s created a cult following among inner-city adolescents worldwide.[5] Japanese *anime* and Hong Kong bloodshed gangster sagas attracted audiences outside their respective diasporic communities in the 1980s and 1990s. What is noteworthy about the current phenomenon, though, is how the mobility of both people and commodities enhanced by the development of technology and communication system, expedite and *intensify* such transactions. Many of the filmmakers and producers, with cosmopolitan backgrounds and educated abroad, actively adopt the global production strategies of Hollywood, while the dissemination of the Internet and digital media makes information about local and national cinemas readily available to the audiences outside the host country.

The regional market is increasingly significant for small film industries such as those in South Korea and Thailand. The industry boom, which is currently taking place in South Korea, was in part triggered by the Bilateral Agreement between South Korea and the United States. The U.S. government demanded that the South Korean government abolish the restrictions on the number of imports and reduce the screen quota allotted for the domestically produced films, and the South Korean film industry underwent rapid conglomeration in order to successfully compete with Hollywood in the domestic market.[6] Lack of sufficient ancillary markets leads the South Korean film industry to seek an export market, with Japan being the biggest customer for the film industry. Similarly, Hong Kong faced a decline in the number of films produced and witnessed the shrinking local audience attendance in the domestically produced films after its return to the People's Republic of China.[7] Co-production of films with an emerging yet neglected film industry such as the one in Thailand provides a viable option to the Hong Kong film industry, while this in turn satisfies the aspiration of Thailand to be positioned alongside the more economically advanced Asian countries, and its hope to be mapped onto the international film scene. Japan was once a self-contained industry, which was able to recuperate the production costs without relying heavily on the overseas market. However, with the stagnation of film studios in Japan, more revenues are earned from the consumption of cinema outside the theatrical venues. The booming film industry in neighboring countries such as South Korea also provides a model for the Japanese film industry to follow, and the Japanese has since attempted to broaden their target audience to include regional audiences. The changing cultural policies in South Korea further provide conditions that facilitate cultural flows within the region. Japanese popular culture had been banned in South Korea for fifty years since 1945, and the ban was only completely lifted in 2004.

As the essays in this volume demonstrate, national specificities are differently manifest in horror films from the East Asian region. In the case of Japanese horror films, technology seems to be the most crucial aspect as iconography and for narrative development, such as the cursed videotape in *Ringu*. The horror films from South Korea are often concerned with adolescent sensibility, which can be seen within the *Whispering Corridors* series

(Park Ki-hyeong et al., 1998–2003), while recent Hong Kong horror films seem to be tied to the Chinese national identity, and reveal Hong Kong's oscillation between desire for and anxiety toward China. Certainly, these themes are not unique to the host countries. Korea's *Phone* (*Pon*, Ahn Byeong-ki, 2002) and Japan's *One Missed Call* (*Chakushin ari*, Miike Takashi, 2003) share the same premise that characters' death are forecast by their cellular phones. Asian societies, despite the uneven economic developments in the region, share similar socio-economic problems and concerns — technology, sexuality, and nascent youth culture — which may explain the prevalence as well as the regional appeals of these themes.

The distribution and consumption of Asian cinema raise issues that are significantly different from those in the production sector. Some of the subtle differences in Asian horror and extreme cinema are discernable to the attuned viewers with cultural knowledge, but might be erased when they are exported and lumped together under a homogeneous category "Asia Extreme," the DVD label launched by London-based distributor Metro Tartan. "Asia Extreme" designates both horror and other films that are, according to Hamish McAlpine of Tartan, "slick and glossy with fast, MTV-style editing . . . and sensibility, typified by . . . over-the-top grotesque[ness] to the point of being surreal."[8] In addition to the Japanese filmmaker Miike, whose films provide prototypical examples of "Asia Extreme" such as *Audition*, directors such as Park Chan-wook (the *Vengeance* trilogy, 2002–2004), Kim Ki-duk (*The Isle*, 2000), and Fukasaku Kinji (*Battle Royale I, II,* 2000–2003), have expanded the category by rendering ultra-violent narratives set against serene portrayals of the troubled psyches of doomed protagonists. The strategic designation "Asia Extreme" has undoubtedly created a regional affiliation among these directors' films, but the category itself is purposefully flexible in order to include a range of Asian cinema that seems exportable.

Classification of "Asia Extreme" deserves critical attention here. The distinction between the production genre and the marketing genre which Paul Willemen draws in tracing out the transformation of the "action" genre would be useful in examining the function of "Asia Extreme" label.[9] "Asia Extreme" is a distribution/marketing term rather than a production category such as melodrama or western, which are largely based on narrative structure and components. In fact, some of the films were released retroactively and categorized as such after the launch of the label. What is worthy of note is how this label is fed back into the production sector. Unlike "Asian Minimalism," which is claimed to have emerged rather independently across East Asia, "Asia Extreme" seems to connote a closer tie, even mutual influences among such directors as Miike, Park, Fukasaku, and Kim.[10] For contemporary Asian filmmakers, the regional label "Asia Extreme" may provide them with what David Desser calls "instant canons" to follow, rework, and transform, depending on their intentions to either be affiliated with the label or differentiate themselves from it.[11] The "time lag" that existed in the invention, renovation, and dissemination of film styles and conventions has been compressed with the immediate availability of cinema from different countries. For the new connoisseurs of Asian cinema, it is not a film's originality, but the detection of allusion and intertextuality, which makes their viewing experience playful and pleasurable.

"Asia Extreme," however, is not merely a marketing label. It also carries a set of cultural assumptions and implications that guides — and sometimes misguides — the viewer in assessing the political and ideological significance of the films. Youth audiences, who would normally be reluctant to watch foreign film with subtitles, are drawn to such films by virtue of their non-mainstream sensibilities and attractions. McAlpine compares such youth audiences, who endorse films imbued with extreme sensibilities, with the art theatre audience of the 1960s, who visited theatres to relish foreign films for their explicit sexual content.[12] There might be a continuity between European art cinema of the 1960s (and even the contemporary) and the Extreme cinema of the 1990s onward in the sense that some of the attractions of foreign films in the U.S. lie in the depiction of subject matters that are not easily permissible within Hollywood, such as sex, gore, and violence.[13] Yet, it also carries the danger of effacing local/national specificities and of fostering aesthetic relativism: "Asia" just becomes a spatial fix or an empty signifier for being cool, rather than providing an entry point for the viewer to be exposed and learn about the originating countries. *Horror to the Extreme* brings to the fore some of the issues of multimedia textuality and the plurality of reception of Asian horror and extreme cinema both within the region and worldwide.

In presenting eleven analyses of recent Asian horror films, this book aims to unravel the complex variety of cultural traffic now flowing across the national, the regional, and the transnational spheres. There is a dramatic shift toward a more diffused pattern of cultural production and consumption, as the Internet and DVD have become the main channel through which viewers encounter local and/or regional products. The authors attempt to map and analyze the historical and cultural conditions underlying such changes, and we hope that our collaboration can be taken by the reader as a meaningful heterogeneous challenge rather than a singular approach to the multifaceted and uncertain cultural sphere of Asian cinema. The eleven chapters, contributed from North America, the United Kingdom, Hong Kong, Taiwan and South Korea, are divided into three sections that bridge the material and imaginary realms of contemporary film culture in genre and industry, national identity, and iconography.

The first section, "Contesting Genres: From J-Horror to Asia Extreme," examines the historical and industrial conditions which have propelled the contemporary Asian horror boom. It also discusses how the respective industry has been transformed to increase the circulation of its products across national borders through co-productions and multimedia formats. The five chapters in this section focus on the horror cinema from Japan, South Korea, Hong Kong, Thailand, and their international distribution under the label of "Asia Extreme." These contributions will foreground the transnational nexus embedded within both regional production of horror cinema and its distribution abroad by delineating how each industry responds to local and global demands.

Mitsuyo Wada-Marciano examines the impact of digital media on J-horror, which gained prominence at the end of the 1990s with the success of Nakata Hideo's horror film *Ringu*. Posed against a background of decline and upheaval in Japan's major film studios, her essay's central question is "How could a low-budget B genre, Japanese horror film, intrinsically linked to regional popular culture become a transnational film franchise?" She focuses on contingencies in the late 1990s between technology and cinema — the rise of digital technology (digital video shooting and DVD distribution) and the popularity of the relatively inexpensive horror genre in Japan — and analyzes the film *Marebito* (Shimizu Takashi, 2004) as a case study. She asserts that the digitalized multimedia format of "cinema," as J-horror exemplifies, expedites its transnational dissemination, yet remains regional on various economic, industrial, and cultural levels in that it has contributed to the regional boom of horror cinema throughout Asia. Wada-Marciano further notes that while academic discourses on the connection between cinema and digital media have increased, there has been little attention paid to the ways regional film movements or genres, such as J-horror, have challenged long-standing patterns of culture, capital, and distribution flows.

Jinhee Choi approaches the commercial success of contemporary South Korean horror films in the domestic market. She examines the niche marketing strategy employed in the horror genre, in particular the targeting of teenage female audiences. The recent success of South Korean cinema has resulted from the steady influx of capital via conglomerates and venture capitalists since the 1990s. While the industrial norm has been an increased commercialization of the cinema bringing about an abundance of high-budget action films, there are mid- and low-budget films catering to the sensibilities of the youth audience. Despite their relatively low budgets, horror films in particular have proven the commercial viability of such niche marketing strategies. Since the unexpected box office success of *Whispering Corridors*, films including *Sorum* (*Goosebumps*, Yun Jong-chan, 2001), *Phone*, and *A Tale of Two Sisters* (*Janghwa, Hongryeon*, Kim Ji-woon, 2003) have demonstrated the genre's popularity particularly within teenage female demographics. Choi argues that the appeal of South Korean horror films to the female audience is tied to their evocation of melancholy and sadness, and examines how such sentiment is produced within the narratives and the visual styles of the *Whispering Corridors* series and *A Tale of Two Sisters*.

Kevin Heffernan's chapter uncovers several significant trends in contemporary Hong Kong horror film including the growing importance of transnational co-productions, export markets, and a fertile cross-breeding of popular genres native to both Hong Kong and other East Asian cinema. Focusing on the hugely successful efforts of independent producer Filmko Pictures (founded in 2000) and its supernatural thriller *Inner Senses* (*Yee do hung gaan*, Lo Chi-Leung, 2002), Heffernan reveals how the Hong Kong film industry, previously threatened by such Hollywood blockbusters as *Jurassic Park* (Steven Spielberg, 1993) and *The Matrix* (Andy and Larry Wachowski, 1999), has attempted to move toward more regionally driven film production. Heffernan draws our attention to how regional film industries such as Hong Kong's have successfully crafted self-consciously pan-Asian films via the horror genre, and have helped transform production strategies.

Equally sensitive to the increasingly pan-Asian, transnational context of Asian horror production, Adam Knee discusses *The Eye*, as a material and metaphoric representation of pan-Asian cultural flows. Knee charts the film as one of the first efforts of Applause Pictures, a Hong Kong-based production company with a transnational focus. While the film manifests the influences of Hollywood cinema such as *The Sixth Sense* (M. Night Shyamalan, 1999) and the tradition of Hong Kong ghost films, Knee underscores its pan-Asian trajectory, particularly when the film changes its setting from Hong Kong to Thailand in the third act. After the protagonist experiences haunting visions following an eye transplant, she investigates their origin by traveling to the donor's home in Thailand. Knee traces "pan-Asian-ness" in *The Eye* and looks at how it is intertextualized with other national cinemas and the film's sequel, *The Eye 2* (Danny and Oxide Pang, 2004). He argues that the power of the film's central narrative trope — the doubling of identity across national borders and temporalities — is reflected in the popularity of such cross-cultural themes (to which Heffernan also alludes in his chapter) throughout Asian horror cinema.

Chi-Yun Shin examines Tartan's flagship trademark "Asia Extreme," with special reference to its relation with recent East Asian horror films. Through interviews conducted with Tartan personnel and detailed research, she examines the company's marketing strategies and its aspiration to expand to global markets including the U.S. Shin problematizes the label's tendency of homogenizing both levels of national cultures (Japan, South Korea, Hong Kong, Thailand, Taiwan, and Singapore) and diverse genres (horror, action, thriller, etc.). Tartan's success is hinged upon the very nature of such ambiguous marketing, but the re-packaging and re-circulation of film products with scarce regard to their national origins gives rise to further questions on the epistemic risk involved in distribution and consumption in the digital age.

In the second section, "Contextualizing Horror: Film Movement, National History, and Taboo," Chika Kinoshita, Robert Cagle, Emilie Yueh-yu Yeh, and Neda Hei-tung Ng discuss the formation and transformation of J-horror, the South Korean "extreme" Film, and Hong Kong horror, by linking each to its cultural as well as political contexts.

Chika Kinoshita is concerned with the regional and national categorization of J-horror, which one can arguably regard as a forerunner of the horror boom in Asia. With her cultural knowledge of J-horror's emergence within the contemporary Japanese film industry, Kinoshita frames it as a film movement instead of a genre. Her fundamental but nonetheless crucial question — "What is J-horror?" — specifies that the category is not inclusive of all horror films shot in Japanese language and/or produced by the Japanese film industry. Rather, it is tied to a specific period and filmic style, and is connected to a close-knit group of filmmakers, critics, and distributors. She highlights Kurosawa Kiyoshi's *Loft* (2005), and analyzes the film's narrative and stylistic aspects that are representative of J-horror. While J-horror is indeed a local phenomenon in the sense that it is a film movement launched by local filmmakers and critics, its stylistic affinity to other national cinemas, as Kinoshita claims, underscores its transnational aspect, or in Kinoshita's words, its "non-originary space." Her concept provides a useful stylistic framework for assessing Kurosawa's film style and enables the reader to discern the intertextual influences that are remote from the local culture and putative "Japanese" aesthetics.

Robert L. Cagle analyzes the issue of violence in recent South Korean "extreme" films, and focuses on three films: *Oldboy*, *H* (Lee Jeong-hyeok, 2002), and *A Bittersweet Life* (Kim Ji-woon, 2005). Starting from the American mass media's dubious cultural link between the assailant, Cho Seung-ho, of the April 16, 2007 shootings at Virginia Tech and these new South Korean extreme films, Cagle questions the simplistic dichotomies of "us" (or "U.S.")

versus "them," "good" versus "evil," and "sane" versus "sick." He tries to see violence in these films from a different perspective. Seeking answers to why so many American viewers and critics have chosen to single out works from South Korea for censure, he compares the three films with Hollywood melodrama. He notes how a "threat" to social order propels the narrative in both the South Korean "extreme" films and Hollywood melodrama, yet the "threat" functions differently in that the moral good is never fully restored in the former. Cagle attributes such a narrative structure to the recent history and national traumas of Korea, and demonstrates that violence in Korean extreme films provides a revelatory moment, in which the sustained moral structure is reversed; the protagonist recognizes the "other" in him or her, dissolving the binary moral opposition between good and evil.

In their essay, Emilie Yueh-yu Yeh and Neda Hei-tung Ng address the question of national identity and social psyche in contemporary Hong Kong, with reference to the treatment of ghosts and ghostly bodies in recent Hong Kong horror cinema. They examine two signature films from Applause Pictures — *Three: Going Home* (Peter Chan, 2002) and *Three Extremes: Dumplings* (Fruit Chan, 2004) — as examples that depart from a long tradition in Hong Kong horror cinema. As Yeh and Ng point out, in the local tradition, zombie pictures (*jiangshi pian*) once took the center stage during the boom years of Hong Kong cinema in the 1980s. Later in the early 2000, with Applause Pictures (as elaborated in Adam Knee's chapter) capitalizing on the phenomenal success of J-horror, ghost films re-emerged as a highly marketable genre. Yet, Yeh and Ng assert that this horror resurrection has less to do with recycling previous narratives or stylistic formulas than it does with an urge to remake horror that relates to the contemporary Hong Kong psyche. The mythical and ghostly presence of Chinese migrants is central to the narrative of the two horror films, and yet China is not a wholly negative presence when it comes to problems of survival, competition, and ambition. Here China resurfaces as a desirable alternative to overcome aging, illness, and mortality. However, the Chinese cultural legacy, such as traditional medical practices, is quickly dissolved and transformed into a monstrous invasion and occupation. Horror, in this regard, displaces the backlash against the market economy's preoccupation with youth, beauty, and fitness.

The chapters in the third section, "Iconography of Horror: Personal Belongings, Bodies, and Violence," explicitly approach questions of sexuality, identity, and violence in the horror films packaged under the label, "Asia Extreme." The aim of this section is to discern the degree to which such aspects in those films stem from certain national and/or regional cultures. The essays also attempt to find out whether the films are simply part of a marketing strategy to essentialize "Asia" as a signifier of the abject unknown, something beyond the ethical consensus in Euro-American societies.

The section begins with Hyun-Suk Seo's investigation of recent South Korean horror films' images of domestic materiality, or women's personal belongings. Seo focuses on the common motifs of "resentment," "jealousy," and "revenge" in such films as *The Red Shoes* (*Bunhongsin*, Kim Yong-gyun, 2005), *Phone, Acacia* (Park Ki-hyeong, 2003), *The Wig* (*Gabal*, Won Shin-yeon, 2005), *Cello* (*Chello hongmijoo ilga salinsagan*, Lee Woo-cheol, 2005), and *Apartment* (*APT.*, Ahn Byeong-ki, 2006). He notes how these films are driven by a female protagonist's attachment to personal objects that once belonged to the dead. Such uncanny objects, Seo claims, emanate both attraction and repulsion, which express the heroine's role within patriarchal discourses that reproduce women's desires and anxieties through phallocentric fantasy. Employing both Freudian and Lacanian concepts of fetishism, Seo analyzes the female bonds and selfhood in these films as vehicles for a male fantasy centered on the fetishistic anxiety. By localizing the depiction of such fetishes, Seo concludes that the genre conventions of recent Korean horror films are built upon the limited roles allotted to women.

In contrast with Robert L. Cagle's emphasis on the extremes in Park Chan-wook's work, in Chapter 10, Kyung Hyun Kim examines Park's "vengeance trilogy": *Sympathy for Mr. Vengeance* (*Boksuneun naui geot*, 2002), *Oldboy*, and *Sympathy for Lady Vengeance* (*Chinjeolhan geumjassi*, 2005) as indicative of the director's stylistic oeuvre. Kim tackles the established discourse on Park's work, which views it as just images empty of meaning, and traces the emergence of a "postmodern" aesthetics in Park's films, that is, a sense of failed political ideologies as well as an aesthetic of flatness with images floating free of their referential meaning. What Park's work offers is not an imprint of reality, but a perception that only mimics the verisimilitude of space and time. Kim analyzes a number of elements that characterize the opaque sensibility of Park's films: the trope of captivity, the video game style of violence, the distinct separation of planes of representation and signification, and the camera's "flat" wide-angle shot. Through these analyses, Kim further challenges the recent criticism, as Cagle describes in Chapter 7, which has conflated the stylized violence of Park Chan-wook's work with nihilistic indifference to violence's aftereffects.

In the last chapter, Robert Hyland examines the violence in Miike Takashi's *Audition*. Hyland links the violence within "Asia Extreme" films to a politics of excess. "Asia Extreme" cinema, for Hyland, is an overtly political cinema, and he finds its evidence in the work of Miike Takashi, whose films represent a challenge to the complacent cinema of the studio system, especially through an aesthetic of "excess" and "a politic of aggression." Hyland points out that Miike's films are not only aesthetically extreme, but they also comprise a radical critique of social values and norms. In the case of *Audition*, he argues that Miike's aesthetic system interrogates the patriarchal roots of the monstrous feminine.

A few notes on transliteration are in order. We have omitted the macron, which typically indicates long vowels in the romanization of Japanese (*Romaji*). We have done so in order to have consistency over what we see as a selective and often arbitrary use of the diacritic. For personal names, we have also followed the authentic order in Japanese, Korean, and Chinese. The family name precedes the given name for most of the filmmakers and actors appearing in this book, and we have used the Anglophone order, that is, the given name preceding the family name, for those whose English transliteration gained currency outside their native countries. As for the Chinese names, we have adopted the most common usage, such as Ang Lee (the given name first and the family name last) and Tsui Hark (the family name first and the given name last). We have often referenced the Internet Movie Database (IMDb) and also accepted exceptional orders and spellings based on the contributors' preference.

I

Contesting Genres:
From J-horror
to "Asia Extreme"

1

J-horror: New Media's Impact on Contemporary Japanese Horror Cinema

Mitsuyo Wada-Marciano

The main objective of this chapter[1] is to scrutinize new media's effect on contemporary Japanese cinema, especially the horror film genre "J-horror." In particular, I would like to examine the ongoing contestation and negotiation between cinema and new media in contemporary Japan by analyzing the impact of new media on the transnational horror boom from Japan to East Asia, and finally to Hollywood. As the case of contemporary J-horror films exemplifies, the new, digitalized, multimedia form of cinema is now a dispersed phenomenon, both ubiquitous and transnational as technology, yet regional in the economic, industrial, and cultural contingencies of its acceptance. While academic discourses on the connection between cinema and new media have been increasing, many of them are following the historical constellation of hegemony and capital in cinema, namely Hollywood as the center of production and distribution. From my perspective the emerging possibilities of new media in cinema have less to do with the progress of CGI (Computer Generated Imagery) effects in such Hollywood franchises as the *Star Wars* series (George Lucas, 1977–2005) than in the ways regional movements or genres, such as Dogme 95, Chinese Sixth Generation Films (typically low-budget films made outside the state-run studios) and J-horror, have challenged the long-standing flow of capital and culture, i.e. the centrality of Hollywood. I argue that such a phenomenon is not entirely new in the history of the cinema, but what makes it most interesting is its vernacular staging within a specific time, locale, and media. How did a low-budget B genre intrinsically linked to regional popular culture become a transnational film franchise? The answer lies in the contingencies of new media's influence at all levels of production, text, distribution, and reception. Simply put, I frame J-horror's emergence since the 1990s as a form of trans-media commodity, one that is based less on theatrical modes of exhibition than on new digital media.

The Shift to Digital Production

The first part of my chapter focuses on the contemporary Japanese film industry and J-horror's production processes, and examines how the J-horror boom is connected to digital or computer technologies. Beginning in 1989, the decline of Japan's once vaunted economy has ushered in widespread cultural change. What has emerged in this period of the Japanese film industry is a reconfiguration at all levels of production, distribution, and reception. The role of film studios has shifted from actual filmmaking to the distribution of films in multimedia formats, such as DVD and cable television. Within the industry's risk-averse environment, most directors have become paradoxically *independent* as filmmakers, and increasingly *dependent* on multimedia financing and distribution by the major film companies. The Japanese film industry has been mainly categorized into two types of filmmaking groups, "major" and "independent," and the former now stands for three film companies: Toho, Shochiku, and Toei, with the rest of the filmmaking productions more or less independent.[2] As Geoff King observes on American cinema, "The term 'independent' has had rather different connotations at different periods."[3] In the case of the contemporary Japanese cinema, the distinction of cinema being independent from the studios is rather meaningless given the current ubiquity of independent filmmakers. This is different from the case of the American cinema from the mid-1980s, which King describes as "the more arty/quirky, sometimes politically inflected, brand of independent cinema [that] began to gain a higher profile and a more sustained and institutionalized base in the broadly off-Hollywood arena."[4] Writing on recent Japanese cinema, Tom Mes and Jasper Sharp offer this description of the independent filmmakers: "These were filmmakers whose attitudes and philosophies of cinema were entirely different from those of the old studio period. They were independent in spirit: artists with nothing to lose, but with everything to gain."[5]

However, given the current economics of filmmaking, Japanese independent no longer means independent production. During the studios' heyday of production, the gap between the major companies' films and those of independents was considerable in terms of budgets, production modes, and aesthetic outcome. In the current "post-studio" period, the dichotomy of major vs. independent has been reconfigured to a symbiotic relationship of the former as financier and distributor, the latter as divisions of production. Independent filmmakers often work with the sponsorship of the major studios and/or produce within an organized production company that is regularly engaged in the making of films and television programs. Conglomerates such as Kadokawa publishing company and Fuji Television often support these independent filmmakers, whose objectives are seldom free from business constraints, in contrast to Mes's and Sharp's idealized notions. For instance, both J-horror film directors Nakata Hideo and Shimizu Takashi are so-called independent filmmakers, and yet *Ringu* (Nakata Hideo, 1998) was produced by Kadokawa and distributed by Toho, and *Ju-on: The Grudge* (Shimizu Takashi, 2002) was produced by Toei Video Co. Ltd. Nakata, as one of the last generation of studio-trained directors, started his career as an assistant director in Nikkatsu Studios in 1985, then made his debut as an independent director in 1992. His first directed works are not films, but three segments for the television series *Real-Life Scary Tales* (*Honto ni atta kowai hanashi,* Nakata Hideo et al., 1992).[6] Shimizu, on the other hand, started out with a short video, produced as his film school project, and he subsequently was offered the chance to direct his first horror program for Kansai Television.[7]

The integration of major and independent has also served to maintain historical tactics employed by the major studios for releasing films in "series" that inculcate audience loyalty. While the majors have steadily decreased their in-house production numbers, they have remained heavily dependent on so-called "program pictures," typically a film series like *Tora-san* with forty-eight episodes (Yamada Yoji, 1969–95) from Shochiku or the *Godzilla* series (Honda Ishiro et al., 1954–2004) from Toho. Each company has nurtured its brand associations with its particular "program picture" built around a specific character and usually the same director, and it releases an installment once or twice a year during the high-profit holiday seasons. The "program picture" has provided a measure of economic stability to the production side, since it functions the same as a genre at fulfilling expectations in the triangular relationship of production, distribution, and reception. J-horror, like many of the films that have come out of the recent independent production system, has often been molded after this pattern of serialization as well. The independent film production company Ace Pictures, for instance, produced *Ringu* and distributed it with another horror film *Ring 2: Spiral* (*Rasen,* Iida Koji, 1998) as a special event. They then made it a series, following the pattern of the "program picture," in the following years as the "Kadokawa Horror

Series," and produced *Ringu 2* (Nakata Hideo, 1999) and *Ringu 0* (Tsuruta Norio, 2000) within three years. As these examples indicate, J-horror grew out of the specific context of the contemporary Japanese film industry — the disintegration of the studio system and a leveling of competition, even increasing affiliations among "major" and "independent" film productions.

In the current post-studio period, many of the Japanese filmmakers are de facto independent, lacking the extensive 35 mm training which many directors once had during the studio production period. Those new filmmakers, however, have been quick to embrace new media, whether through digital video or computer editing, in order to trim their production budgets and schedules. For instance, the director Shimizu Takashi shot his film *Marebito* (2004) in just eight days, between the production of *Ju-on: The Grudge 2* (2003) and the Hollywood remake, *The Grudge* (2004).[8] J-horror filmmakers' prolific production, both in speed and number, has been a major reason for the genre's success, and their productivity has been made possible by new media technologies. More importantly, the abundant growth in production was not simply related to film and its theatrical release, but also to an alternative venue for marketing, namely the DVD, another new technological influence since the late 1990s. What then, is the result of this technological conversion to digital on the level of filmic or post-filmic texts?

New Iconographies and the Rhetoric of New Media

The appeal of J-horror films can be seen in their textual elements drawn from the urban topography and the pervasive use of technology, elements which are, at once, particular and universal. In the current post-studio climate, the conditions of low-budget and studio-less production are imprinted on new filmmakers' work, especially with reference to location shooting that frequently captures a sense of Tokyo urbanity. J-horror has often effectively used this dense topography to represent a uniquely urban sense of fear attached to the possibilities of the megalopolis and its mythos. The images of Tokyo and the surrounding locales tied with the city dwellers' lives have been significant motifs in J-horror. *Ringu*, for example, uses mainly three locales: Tokyo, Oshima island, and Izu peninsula. Oshima island is sixty miles south of Tokyo, where the film's female "monster" Sadako (Inou Rei) was born, and Izu is southwest of Tokyo, where she is now confined in an old well and waiting to extend her reach. Both Oshima and Izu are usually considered weekend resort areas for Tokyo dwellers. The mix of familiarity and relative remoteness of these areas gives the film a sense of spatial and temporal reality as well as a mythical undercurrent related to the remnants of pre-modern culture lurking in rural locales. Besides *Ringu*, many of the J-horror films use Tokyo as their spatial backdrop and even as a causal aspect for a character's isolation. As one can see in *Audition* (Miike Takashi, 1999), the female "monster" Asami's (Shiina Eihi) residence is an old and drab apartment in Tokyo, and her isolation is suggested by the space, largely unfurnished except for a telephone. *Audition* also draws upon various Tokyo locales, such as the subterranean, run-down bar (in Ginza), where its owner was killed and chopped to pieces, and the former ballet studio (in Suginami Ward), where Asami, as a child, was molested by her stepfather. Those spaces in Tokyo give both feelings of familiarity and repulsion in Julia Kristeva's sense of "abjection," the concept of letting go of things that one would still like to keep.[9] The old capital Tokyo, indeed, has a number of these derelict spaces, which enrich the megalopolis with history and nostalgia, and yet they are also dysfunctional and archaic, waiting to be discarded in order to introduce something new. The "abject" space can be depicted as "uncanny" as well; it is familiar, but at the same time "foreign," a relic of disappearing history. In the case of the *Ju-on* series, the film uses an abandoned and haunted house that conjures J-horror's dual sensibility of space that is both ordinary and familiar, and yet isolated, neglected, and dreadful. A sense of claustrophobia is created by the use of an actual house, with the camera work dictated by the tight dimensions of a typical Japanese residence. When the director Shimizu made the Hollywood version *The Grudge*, he even built a replica of the house in Tokyo, with its compartments and alcoves, in order to keep the sense of spatial banality and the feeling of claustrophobia.

It is revealing to compare the aspect of locality in *Ringu* and its Hollywood adaptation *The Ring* (Gore Verbinski, 2002). In the Hollywood version, geographical specificity is transferred from Tokyo to Seattle. The film demystifies locations and does not use the dual sensibility of space to conjure familiarity and abjection, relying instead on more firmly established characters and narrative causality. For instance, the "Moesko Island Lighthouse" that Rachel (Naomi Watts) visits is a fictional name for a real lighthouse located in Newport, Oregon; the Seattle setting is actually Vancouver.[10] What the film creates with its locales is not a simulation of an urban dweller's actual topography, but only a geographic plot device for the narrative development. Strengthening the characters and the narrative causality makes *The Ring* more rational and expository than the original, and consequently the film allows the audience to identify with the characters and their predicament rather than *Ringu*'s identification through the shared knowledge of topography.[11] *Ringu*, for its part, presumes a level of regional sophistication from its audience, an understanding of the spatial and temporal logic underlying the film's schemata, and the time and the distance that the characters have to travel in their attempt to ward off Sadako's curse. Still, *Ringu*'s appeal to international audiences rests on the realism of its depiction of locales, images that resonate with a sense of Japan as a repository of the "antiquated" and the "mysterious." The independent distributor Rob Straight, for instance, points out that the attraction of Asian horror films is their well-received original stories and culturally inflected images. "Many of the films that we've handled . . . are terrifying in a cerebral kind of way. Asian cultures provide supporting mythologies of spirits and demons that are new to us and that make the terror feel more rooted, less arbitrary. They are not the usual kind of slash-and-cut horror films, and I think people were ready for a change."[12]

Despite the transformation of locale, *The Ring* accurately follows the original's use of technology as a medium for the horrific.[13] The indispensable gadgets of urban life such as televisions, videos, cell phones, surveillance cameras, computers, and the Internet augment the anxious reality that J-horror films produce. Various J-horror films, including *Ringu* and the *Ju-on* series, play with the conceit of that technological fluency. A character often becomes the target of an evil spirit by a mistaken belief in his or her ability to read the texts emitted from electronic devices that unexpectedly become conduits of spirits. *Ringu*'s sense of the horrific derives from the idea that a curse is disseminated through trans-media, such as Sadako crawling out of a television screen, a notice of death via telephone, and videotape functioning as a medium for transferring the curse to others. All of these cases have, as their basis in reality, the possibility of a destructive force spreading through media traffic like a computer "virus." Like an epidemic spiral, the more these everyday technologies are diffused, the more the horrific spreads along with them. *Ringu* carefully overlaps the frame of the television screen with that of the film itself when it displays the sequence of the cursed videotape. The gaze of the character in the film thus completely overlaps with the camera's gaze and then the audience's as well, and thus becomes the perfect identification between the victim and the film's spectators. The whole scheme is to create the illusion that the film itself is the medium to transmit the curse.

Likewise, Kurosawa Kiyoshi's *Pulse* (*Kairo,* 2000) deploys the Internet as a medium for transmitting a curse.[14] The film presents a succession of suicides among Internet users, and subverts the subject–object relation between human and computer by depicting the Internet images persisting in logging on even after the user shuts off the computer. Kurosawa broke through with *Cure* (1997), so he has often been described as a forerunner of J-horror. However, he has stated that his later film *Pulse* is the first and only work that he consciously associated with the J-horror boom.[15] Kurosawa points out that the boom of J-horror actually started in the early 1990s, with so-called "original video" (straight-to-video) films by filmmakers such as Konaka Chiaki and Tsuruta Norio. The distinct characteristic of these early J-horror films, according to Kurosawa, was the cheap, flat, home video aesthetic due to the fact that they were originally produced on videotape. Placing something extraordinary in those ordinary looking video images, such as the image of a dead person appearing in one's home videotape, was the charm of the contemporary Japanese horror films.[16] Their methods of making a horror film were distinctly different from both Hollywood's more expensive film productions and the pre-1970s Japanese classical horror films, which used elaborate studio sets and classical narratives, such as *Ghost Story of Yotsuya* (*Tokaido Yotsuya kaidan*, Nakagawa Nobuo, 1959) and *Kwaidan* (*Kaidan*, Kobayashi Masaki, 1964).[17] In this sense, *Pulse* shares the characteristic of J-horror's juxtaposition of the extraordinary with the ordinary, in the device of using the Internet and seeing the already dead person's images in it.

I have discussed how the new technologies have influenced J-horror films in terms of iconography, such as the Internet in *Pulse*. J-horror films also take advantage of digital editing to create new styles on the level of aesthetics and narrative structure. Many of the films use the rhetoric of new media, and in the dialectic relationship between film and new media, the genre takes on the role of a storyteller appealing to younger audiences who are already steeped in a variety of digital technologies including computer games, DVDs, and home theater systems. Moreover, they are used to the repeated viewings made available by these technologies. *Ju-on: The Grudge* uses the concept of "modularity," in which the narrative is constructed of multiple modules or narrative segments, each one titled with a victim's name. This structure simulates the "chapter" format of the DVD, which is typically used to cue an exact sequence, either for a repeat viewing or to watch the text intermittently. The majority of home theater viewers tend toward an interrupted pattern of spectatorship rather than watching a film straight through as in a movie theater. As Timothy Corrigan puts it, watching movies at home becomes "a combination of . . . visual 'grazing' and domestic 'cocooning.' "[18] The fragmented format of the film *Ju-on: The Grudge* is perfectly suited to this type of spectatorship, one predicated on the need for immediate satisfaction, fulfilled by the placement of a horrific moment within each short segment. This structure was eliminated in the Hollywood remake *The Grudge*, a fact that reveals the shift of the targeted audience from the DVD home viewers to audiences in a movie theater.

The director Shimizu Takashi is especially keen to create horror films using the rhetoric of new media. Shimizu's aforementioned film *Marebito* — digitally shot, edited, and distributed — is one of the best examples that bares the influence of new media rhetoric in its narrative structure and aesthetics, and takes advantage of the spatializing properties of digital editing (see Figure 1.1). *Marebito*'s non-linear narrative appears as the result of digital editing, and the film even simulates "digital error," a range of techniques that use the disrupted flow of image or sound, popular among digital video artists. The film was originally a straight-to-DVD, having been released theatrically only in New York and Los Angeles in late 2005. The narrative concerns a freelance video cameraman (Tsukamoto Shin'ya) working for television news programs who is obsessed with finding the most dreadful horror one can possibly see. He engages with the world largely through a video camera, and the boundary between the reality in his life and the reality captured by his camera is increasingly blurred. One day, he discovers an entrance to the underground, where he encounters mysterious creatures called "Deros" (detrimental robots). He takes a female Deros (Miyashita Tomomi) back home and confines it like a pet (see Figure 1.2).

Figure 1.1   The DVD cover image for *Marebito* (Shimizu Takashi, 2004)
(Source: Eurospace)

Figure 1.2 The freelance video cameraman (Tsukamoto Shin'ya) and the captured female Deros (Miyashita Tomomi) (Source: Eurospace)

As in recent science fiction films with CGI such as *The Matrix* (Andy and Larry Wachowski, 1999) and *eXistenZ* (David Cronenberg, 1999), *Marebito* deploys double layers in its narrative: a real world and an underworld. The doubling of spatial layers is deepened by a matching sense of the protagonist's double selves, one governed by his sane cognition and the other by emerging paranoia. The film deviates from a linear narrative development, using instead fragmented time and space to develop the complex layers. Time skips back and forth, following the oscillation of his mental state. The sequence of a seemingly disturbed woman pursuing him is repeated; only later is she revealed to be his ex-wife. The "rhizomatic" narrative — the multiple and non-hierarchical collection of narrative segments — represents narrative expansion within a temporal and spatial mesh. The film's combination of stratified and nonlinear narrative strands can be seen as the product of its dependence on digital editing, which allows more spatial extension than is typical of analog editing. Laura U. Marks describes such digital editing as an "open form," and notes that the advantage of digital editing is "to multiply the opportunities for flashbacks, parallel storylines, and other rhizomatic narrative techniques, producing a story that is so dense it expands into space as much as it moves forward in time. Experimental video remains the pioneer of the digital open form, as it is more free of narrative cinema's will to linearity."[19]

The film also mimics "digital errors," the now familiar innovations of electronic musicians and video artists. They "intentionally mess with the hardware: turning the computer on and off, or plugging the 'audio out' into the 'video in,' liberating the electrons to create random effects,"[20] and they try to subvert or challenge already existing music or images with techniques such as "stutter," repeating the same sound or image as if it is caused by a technical mistake, and "breakdown," shutting down the sound or image abruptly. In the film *Marebito*, the latter technique is used for the sequence called the twelve-seconds' mystery. The protagonist monitors the Deros with two surveillance cameras when he is out, and on returning home he finds that the Deros is near death. He then rewinds the surveillance tapes to find out what happened to it. However, once both tapes reach the same point, they inexplicably show only blank screens. Twelve seconds later, the monitoring images come back, and there is the Deros in convulsions. This breakdown of images works by extending the protagonist's inner state to the audience, blurring the boundary between reality and the video world and threatening him/us with the nightmarish proposition that there is no reality when it is not recorded. What *Marebito* accomplishes in near poetic symmetry of narrative and form is an exploration of the human tendency to apprehend reality through the prosthetic of technology. As our dependence on technology increases and what passes for reality consists of mediated images, there is a corresponding loss of subjectivity, an inability to grasp "the real." The film's digital rhetoric effectively simulates the prosthetic connection between a subject and a camera, a viewer and a screen, the now privatized scale of experience that is characteristic of digital and computer technology.

A surveillance camera or its aesthetic is often used in works that are digitally shot, whether they are films or video art. *Timecode* (Mike Figgis, 2000) deploys four screens, continuously and simultaneously shot by four digital cameras. *Dead End Job* (Ryan Stec, 2003) uses the actual images from surveillance cameras and edits them into a hallucinatory collage. The device allows for an exploration of real-time recording, albeit to different effect than J-horror. A significant number of J-horror films use surveillance camera images to create a moment of shock through the intrusion of something extraordinary within the banality of the ordinary. Shimizu's *Ju-on: The Grudge* has a sequence of a ghost appearing in a surveillance monitor, where the film skillfully uses continuous short cuts and slowly leads the spectator's point of view to the full size of the monitor image. The "chapter's" victim Hitomi (Ito Misaki) witnesses, first, the image of an office hallway, partially distorted with static interference appearing on the screen; then, a security guard is gradually enveloped by the ghost's shadow. After the cutback to Hitomi's reaction (she freaks out and runs away), the last shot in the monitor displays the usual image of the same hallway, only now the guard has disappeared. The film cleverly reduces the visual information in the sequence; first, reducing its color to black and white, which *Ringu* also used for the cursed videotape, and, second, lowering the visual resolution by blowing up the image of a small surveillance television monitor onto the full screen. The film undermines our preconception that the image of a surveillance camera is objective reality, and, as the director Kurosawa pointed out, it creates J-horror's idiosyncratic moment, in which the ghost's extraordinary figure appears (through CGI in this case) in the mundane space of the monitor.[21] Moreover, the principle of reduction in order to create an eye-catching image is strongly tied with the use of digital cameras, with which anyone can take a well-lit, focused image, and even with synchronous sound; thus, to create a less distinct image, one needs to find a way to *reduce* what the camera captures. Digital shooting represents an aesthetic regime of reduction that is markedly different from conventional filmmaking, in which one needs to *add* the necessary elements, such as by enhanced lighting and sound, in order to grant the image a degree of verisimilitude.[22]

As a result of using digital video cameras and computer editing, the contemporary Japanese horror films have a "new" look. It is certainly not only in the case of horror, as one can also see this stylistic transformation in other genre films, such as the comedies *Yaji and Kita: The Midnight Pilgrims* (*Mayonaka no Yaji-san Kita-san,* Kudo Kankuro, 2005) and *Takeshis'* (Kitano Takeshi, 2005), and the drama *Distance* (Kore'eda Hirokazu, 2001). Yet only J-horror has managed broad commercial success with global audiences through the alternative distribution of DVD, rather than depending on international theatrical release. Both Kore'eda and Kitano, on the one hand, brought their films to the Cannes Film Festival, and tried to extend their distribution to international markets. Kudo's comedy, on the other hand, was only targeted at the domestic box office by following the industrial commonplace that comedy does not cross cultural boundaries well. It bears repeating that the boom of J-horror occurred alongside the cultural contingency of independent filmmakers' affinity with digital technology. Moreover, J-horror has been especially successful in tapping the aesthetic of new media, in particular, the digital regime of fragmentary narrative, highlighted attention to the disrupted electronic image, privatized spectatorship, and aesthetic reduction. J-horror's appeal to global audiences is due to both this "new" look and how the filmic content is packaged and distributed, as I will outline in the following section.

DVD and the New Paradigms of Distribution and Consumption

J-horror's emergence parallels the rise of the DVD market in Japan. The timing of its appearance was fortuitous, since the genre had both a sufficient mass of existing narrative content in novels, *manga* comics, and television programs, and speed in generating new content, whether shot on film or video, to meet the demand of the growing DVD market. Indeed, one difficulty in discussing J-horror is due to the genre's symbiotic relation with the new digital technology, which leads the film genre into a tangle of cross-media traffic. Simply put, the centrality of film as the primary medium for production, distribution, and consumption has shifted with the emerging predominance of DVD. Consequently, a discussion of J-horror must be placed within this transitional stage of cross-media consumption. Shimizu Takashi, for example, has serialized his original video *Ju-on* (1999), in a number of films and videos, as well as Japanese and Hollywood feature film versions. Shimizu has already directed six *Ju-on* videos/films: *Ju-on* (video), *Ju-on 2* (video, 2000), *Ju-on: The Grudge* (film), *Ju-on: The Grudge 2* (film), *The Grudge* (film), and *The Grudge 2* (film, 2006). The seventh work *Ju-on: The Grudge 3* is scheduled to be produced, though Shimizu might not be the director.[23] The multiple versions of *Ju-on,* whether originally video or film, are available as separate texts in the DVD format. J-horror's affinity with the extra-filmic products of DVD (and television programming for the domestic Japanese audience), has, indeed, fueled the J-horror boom both inside and outside Japan. In other words, the genre is constructed of a number of media products, only one of which is in the traditional form of theatrically released feature film.

The profusion of horror omnibuses is the best example of J-horror's compatibility with new media, especially DVD. They often circulate in the DVD market without depending on the theatrical release at all, and they are either re-edited from already existing television programs or produced straight-to-DVD. The DVD, *Dark Tales of Japan* (*Nihon no kowai yoru,* Nakamura Yoshihiro et al., 2004), for instance, is an omnibus of five television programs, which were originally broadcast in September 2004. Shimizu Takashi directed one of the five episodes, "Kinpatsu kaidan/Blonde Kwaidan," and in the narrative he mockingly intertextualized Hollywood's rush for adaptation of J-horror films, including his own *The Grudge.* These omnibuses function as a system for creating and sustaining the J-horror boom in three principal ways: (1) relatively young and inexperienced filmmakers can start making a short film as practical directorial training; (2) horror films on DVD find alternative distribution without the expense of theatrical release marketing; (3) it facilitates cross-media, intertextual references to contemporary popular cultures. Distribution only on DVD makes economic sense, especially given the contemporary dearth of theatrical venues that has caused the shelving of many unreleased films. As the film producer Kuroi Kazuo states "although the mass media has been fussing by saying that the Renaissance of Japanese cinema has come, there are about one hundred films still unreleased and put up on the shelf. . . . There are a limited number of screens, and too many films."[24]

In terms of the third aspect, the practice of referencing or even adapting from other media such as comics, television programs, and novels, secures an already existing audience for both films and DVD. The omnibus format in the horror genre has indeed a long history as we can see in various examples. *Three Tales of Terror* (Jacob Fleck et al., 1912, Austria/Hungary) has three episodes directed by Jacob Fleck, Luise Fleck, and Claudius Velée; *Tales from the Crypt* (Freddie Francis, 1972, UK/US) is based on the same-titled comic book series, and the film has the omnibus format of five people, trapped in a crypt and shown their futures. *Two Evil Eyes* (*Due occhi diabolici,* Dario Argento and George A. Romero, 1990, Italy/U.S.) is composed of two horror segments based on Edgar Allan Poe stories "The Facts about Mr. Valdeman," directed by Romero, and "The Black Cat," directed by Argento. As evinced by the omnibus format, the horror film genre, in general, has developed under the influence of short stories or comic book segments. This format is even more suitable for the DVD medium since its chapter structure allows one to watch an individual segment or skip to another episode. In the case of J-horror, one of the most significant intertextual references for those omnibus DVDs is *manga* comics, as illustrated by the horror omnibuses *Hino Hideji's Mystery Theater DVD-Box* (*Hino Hideji kaiki gekijo DVD-Box,* Shiraishi Koji et al., 2005) and *Umezu Kazuo's Horror Theater* (*Umezu Kazuo kyofu gekijo,* Kurosawa Kiyoshi et al., 2005). The Umezu omnibus includes six shorts, all based on the comic artist Umezu Kazuo's horror *manga* comics. While a few of those films had limited theatrical release in Tokyo (Shibuya CinemaVera in June 2006) or at film festivals (Fukuoka Hero Festival, November 2006; Sapporo Film Festival, November 2006), the series was packaged for the DVD market. The *Tomie* series (Oikawa Ataru et al., 1999–2005) is also based on the *manga* comics of the same title by the artist Ito Junji. This series has a television version as well, which is repackaged on DVD in the form of an omnibus, titled *Tomie: Another Face* (Inomata Toshiro, 1999). The original comic's narrative device for serializing a story with the main character Tomie (Nagai Runa) as a clone, having an ability to regenerate her body even after her murder, is not just timely as a topic, but also works for extending the series.

From the industrial point of view, the central force enabling J-horror's entry to the world market has been its integration with the DVD format. The rise of new media, DVD in particular, has altered the trajectory of cultural flow worldwide toward a decentralized model of multiplied venues that are less beholden to the theatrical screen. The concept of "global cinema" has been changing along with the distribution of cinematic content in multimedia formats. Fewer regions like India or the U.S., where the film industries are still considered thriving businesses, can manage to sustain the hierarchical notion that theater screening is the center of cinema circulation. Even in the U.S., the state of cinema has been gradually changing with the improvement of the home theater as the steep curve tracking the numbers of DVD players indicates. As Barbara Klinger notes, "[r]ising from a 2 percent to a 30 percent penetration of U.S. homes from 1999 to 2002, DVD players have inspired owners to upgrade their entertainment equipment so that the superiority of DVD picture and sound can be fully realized."[25] Film studies itself is still struggling to assimilate the fact that film is no longer simply represented by movies in theaters. David Bordwell writes that "a truly global cinema is one that claims significant space on theater screens throughout developed and developing countries. . . . The only global cinema comes from America. Blockbusters like *Independence Day* (Roland Emmerich, 1996) and *Titanic* (James Cameron, 1997) are international media events. . . . The Hollywood of the East is Hollywood."[26] While the Hollywood blockbuster might still command such attention, it should be emphasized that the examples Bordwell cites here are films produced when DVD had only recently entered the market. Moreover, since the mid-1980s, more people were watching Hollywood films at home than in theaters.[27] *Titanic*'s gross for rentals in the U.S. ($324,425,520) is much higher than its box office total ($128, 099, 826) as of December 1998.[28]

Japanese Cinema in the Global Marketplace

Until the advent of J-horror, Japanese cinema has never been a "global cinema" except for *anime* (Japanese animation) and some *auteur* films circulated via various international film festivals. J-horror's border traffic represents a significant departure from the cinema's long-standing failure in foreign markets. The history of Japanese exported film (*yushutsu eiga*) has largely been a series of misfires which, despite an often-favorable critical reception, failed to reach wide theatrical release and box office profits. Outside of the occasional art-house film, there have been few attempts to export Japanese cinema in a commercially viable way, much less create a global cinema. The influence of Japanese popular culture has, instead, largely been in the commodities targeted at children, such as television animations and video games. "Japanese 'cool' is traveling popularly and profitably around the world and insinuating

itself into the everyday lives and fantasy desires of postindustrial kids from
Taiwan and Australia to Hong Kong and France."[29] The historian William
Tsutsui agrees:

> Japanese popular culture exports have had a profound influence in
> America (and indeed, throughout the world) in the decades since World
> War II. From Godzilla in the 1950s through Astro Boy in the 1960s,
> Speed Racer in the 1970s, and the more recent phenomena of the
> Mighty Morphin Power Rangers, Hello Kitty, Nintendo, and Pokemon,
> creations of the Japanese imagination have been high profile and big
> business in the United States.[30]

As Tsutsui's examples indicate, Japanese cultural exports to the U.S. have
specifically flourished in the categories of monster and animation products,
but seldom in the cinema. However, there were a few periods when the
Japanese film industry tried to intensively promote their films abroad even
before the Second World War.

The Japanese cinema was, arguably, first introduced in the U.S. in 1904,
when the producer Kawaura Ken'ichi screened the newsreels from the Japan-
Russia War at the exposition in St. Louis, Missouri.[31] Later, a number of
bunka eiga (cultural films)[32] were shown at the New York Exposition, and
most of the films served to introduce Japan to foreign audiences as indicated
by such titles as *Nara and Kyoto* (*Nara to Kyoto*, 1933), *Festivals in Japan* (*Nihon
no matsuri*, 1934), *Japan in Four Seasons* (*Shiki no Nihon*, 1933), and *Glimpses
of Japan* (*Nihon bekken*, 1936), all produced by the Japanese International
Tourist Bureau.[33] Although the director Murata Minoru's attempt to promote
his film *The Street Magician* (*Machi no tejinashi*, 1925) in Europe failed in 1925,
another director, Kinugasa Teinosuke, succeeded in marketing his film
Shadows of the Yoshiwara (*Jujiro*, 1928) in Germany. The well-known producer
Kawakita Nagamasa made two multinational production films *The New Earth*
(*Atarashiki tsuchi*, Arnold Fanck and Itami Mansaku, 1937, Japan/Germany)
and *The Road to the Eastern Peace* (*Toyo heiwa no michi*, Suzuki Shigeyoshi,
1938). Naruse Mikio's film *Kimiko* (*Tsuma yo bara no yo ni*, 1935) was shown
in the U.S. and harshly reviewed by the *New York Times* in 1937.[34] The
breakthrough of Kurosawa Akira's *Rashomon* (1950), which won an award
at the Venice Film Festival in 1951, opened the way for many Japanese films,
especially "art films," to be accepted at various international film festivals and,
hence, seen by potential foreign buyers.

One might argue that the overall resistance within the Japanese film
industry to produce more exportable commercial products is based on an

intrinsic condition of Japanese cinema's coexistence with Hollywood: only those Japanese films that were distinguished by culturally specific genres could compete with the dominant Hollywood films in the Japanese market, and due to the cultural specificity of these films the industry assumed that they were unsuitable for export. J-horror, exemplary of Japanese genre cinema, would change those assumptions. Thanks to DVD distribution, it managed to traverse the historical boundaries that shaped Japanese cinema as a fundamentally domestic product. J-horror, thus, followed the model of Japanese *anime* videotapes of the 1980s.

Since the 1980s, *anime* crossed the boundaries between Japanese and global markets due to its capacity for modification on levels of both text and media. It is easily redubbed and reedited to make it more universal, and it was highly mobile in the form of videotape. As Tsutsui's recollection indicates, the animations *Astro Boy* (*Tetsuwan Atom,* Fuji Television, Tezuka Osamu et al., 1963–66) in the 1960s, *Speed Racer* (*Mahha go go go,* Television Tokyo, Yoshida Tatsuo et al., 1967–68) in the late 1960s, and *Pokémon* (*Poketto monsta,* Television Tokyo, Yuyama Kunihiko et al., 1997) in the 1990s, found success abroad in dubbed and reedited versions on television worldwide, and it is likely that the majority of the viewers did not even recognize that those animations were from Japan. *Anime*, at the same time, has characteristics that are culturally specific, due to its jerky movement, typical of limited animation techniques. Still it has managed to reach audiences of varying age, gender, and culture, primarily through its multitude of texts, subject diversity, and variations in quality.

Similarly J-horror's assimilation with new digital technology enabled it to cross market boundaries, despite its culturally specific images, such as a ghost with a white painted body theatrically stylized like a *Butoh* dance performer and a vengeful woman figure with long black hair. Such cultural specificities are, on the one hand, generally diminished in Hollywood remakes, reflecting the calculations of marketing to a generic worldwide audience, and on the other hand, they are highlighted in the DVD packaging of J-horror films that aims at a cult fan demographic with an appetite for the culturally authentic and macabre violence. Both *anime* and J-horror demonstrate a formidable capacity for variegated production targeted toward diverse consumers with products that range from high to low quality. One can, for instance, find 1,000 *anime* DVDs and more than 350 J-horror DVDs by using combinations of the key words "animation" and "Japan," and "horror" and "Japan," at one of the most popular Asian film Internet sites, HKFlix.com.[35]

DVD is inextricable from the enriched flow of cinematic commodities away from the Hollywood-centered film distribution model to more region-oriented models. Worldwide, DVD has extended the film industry's market models beyond the theatrical release to address diverse, private, and home-based reception patterns. The excessive price of going to a movie in Japan (approximately US$15 per adult, or ¥1,800) and the industrial strategy for marketing certain B genre films solely in DVD formats have spurred the tendency to purchase films on DVD. Its high information capacity with multiple languages in dubbing and subtitling has also expanded the marketing potential of J-horror across national boundaries. The worldwide success of J-horror is illustrative of how digital media have extended cinema's reach as a global commodity through both official and unofficial channels, such as downloading films from the Internet, file sharing, and piracy. Indeed, the regional boom of the genre has been largely a matter of unplanned cultural contingencies, the intersection of digital media and mobile culture.

In the case of *Ringu*, for instance, the executive producer Hara Masato attributes the unexpected success of the series to the technological fluency of schoolgirl culture. Originally, the production side planned to market *Ringu* as a "date film," but it turned out that many female high school students came to see the film and the positive word-of-mouth generated by their cell phone text messaging contributed to the success of the series. *Ringu*'s gross sales were more than ten million U.S. dollars, and *Ringu 2* in the following year doubled its sales.[36] The income is, of course, not only from theatrical release, but also includes video and DVD sales. *Ringu*'s release was especially timely, since it came right after DVD was legally licensed in Japan in 1996, and the promotion of both DVD software and hardware encouraged the purchase of films. The same strategy was used in the U.S. later, and *The Ring* DVD sold more than two million copies in the first twenty-four hours of video release.[37]

The global circulation of J-horror has indeed depended on the less controlled cultural contingencies linked to the rise of digital networking and film piracy concurrent with the popularization of DVD since the late 1990s. As Shujen Wang notes, "[t]he rapidly changing spatiotemporal dynamics and configurations afforded by these new [digital] technologies have radically changed the nature of 'property' and market, the balance of power, and the relations and means of production, distribution, and reception/consumption,"[38] J-horror, in its upending of the existing hierarchy of film distribution, is one of the best examples of this potential of new digital technologies. Global audiences, who are more equipped technologically than ever before and better informed about new trends in software and films through instantaneous Web-casting, are no longer content to wait for the local release of films when they can purchase the film's DVD on the Internet or download it from a sharing file. While safeguards such as region codes exist to prevent the cross-national flow of DVD from one region to another, multi-region DVD players are cheap and widely available. An audience segment of high techno-literates, then, creates a perfect market for such pirated products. Not only that, they directly promote local digital products, such as B-movie films like J-horror through their own Weblogs. The phenomenon of such alternative distribution subverts the long-standing economic calculations of major studios and distributors, especially since it has renewed interest in genre films, which historically were not often exported to "central" markets, such as the United States.

Digital networking is much faster and more flexible when compared with the containment strategies of law enforcement or its legitimate counterparts (such as Hollywood or other national film industries). J-horror's regional boom is largely a matter of the contingencies of DVD distribution in Asia, a model that is functionally different from Hollywood's traditional scheduling of its film release dates. Such an exercise of global control has never been tenable for regional or national cinemas, but digital networking has enabled these cinemas to de-center the pattern of cultural globalization vis-à-vis Hollywood. The newly emerging geography of digital cinema thrives on its center-less quality, a dynamic that also allows for the uncontrolled circulation of its products. In the case of *Ringu*, the film was released in Japan on January 31, 1998. Intriguingly, in South Korea, the local Korean film production company AFDF produced an adaptation of the film titled *The Ring Virus* (Kim Dong-bin, 1999) and released it on June 12, 1999 — six months before the original Japanese film was released in South Korea on December 11, 1999. The Japanese DVD was, of course, available on the Internet in June 1998; moreover, the film had already been released in other East Asian markets, such as Hong Kong, in April 1999. Such accelerated circulation of film (as content, whatever its form), caused by the ubiquitous digital technology, has started to reshape the flow of culture and the balance of power in different media. As Wang points out in the case of Ang Lee's *Crouching Tiger, Hidden Dragon* (*Wo hu cang long,* 2000), this circulation reverses the usual directional flow of commodities from Hollywood to global regions: "This Hong Kong-Taiwan-China coproduction was released in Asia five months before its U.S. premiere . . . [P]irated video copies of the film were circulating in the U.S. market long before the film's formal U.S. release in December 2000."[39] In another case of reverse cultural flow, not only at the "illegitimate" level, but also as an act of "legitimate" global acceptance, J-horror's circulation gave rise to the subsequent horror boom in Asia and, ultimately, accelerated the export of both adaptations and new filmmakers to Hollywood.

J-horror is well suited for the circumstances of industrial transition and the new economics of small screen movie viewing. The genre targets younger audiences, who would rather rent or purchase DVDs than pay exorbitant ticket prices at movie theaters in Japan. The tactics of emphasizing DVD sales also suits the current circumstances of the Japanese film industry, in which the "digital cinema" has not grown as fast as DVD's popularization. Digital cinema refers to the use of digital technology to distribute and project films. Movies are distributed through hard drives, DVDs or satellite, and are projected using a digital projector instead of a conventional film projector.[40] In contrast with the rapid spread of DVD acceptance since the late 1990s, the Japanese film industry has been experiencing a difficult time digitalizing its distribution and projection systems. Computerizing the system and purchasing a digital projector for each theater is about four or five times more expensive than the traditional film projection system.[41] For the majority of movie theaters, investing in the digitalization technology guarantees neither an increase of audience nor revenues. Moreover, theater owners are hesitant to convert to digital until the format and regulation of the system is standardized. T-JOY, funded by Toei in 2000, is one of the few companies that accept digital cinema, but it has only fifteen entertainment complexes throughout Japan.[42]

Critical Reception and the Loss of Filmic Context

J-horror's proclivity for crossing borders of media and patterns of reception has made the genre fertile ground for airing problems in film studies' assimilation of the transitions occurring in cinema. The genre represents what I see as the dual potentialities of new media: on the one hand, a greater access to a multiplicity of texts, and on the other, the power of digitalization to erase historical context. Because of the genre's affinity with the DVD format, J-horror has extended its reach through an enormous amount of works and broadened its parameters. This reconstruction of the J-horror genre as a pragmatic category in the DVD market has led to a shuffling of media (i.e. the erasure of content-origin as films, the production of straight-to-video films, and the formatting of television programs into DVD) and history (i.e. repackaging non-horror films of the 1960s as precursors to J-horror). The materiality of the genre, whether it is film or DVD, now needs to be specified if one is to analyze the genre in the context of film history. The identification with each medium has become crucial to the analysis of a text since the antiquated hierarchy among media — that film is the ultimate product and other post-filmic products are simply spin-offs — has been subverted, especially in the case of J-horror.

For instance, the anthology *Japanese Horror Cinema*, edited by Jay McRoy, displays a glaring need for clarification on horror cinema's materiality. As the anthology's "filmography" reveals, what the book considers as film is actually DVD, and this substitution causes the reconfiguration of the horror genre itself. Although the act of analyzing a film in different formats has been indispensable to film scholars since the 1980s, the critical problem here is that in blurring the distinction between those media, the contributors to the anthology take an expansive view of what constitutes Japanese horror cinema, far beyond the historic context of the genre. A number of films that are dealt with in the anthology, such as *Ugetsu* (*Ugetsu monogatari*, Mizoguchi Kenji, 1953), *Throne of Blood* (*Kumonosujo*, Kurosawa Akira, 1957), *Blind Beast* (*Moju*, Masumura Yasuzo, 1969), *In the Realm of the Senses* (*Ai no korida*, Oshima Nagisa, 1976), *Tetsuo, the Iron Man* (*Tetsuo*, Tsukamoto Shin'ya, 1989), *Freeze Me* (Ishii Takashi, 2000), and *Battle Royale* (Fukasaku Kinji, 2000), were never associated with the horror genre at all with reference to either the films' production or distribution in Japan. They were distributed and discussed within the regimes of the *auteur* (Mizoguchi and Kurosawa) or other genres, such as *jidaigeki eiga* (period film) and *bungei-mono* (literary adaptation) in the case of *Blind Beast*, the porno film in the case of *In the Realm of the Senses*, the cyberpunk film in the case of *Tetsuo*, and the psycho thriller in the case of *Freeze Me*. Or simply, they have been viewed as topical films in connection with bestselling novels as in the case of *Battle Royale*. Peter Hutchings is right about the difficulty of defining horror when he notes, "[i]f one looks at the way that film critics and film historians have written about horror, a certain imprecision becomes apparent regarding how the genre is actually constituted."[43] I do not think, however, that the issue is solely a matter of genre categorization in the case of *Japanese Horror Cinema*. Rather, it is the failure to acknowledge the connections among a text, its historical context, and the discursive subject. Such connections are ever more crucial in my view, given that new media have the tendency to encompass and reposition the old media and the past as well.

If one visits any Internet site that promotes and distributes Japanese horror films, he or she will find that the films mentioned above are actually categorized as "horror." At HKFlix.com, for example, *Battle Royale* is included in both the "horror" and "thriller" genres, and other keywords are "action," "children," "teen[-pic]."[44] DVD distributors and countless Internet retailers categorize their products by following their own marketplace imperatives. The difference between film and DVD genre categories is also reflected by the shift of target audience/consumer from regional movie theater audiences to global DVD consumers. In the case of J-horror, the dominance of DVD in the marketplace has produced a new genre system in post-filmic distributions. It is a system with more generic terms, but at the same time it resembles the genre categories of Hollywood cinema. Amidst this process, local generic terms such as *jidaigeki eiga* have been erased. Rick Altman indicates that "the technological and representational explosion of recent years only reinforces earlier patterns of alienation and lost presence. . . . While genres are certainly not as simple as most people think they are, many a placebo has provided a successful cure. Because people see safety in the apparent stability of genre, they find genre films useful as signs of successful constellated community communication."[45]

This shifting of genres between film and DVD highlights the difficulty of connecting a filmic text with its historical cultural context. With the help of digital technology, visual content is released not only in multiple formats but also with multiple layers of ownership rights. The content is often manipulated (from black and white to color, reedited as a director's edition, and so on) and repackaged. Recently, the director Shindo Kaneto's film *Onibaba* (*Onibaba'a,* 1964) was released on DVD in region one (the U.S. and Canada) on March 16, 2004. Although Criterion, one of the most representative DVD distributors for canonical classic films, makes no connection between "horror" and its newly packaged *Onibaba,* one finds that "horror" has gradually sneaked into the marketing of the DVD. Amazon. com's editorial review, for instance, begins its description of the DVD with: "[A] curse hangs over Kaneto Shindo's primal Japanese classic like a looming storm cloud, but the supernatural has got nothing on the desperation and savagery of the human animal trying to survive the *horrors* of war." IMDb (Internet Movie Database) categorizes the film as "Drama/Horror" and includes a link to Amazon.com DVD shopping.[46]

Once analyses of the film appear in academic discourses in the U.S., it is, without any hesitation, categorized as horror, as we see in Jyotsna Kapur's essay "The Return of History as Horror: *Onibaba* and the Atomic Bomb," and Adam Lowenstein's chapter "Unmasking Hiroshima: Demons, Human Beings, and Shindo Kaneto's *Onibaba,*" in his book *Shocking Representation: Historical Trauma, National Cinema, and the Modern Horror Film.*[47] Kapur "focuses on haunting histories and regional gothics" and reveals that "the traditional Japanese horror film . . . is a radical reworking of this genre into a political allegory of survival in conditions of scarcity amidst class antagonism ruled by war."[48] Lowenstein "examines Shindo's horror film *Onibaba* as a means of refiguring how cinematic representations of Hiroshima are legislated theoretically, with particular attention to the political issues of victim consciousness, war responsibility, and the construction of gendered models of Japanese national identity."[49]

It has been a while since Frederic Jameson's allegorical reading on "Third World Literature" was criticized due to its lack of specificity and its ahistorical tendencies.[50] I have no interest in directing the same criticism toward these scholars' allegorical approach to Japanese cinema, but I must indicate the gap between the regional, journalistic discourses, which followed the film's release in 1964 and their post-DVD academic discourses. None of the advertisements, film reviews, and interviews at that time connected the film with the horror genre. The generic categories that these regional discourses associated with the film were either *minwa-mono* (folktale genre) or *dokuritsu puro eiga* (independent film).[51] When *Onibaba* was released on November 21, 1964, an advertisement for the film highlighted three aspects of the film: it was directed by Shindo Kaneto, who was already well known as a realist filmmaker; it was submitted to *geijutsusai* (Arts Festival), a wide-ranging annual festival (including theater, film, television programs, music, dance, performance, etc.) sponsored by the government since 1946; it was distributed nationwide by Toho, one of the country's major film companies.[52] *Onibaba* was recognized as one of the new independent films in the mid-1960s.[53]

The year 1964 was actually the turning point for both independent filmmakers and major studios. As the film industry started to see declines in both revenue and number of viewers in the early 1960s, the major studios dropped their policy of excluding independent films from their distribution channels in order to reduce production costs and increase profits from their distribution. *Onibaba* was one of three independent films in that year (the other two were *Woman in the Dunes* [*Suna no on'na,* Teshigahara Hiroshi, 1964] and *Kwaidan*) which were distributed by Toho and made large profits for the company. As a result, the regional discourses in both advertisements and film reviews naturally focused on *Onibaba*'s aspect as an independent film. Shindo himself commented on this: "It has become common knowledge that one cannot make a film if he/she leaves a major film studio. So the fact that I showed that one can still make a film outside of the major studios, is some sort of contribution of this film."[54]

Conclusion

The history of *Onibaba* and *Kwaidan* (its DVD was also released in October 2000 in the U.S.) has been reconfigured by their DVD release within the context of the recent horror boom. Similarly, as obscure films are revived through DVD, a greater access to film has occurred; or, put differently, the fact that the film medium has been subsumed within multimedia has multiplied the connections between texts and their histories. As Jan Simons indicates, "[m]ultimediality in itself, however, [is] neither unique nor new, and the novelty of new media mainly and most importantly consists of a repositioning and redefinition of old media." He continues, "[a] film's content can be redefined as 'information' that can be conceived of as a collection of data that can be organized in various ways, out of which a film's particular narrative is just one possible choice."[55] As a film is located as information within the digitalizing process, the notion of cinema — films shown in movie theaters — becomes only one particular interface to that information. The concept of film as an immutable, superior material may be preserved only in the specific nostalgic sense of "aura," as we now recognize in the sound of vinyl records.[56] Kapur's and Lowenstein's allegorical readings of *Onibaba* is, after all, results of their interfacing with the text, and while one may also view the film as a precursor of J-horror, neither view is supported by the film's historical context. Such connections only seem plausible once the film is wrenched from its historical materiality.

2

A Cinema of Girlhood: *Sonyeo* Sensibility and the Decorative Impulse in the Korean Horror Cinema

Jinhee Choi

Park Ki-hyeong's surprise hit *Whispering Corridors* (*Yeogo geodam*, 1998), a horror film set in a girls' high school, helped initiate the most recent horror cycle in the South Korean film industry. Highly successful at the box office, *Whispering Corridors* ranked third among domestically produced films for the year, following *Letter* (*Pyeonji*, Lee Jeong-kuk) and *A Promise* (*Yaksok*, Kim Yu-jin).[1] Three sequels have followed so far — *Memento Mori* (*Yeogo Geodam II*, Kim Tae-yong, Min Kyu-dong, 1999), *Wishing Stairs* (*Yeogo Geodam III: Yeowoo Gyedan*, Yun Jae-yeon, 2003) and *Voice* (*Yeogo Geodam IV: Moksori*, Choe Ik-hwan, 2005). The commercial success of the recent Korean horror cycle demonstrates the case of a niche marketing strategy adopted by the Korean film industry, as it continues a process of conglomeration that began in the late 1980s. More importantly, the attempts by the makers of these films to appeal to adolescents and portray their social circumstances not only bring to the fore the consequences of the Korean education system but also seemingly authorize a culture of adolescent sensibility.

This chapter attempts to examine the industrial, ideological, and aesthetic significance of a *sonyeo* (girls') sensibility to the Korean horror cycle of the late 1990s and early 2000s. How is the *sonyeo* sensibility that is represented in the Korean horror cycle culturally specific? What are some of the reasons that ghost stories are recited among teenagers in South Korea? How is such discourse encoded into the horror genre? How is adolescent female sensibility shaped and trampled by Korean institutions such as the family and the education system? How does the excessive decorative impulse, a symptom of the *sonyeo* sensibility, function to foreground the lack of, or change of, private space in the *Whispering Corridors* series and *A Tale of Two Sisters* (*Janghwa Hongryeon*, Kim Ji-woon, 2003)?

The emergence of the horror cycle in South Korea has not been an isolated phenomenon. The attention given to the horror genre and its revival in general occurred in tandem with a growing popularity in horror cinema within the region as well as across the globe. However, the cultural and aesthetic significance of this distinctly Korean horror cinema should be located within both a changing mediascape and the film policies that propelled the restructuring of the Korean cinema industry. The linked production-distribution quota in place since 1966 had been protecting the domestic film industry from the encroachment of foreign films. The Korean government limited the number of imports in any given year to one-third of the number of domestically produced films.[2] In 1986, an amendment to the Korean Motion Picture Laws removed this quota and allowed for the open import and direct distribution of films by the Hollywood majors. Relaxations on production and distribution regulations led to the emergence of new independent production companies. Korean conglomerates, interested in the growing video market, also took the opportunity to enter the motion picture business.[3] Although the business interest of these conglomerates proved short-lived initially due to the economic crisis in Asia during the mid-1990s, it ignited the urge to produce films that could actively compete with Hollywood cinema and other national cinemas in the domestic market. New production companies such as Shin Cine, Kang Woo-suk Film (now Cinema Service), and Myung Film (which merged with Kang Je-kyu Film to form MK Pictures), produced box office hits such as the romantic comedy *Marriage Story* (Kim Ui-seok, 1992), the buddy cop/gangster comedy *Two Cops* (*Tukabseu*, Kang Woo-suk, 1993) and the romantic melodrama *The Contact* (*Jeobsok*, Chang Yoon-hyun, 1997). After the first wave of conglomerates pulled out of the film business in the end of 1990s because of regional economic conditions, the second wave of conglomerates and venture capitalists returned to the Korean film industry in 1999 approximately.[4] With the aid of new financiers, consisting mostly of venture capitalists, the film industry has created the Korean blockbuster trend, which has boasted of box office draws comparable to Hollywood cinema within the Korean domestic market.

The rising dominance of conglomerates in the Korean film industry has led to a demand for commercially oriented filmmaking. Prior to the revival of horror, which was absent in the Korean film industry throughout the 1980s, comedy and melodrama had dominated the industry. Horror cinema, because of its relatively low production costs, offered a viable option for independent companies such as Cine 2000, the production house for the *Whispering Corridors* series. In an interview, Lee Chun-yeon, the production head of the company, explains that each installment of the series has been directed by a first-time director with casts of relatively unknown or new actresses.[5] *Whispering Corridors* cost only US $600,000 to make and completed its shooting with only 28 set-ups.[6] In so doing, Cine 2000 lowered its production costs and targeted its product to a younger generation audience.

The increasing number of multiplex theaters and the revival of midnight screenings have also contributed to the popularity of the horror genre. The first chain of multiplexes, CGV — a co-venture of Korean conglomerate CJ Entertainment, Hong Kong's Golden Harvest, and Australia's Village Roadshow — opened with an 11-screen theater in April 1998.[7] The success of CGV, along with Cine Plus, triggered the emergence of multiplexes, not only in Seoul, but nationwide as well. Between 1999 and 2000 alone, the number of movie screens rose by 42 percent, but the number of individual theaters actually dropped by 33 percent.[8] *Whispering Corridors* was released in May 1998 shortly after the multiplex boom started within the Korean film industry, securing eight of the eleven screens at CGV alone.[9]

The box office success of *Whispering Corridors*, along with *Soul Guardians* (*Toemarok*, Park Kwang-chun, 1998) and the horror comedy *The Quiet Family* (*Joyonghan gajok*, Kim Ji-woon, 1998), offered production companies an incentive to create sequels and gave rise to the subsequent horror cycles. *Memento Mori* (Kim Tae-yong, Min Kyu-dong, 1999), the second installment of the *Whispering Corridors* series, was applauded for showcasing a nuanced portrayal of character psychology with keen female sensitivity, although it proved merely a lukewarm box office draw.[10] *The Ring Virus* (Kim Dong-bin, 1999), the Korean remake of Japanese *Ringu* (1998) appeared in the summer of 1999, six months before the theatrical release of the Japanese original in Korea.[11] Until 2004, when the Korean film market completely abolished its longstanding regulation over Japanese imports, Korean film policies had limited the theatrical release of Japanese films to only those that had won awards at any of seventy or so international film festivals. Therefore, the showing of original Japanese *Ringu* was delayed until 1999, after the film had won the Golden Raven award at Brussels International Festival of Fantasy Film. The most successful horror film in the Korean domestic market in 1999, however, was *The Sixth Sense* (M. Night Shyamalan), which snatched the seventh seat at the domestic box office for the year.[12] After the critical attention given to horror films such as *Sorum* (Yun Jong-chan, 2001), as well as sporadic box office successes, such as the 2.6 million admissions of Ahn Byeong-ki's *Phone* (2002), an attempt to aesthetically elevate the horror genre was witnessed in Kim Ji-woon's *A Tale of Two Sisters* (2003). [13] Co-produced by Oh Ki-min and the production company B. O. M., *A Tale of Two Sisters* replaced the raw aesthetics of low-budget horror cinema with a carefully controlled, meticulous mise-en-scène. The film was welcomed by Korean audiences and it broke the all-time box office record for Korean horror cinema with 3 million admissions. [14]

The emergence of the horror cycle in South Korea may be both a consequence of globalization in the Korean film industry and a byproduct of the regionalization of screen culture. However, one of the specificities of Korean horror cinema can be found in its foregrounding of a *sonyeo* sensibility. This chapter attempts to delineate the *sonyeo* sensibility portrayed in the *Whispering Corridors* series and *A Tale of Two Sisters*. "Sensibility," I would argue, provides a concept alternative to "sexuality," on which many of the previous approaches to the horror genre have been based. As Rhona Berenstein and Harry Benshoff convincingly argue, monsters in both classical and post-classical Hollywood horror cinema cross boundaries of multiple categories — between human and non-human, male and female, heterosexual and queer, and hegemonic and marginal — thus encouraging a fluid spectatorship instead of pigeonholing one over the other. [15] The characterization of monstrous figures as exclusively one or the other within each pair would undermine the transgression — both ideological and sexual — embodied by them. Furthermore, an essentialist approach that examines a viewer's identification with monsters based on sexual affinities or shared gender traits would fall short of delineating the range and processes of the viewer's engagement with horror cinema overall. [16]

Although both Berenstein and Benshoff propose theories of fluid spectatorship — via concepts of "spectatorship-as-drag" and "queer sensibility" respectively — sexuality remains central to their framework. Benshoff, for instance, defines "gay sensibility" as "the sensibility of a man who recognizes his status as a sexual outsider, someone who acknowledges his difference from the heterosexualized hegemony, and uses that distanciation as a way to comment upon it." [17] Here sensibility is mainly construed as a self-reflexive, political stance toward one's own sexuality. In my view, sensibility is more of an inclusive term than sexuality or an attitude toward it. It encompasses both emotional predilections, psychological dispositions and behavioral tendencies. It is often conceived of as a collective trait associated with a particular demographic and/or subculture. Sensibility may be an innate disposition to a certain extent, but it can also be cultivated and sometimes exploited by a cultural industry. Production and marketing strategies are closely tied to capturing and appealing more to sensibility than to sexuality, as shown in the case of the Korean horror. A focus on sensibility, then, provides us with a way to analyze any links or disparities between production strategies within the industry and actual audience reception of their products. In addition, audiences can share a similar sensibility beyond a specific demographic group and push beyond cultural and national boundaries from which they initially originated. Fluid spectatorship, or "allo-identification" as Fran Martin puts it,[18] is what propels cultural exchanges across national, ethnic, racial and gender boundaries; an examination of shared sensibilities can therefore serve as a starting point for an understanding and appreciation of a subculture and of the audience's engagement with characters beyond gender and/or nation-bound identification.

Sensibility, Sexuality, and Monstrosity

Oh Ki-min, the producer of the first two installments of the *Whispering Corridors* series — *Whispering Corridors* and *Memento Mori* — and *A Tale of Two Sisters*, claims that he hopes to depict female adolescent psychology in the films that he produces: "neurosis, imperfection, vulnerability, and mystery."[19] Oh underscores the need to appeal to female adolescent sensitivity and sensibility in the horror genre, by reference to "sonyeo-jueui," a term coined by Oh himself. It literally means "girls" and "-ism" in Korean, and can be roughly translated as a "cinema of girlhood" — a cinema that targets female teenage audiences by dealing with problems that are pertinent to teenage girls and by evoking an overall mood rather than emotions. It has become a staple for the Korean horror genre, counterbalancing trends toward more male-oriented genres. If adolescent male protagonist-centered films, such as *Beat* (Kim Sung-su, 1997), *Friend* (*Chingu*, Kwak Kyeong-taek, 2001), and *Once Upon a Time in High School* (*Maljukgeori janhoksa*, Yu Ha, 2004), tend to underscore masculinity and portray the pursuit of and suffering from a distorted ego ideal, the films produced by Oh, including *Take Care of My Cat* (*Goyangireul butakhae*, Jeong Jae-eun, 2001), counterbalance such a trend by featuring female protagonists and disclosing the subtle psychology of these characters.

One of the peculiarities of *the Whispering Corridors* series is that these films are set in *all-girls* high schools. In the last decade, high school has provided a major setting for both Korean and Japanese cinema as well as TV drama series across genres: *Volcano High* (*Hwasango*, Kim Tae-gyun, 2001), *My Boss My Hero* (*Dusabu ilchae*, Yun Je-gyun, 2001), *Romance of Their Own* (*Neukdaeui yuhok*, Kim Tae-gyun, 2004), *Battle Royale* (Kinji Fukasaku, 2000), *All about Lily Chou Chou* (*Riri shushu no subete*, Iwai Shunji, 2001), and *Suicide Club* (*Jisatsu saakuru*, Sono Sion, 2002). The high school period might bear more weight in rigid societies like Japan and Korea, where social latitude and flexibility are still not fully granted. But one may speculate some of the reasons for selecting such locations for the Korean horror genre on both realistic and generic grounds. Students in Korea are encouraged by school officials to stay and study in school until late at night. Such a policy provides a prime location and time for the recitation of ghost stories. Within such ghost talk, the school becomes the site of the uncanny and dread, a place that both distances and draws students. *Memento Mori* begins with Hyo-shin's description of the previous six suicides committed in her school, and it is when students are about to leave the building after studying into the night that Hyo-shin's ghost locks the entire school, preventing both students and teachers from leaving. *Voice* (Choe Ik-hwan, 2005), the fourth installment of the series, begins with a scene showing students being dismissed at night.

In addition, co-education at the level of junior high and high school is less common than either all-boys or all-girls high schools. Beneath such gender segregation can still be found the Confucian ideology that distinctive social and gender norms need to be taught to boys and girls. On the wall of one classroom of *Whispering Corridors*, we see a portrait of Shinsaimdang (1504–1551), a historical figure who is widely taught in girls' schools as the emblem of ideal womanhood in Korea. Toward the end of the film, the camera cuts back to the portrait, this time covered with blood tears, shed by the ghost Jin-ju as she finally decides to leave the school. Such a scene may indicate that this rather outdated and vacuous cultural icon has lost its footing with contemporary Korean adolescents. Also palpable under the current education system is the attempt to suppress adolescent sexuality at the institutional level by prohibiting direct encounters between boys and girls in the learning environment. Teen courtship is allowed only outside the institution. In the *Whispering Corridors* series, sexuality is often replaced by exclusive friendships among the same sex, sometimes more explicitly imbued with homosexuality.

An all-girls high school would generically render a more natural setting than an all-boys high school for the adoption of the ghost story formula. Narrative conflicts set in boys' high schools are often resolved by recourse to physical violence, as seen in *Once Upon a Time in High School*. In a girls' high school, by contrast, students may be more likely to be forced to endure or internalize conflicts with their teachers and peers, rather than confronting them or resolving them in physical terms. In such an environment, the supernatural, fantastic elements of horror cinema can appeal to teenagers by providing symbolic solutions to teen problems and thus vicarious pleasures to teenage audiences. In *Whispering Corridors*, Ji-oh has to endure Mr Oh's sexual harassment as well as physical abuse. It is the ghost Jin-ju that murders him out of loyalty to Ji-oh after he beats Ji-oh over one of her paintings.

Both traditional and contemporary Korean horror films employ the ghost-revenge plot, but the latter departs from the former in terms of the motivation for the revenge. In the horror cinema of the 1960s and 1970s, a threat to heterosexual union or family drives the narrative, triggering female rivalry and consequent death: two or more women share an object of desire and one kills the other to take her place. The female protagonist often kills herself out of fear of being raped by a villain or is murdered when she is falsely accused of being an inadequate wife. The ghost of the female victim then, in revenge, haunts her nemesis. In *A Devilish Murder* (*Salinma*, Lee Yong-min 1965), the wife catches sight of her mother-in-law having an affair with a family physician. However, the mother-in-law and the wife's cousin attempt to frame the wife as being unfaithful. When the wife is drugged and about to be raped by a painter, she kills herself and takes revenge on both the mother-in-law and her cousin. A variation of this cycle can be found in the film in *The Public Cemetery under the Moon* (*Wolhaui gongdongmyoji*, Kwon Cheol-hwi, 1967), in which a dead mother haunts a stepmother in order to protect her child. The title character Wol-ha becomes a *gisaeng*, comparable to a certain extent to a geisha in Japan, in order to support her fiancé and her brother, who are both imprisoned. She marries her fiancé when he is released from jail. Wol-ha, however, gets accused of having an affair and is poisoned by her mother-in-law and the lustful nanny. As Wol-ha's son is also about to be murdered, the ghost of Wol-ha returns to protect her son.

In the *Whispering Corridors* series, on the other hand, what needs to be protected is not kinship, but friendship. A threat to friendship causes the ghosts to exercise their supernatural powers. In *Whispering Corridors*, Jin-ju has been killed in an accident, but she resents the fact that her friend Eun-young did not stand up for their friendship to the other girls of the school. The ghost kills Ms Park just as she is about to discover that the ghost of Jin-ju had been attending school under other names for nine years. Such a discovery would endanger Jin-ju's newly developed friendship with Ji-oh. In *Memento Mori*, Hyo-shin commits suicide when her friendship with Shi-eun comes to a dead end. *Wishing Stairs* (Yun Jae-yeon, 2003) portrays a friendship between Jin-seong and So-heui that later turns into a rivalry. So-heui suffers injuries to her legs in an accident, which ultimately causes her to commit a suicide. Her spirit haunts and punishes several characters including Jin-seong. A threatened friendship, again, becomes the reason for the ghost to murder Cho-ah in *Voice*. The *Whispering Corridors* series also violate the protective relationship of family, especially between parents and children. Although parents often remain off-screen in the first three installments, in the last installment, *Voice*, there is a surprise revelation in that Young-eon had hoped for the death of her mother, who has been ill and hospitalized for a long time.

One may find an explanation for such a shift in terms of changing family relationships in contemporary Korean society. Friendship may be seen as a form of displacement from heterosexual or homosexual union in that these relationships demand "exclusivity" from a partner. This friendship can only be shared by the two people involved, and thus is impossible to be extended to or replaced by another, as witnessed in the relationship between Shi-eun and Hyo-shin in *Memento Mori* or between So-heui and Jin-seong in *Wishing Stairs*. Such an exclusive relationship is portrayed as the key to enduring the hardships of the high school period, often depicted via metaphorical extremities — the life or death of a character. The sheer amount of time that students spend with their peers in high school and the pressures they face from their parents to enter prestigious colleges or succeed in future career make students value friendship over family. Exclusivity is further secured by communication methods inaccessible to others: Shi-eun and Hyo-shin in *Memento Mori* keep a secret diary between themselves and read each other's mind via telepathy, while Sun-min in *Voice* can hear the voice of her deceased friend Young-eon.

Situating the school as the prime location for plot development in the *Whispering Corridors* series has several narrative consequences. First, students are entirely removed from home, and the conventional divide between public and private space has broken down. Both the school and the home become sites of oppression and cause psychological burden. The "private" spaces for students in these films are still to be found within the public sphere, often merely in the places neglected by or hidden from school authorities: a piano, a basement, a storage room, a rooftop. Jin-ju and Ji-oh find their own space in an abandoned building believed to be haunted. Hyo-shin and Shi-eun hang out on the rooftop. But these "private" spaces are soon invaded or become a place of haunting, as both Hye-ju's basement art studio and Jin-seong's dorm room in *Wishing Stairs* are haunted by So-heui's ghost. *Voice* is the only film that shows a glimpse of characters' home, but Young-eon's crummy apartment is shown as an abandoned place rather than place of comfort and love.

Second, private space, or lack thereof, is replaced by and reduced to elements of the mise-en-scène, especially a character's decorative impulse, as manifest in her personal belongings. When Ji-oh has a glimpse of Jin-ju's diary, she finds it filled with girlie comic book characters — with big eyes and long curly hair — except the supposed portrait of Ji-oh. In *Memento Mori*, the pre-credit sequence is intercut between a scene of Hyo-shin writing and decorating her diary and a scene showing Hyo-shin and Shi-eun clad in their school uniforms and sinking in a swimming pool with their legs tied together. Hyo-shin's affection toward and obsession with Shi-eun is manifest in the excessive decoration of their exchange diary, while the imaginary swimming scene foreshadows the tragic ending to their relationship. As Min-ah traces the trajectory of the relationship between Hyo-shin and Shi-eun, Min-ah discovers the piano, the bottom of which is filled with presents and memorabilia of Shi-eun. The drawings in Hye-ju's diary of *Wishing Stairs* not only show her being ostracized by her peers, but also represent her belief in the myth that the stairs near the dorm would fulfill her dear wish to be thin.

How is it, then, that the *sonyeo* sensibility represented transforms the generic norms of the horror genre? Female ghosts in the *Whispering Corridors* series may be regarded as monsters in terms of Noël Carroll's definition: ghosts are supernatural, conceptually hybrid entities that threaten the community.[20] Characters are portrayed as "aberrant" in that they challenge the norms. In a flashback in *Memento Mori*, the viewer learns that Hyo-shin became ostracized by her classmates after reciting her poem negating the binary oppositions between existence and non-existence and truth and lie. Hyo-shin earns praise from her literature teacher and becomes the object of other students' jealousy. When Hyo-shin has a beer with Mr Goh, she also questions categorical imperatives such as "you shall not kill people." She denies the absoluteness of such a dictum by recourse to a situational ground, claiming that one simply does not know unless one has the first-hand knowledge of such a situation.

Hyo-shin's sexuality — homosexuality or bisexuality — further isolates her from her peers, and her kiss with Shi-eun in public is indeed a suicidal act that literally leads to her suicide within the plot. Despite Hyo-shin's deviance from, or violation of, social norms, she is portrayed as a victim rather than as a threat. Andrew Grossman and Jooran Lee aptly note that the ghostly nature of homosexuality in *Memento Mori* "remains a method intensifying eros rather than stigmatizing it."[21] Furthermore, Hyo-shin's affair with the male teacher helps underscore the fact that teachers as much as students are the victims of the same system. Her sexual relationship with him should not be attributed to her attraction, or curiosity, toward him; rather, it resides in her sympathy toward him. In one scene in an empty classroom, we see Hyo-shin stroking Mr Goh's hair, underscoring the reversed relationship between the two: Hyo-shin acts like a caregiver rather than a student/lover.

Homosexuality is often linked to monstrosity in horror cinema in that both are deemed as "other," and both diverge from the conventional norm (or "normality"). However, as Benshoff carefully traces out, the portrayal of the homosexual as "other" has been ambivalent throughout the history of Hollywood horror cinema — and this "other" can be portrayed either as a threat to the moral standards of a community, or a victim that can evoke a sympathetic response from the viewer.²² The homosexuality in the *Whispering Corridors* is portrayed more as an act of resistance to conformity rather than as a sign of monstrosity. The real monstrosity resides in the school itself and, more specifically, the Korean education system, which deprives students of their individual freedoms and happiness. In the first installment, So-young claims that her goal is to enter the top university in the country. Higher education loses its purpose; it is not a means to find and develop one's dreams but becomes the end in and of itself. One way to survive within such a system is passivity, to remain "unnoticed" as the ghost Jin-ju wishes. She was not even recognized by her own teachers and was able to remain in school for nine years as a ghost. The first two installments bring to the fore that the deplorable traits of teachers, in part, result from the system itself, as indicated by Ji-oh's rather didactic speech about her portrait of Ms Park. Such an idea is visually reinforced when another student, Jung-sook, commits suicide. Ms Park and Jung-sook, both hanged from the same walkway, are visually linked via similar camera movements and shot compositions (Figures 2.1 and 2.2). When Ji-oh first finds Ms Park's body, Ji-oh puts her hands on Jin-ju's face to keep Jin-ju from seeing Ms Park. There is a montage of student reactions, including Ji-oh and Jin-ju and two others students. When the camera cuts back to Ji-oh and Jin-ju, and tilts up, we see Jung-sook by the window witnessing the death of Ms Park. Later in the film, the camera reveals Jung-sook's body in a similar manner, when her body is found by another student at night. The establishing shot renders Jung-sook's body comparable to that of Ms Park and the probing camera moves from her legs to reveal her face. The maladjustment experienced by newly employed teachers such as Eun-young and Mr Goh in the first and the second installment, respectively, further underscores the fact that both teachers and students are victims of the same education system.

Figure 2.1 Death of Ms Park, *Whispering Corridors* (Park Ki-hyeong, 1998)

Figure 2.2 Death of Jung-sook, *Whispering Corridors* (Park Ki-hyeong, 1998)

Even for those characters with apparent agency, such as Hyo-shin in the second installment or Jin-seong in the third, their agency is not sustained at the level of both narrative and style. Character actions are not seen in their entirety, their integrity being constantly interrupted by the camera or the look of classmates. For instance, after Shi-eun and Hyo-shin decide to "go public," we see Shi-eun and Hyo-shin holding hands. A teacher slaps Shi-eun's face, and Hyo-shin storms out of the classroom with her diary. The camera arcs around the classroom, underscoring the uniformity of shunned reactions of classmates, and awaits Hyo-shin's entrance through the backdoor. Then the camera zooms in on Shi-eun, as Hyo-shin runs toward her. Instead of using a 360-degree arcing camera shot, which is often used to shoot kisses between lovers, the kiss between Shi-eun and Hyo-shin is disrupted as Shi-eun tries to push Hyo-shin away, until the two are broken apart by one of their classmates with the help of the teacher. But their kiss is also disrupted stylistically, shifting between extreme-long shots and close-ups of their faces. The kiss here is not a token of affection, but an act of resistance. This is an exemplification of Hyo-shin's refusal to be assimilated with her classmates. A less elaborate case is found in the scene where Jin-seong and So-heui skip practice to attend a music concert, but only Jin-seong gets punished and humiliated by her teacher in front of her peers. We see a close-up of Jin-seong's feet heading toward screen left, followed by a close-up of her face looking in the opposite direction (Figures 2.3 and 2.4). The visual punctuation here not only indicates Jin-seong's anger and frustration about unfairness and favoritism. Her disintegrated body also conveys her conflicting desires, and how she was torn between her cherished friendship with So-heui and her wish to win the competition.

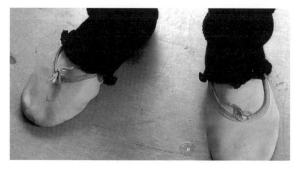

Figure 2.3 Jin-seong's truncated body, *Wishing Stairs* (Yun Jae-yeon, 2003)

Figure 2.4 Visual punctuation, *Wishing Stairs* (Yun Jae-yeon, 2003)

The incorporation of the ghost story formula is not unique to Korean horror cinema. However, the *Whispering Corridors* series successfully encodes the horrific and traumatic high school experiences specific to Korean students by selectively adopting the horror genre icons and conventions. Perhaps some of the reasons that *Memento Mori* was less successful at the box office than the other installments — even though it was critically acclaimed both at home and abroad — can be found in the film's imbalanced treatment of the elements it incorporates from from coming-of-age movies and those of the horror genre. Unlike the first and the last installments, which follow a "whodunit" plot structure, the film foregrounds the emotional trajectory of the two protagonists across the plot. In the beginning of the film, *Memento Mori* imitates conventional horror film style by providing the viewer with false cues through disjointed camera and figure movements, with the camera constantly passing by Shi-eun, who is practicing on the track. In horror films, such a style often misleads the viewer to suspect the presence of a ghost or a stalker. As the camera cuts to inside the classroom to introduce Ji-won and Yeon-an, the unstable camera temporarily confirms the viewer's hunch, which is then instantly undercut when Ji-won is shown operating a camcorder. The film, however, fails to sustain both stylistic and narrative suspense after the death of Hyo-shin. Hyo-shin's ghostly presence is clearly marked by her reincarnation into a red bird or a shifting in color tone. The film is more preoccupied in building up to the emotional climax, while the need to resolve narrative conflicts is nearly absent. The film's climax is neither the confrontation between the ghost of Hyo-shin and the people who used to bully her, nor the revelation of how Hyo-shin died. Rather, it coincides with the lowest point of the emotional trajectory between Hyo-shin and Shi-eun: Shi-eun once again rejects Hyo-shin, who seeks reconciliation. Carroll writes that the two emotional overtones of horror films are fear and disgust.[23] But the emotional overtone of *Memento Mori* is neither fear nor disgust, but sadness.

The Korean high school system, which is solely dedicated to preparing students for college admission, blocks anyone from cultivating his or her own sensibility. Within such a system, the *sonyeo* sensibility is completely stifled, and friendship, the only recourse for students to go to high school, becomes unsustainable at the level of the narrative. In the next section, I turn to *A Tale of Two Sisters*, and discuss how the shift in setting from school to home results in the establishment of personal space.

Home "Sweet" Home: Space and mise-en-scène in *A Tale of Two Sisters*

A Tale of Two Sisters was one of the films that started the production trend of "well-made" films. In the early 2000s, the term "well-made" started to circulate within the Korean film industry as well as in the critical discourse, thus designating this production trend. Bong Joon-ho's sophomore feature, *Memories of Murder* (*Salinui chueok*, 2003), signaled the beginning of this trend, followed by Lee Je-yong's *Untold Scandal* (*Scandal-Joseon namnyeo sangyeoljisa*), and Kim Ji-woon's *A Tale of Two Sisters*, both of which were released in 2003. This slightly awkward term expresses both the dissatisfaction of filmmakers with the heavily commercialized Korean film industry and their efforts to bridge the gap between the economic and aesthetic ambitions of a commercially driven industry. The success of lowbrow gangster comedy, such as *My Wife Is a Gangster* (*Jopok Manura*, Cho Jin-gyu, 2001), *Hi! Dharma!* (*Dalmaya Nolja*, Park Cheol-kwan, 2001) and *Marrying the Mafia* (*Gamunui yeonggwang*, Jeong Heung-sun, 2002), and the box office failure of many blockbuster films, such as Jang Sun-woo's *The Resurrection of the Match Girl* (*Sungnyangpali sonyeoui jaerim*, 2002), *Yesterday* (Jeon Yun-su, 2002), *Tube* (Baek Woon-hak, 2003), and *Natural City* (Min Byung Chun, 2003), gave rise to anxieties within the Korean film industry. A middle ground between high-budgeted blockbusters and low-budget comedies was sought. With the success of *A Tale of Two Sisters*, the horror genre, which had been associated with low-budget filmmaking, came to occupy the middle ground within the bipolarized industry trends.

However, the term "well-made," when applied to commercial cinema, carries an unwanted connotation which suggests that previous commercially successful films did not deserve such warm reception. The industry's attempt to reconcile commercial sensibilities with the aesthetic qualities of a film — even though it fosters a mistaken equation between the aesthetic value and popularity of a film — manifests an attempt to defy the old conception that commercial cinema exists first and foremost for its entertainment value. With this vague term, the Korean film industry and critics promote mid-budget, less-spectacle-driven films with new subject matter and artistic value, urging the audience to appreciate aesthetic achievements of Korean cinema.

A Tale of Two Sisters, along with *Untold Scandal*, was produced by B. O. M., a company known for its employment of immaculate mise-en-scène. Except the exterior shots, the film is entirely shot in a set, unlike *Whispering Corridors*, which was shot mostly on location. This third feature by Kim Ji-woon shares only a vague resemblance to *Janghwa, Hongryeon*, the Korean folktale that the original Korean title of the film references. The narrative conflicts in both stories arise from familial relationships. The ages of two protagonists — the overbearing Su-mi and the naïve Su-yeon — are left unspecified. The setting is a country house — far from school — and the trauma that propels the narrative is hardly the hardship of high school life. But nevertheless, *A Tale of Two Sisters*, like the *Whispering Corridors* series, promotes the *sonyeo* sensibility. The costumes of Su-mi and Su-yeon further accentuate their girlishness and vulnerability. The film starts with an abstract hospital scene that relocates to a scene of Su-mi and Su-yeon arriving at the house. As they exit, the two are seen in sweaters and skirts with flowery patterns. Just as Hyo-shin's obsession with Shi-eun is manifest through her decorative impulse — the secret diary and the piano filled with small presents and memorabilia — Su-mi's neurosis and psychosis are externalized onto mise-en-scène. The multiplicity of personal belongings, such as the two sets of diaries or half a dozen of the same dress hung in the closet, signals the multiple personality of Su-mi. In *A Tale of Two Sisters* the character's troubled interiority is further reinforced by interiors: wallpapers, antique furniture, and the overall visual tone of each space.

If, in the *Whispering Corridors* series, character interiority is rendered metonymically via personal objects, *A Tale of Two Sisters* blends characters' actions into the mise-en-scène, transforming them as an object within the externalized interiority. Shallow space, created via the camera's positioning perpendicular to the axis of action, and the lack of strong backlight that often separates figures from background, renders the image quite flat. Consider the first dining sequence in the beginning of the film. After an establishing shot of the family at the dining room table, with the father's back shown, the camera cuts between the stepmother and the two sisters, Su-mi and Su-yeon, both of whom appear to blend into the background (Figure 2.5). When characters are staged in depth, characters often walk in and out of light, which helps the characters to be absorbed into the space and to reduce their prominence from the mise-en-scène. When the stepmother first greets Su-mi and Su-yeon, for instance, she walks from the far background toward the foreground, coming in and out of light. A similar shot is used when Su-mi comes downstairs in the middle of the night to find the television on in the library.

Figure 2.5 Dining scene, *A Tale of Two Sisters* (Kim Ji-woon, 2003)

Moreover, in some of the film's most impressive shots, the mise-en-scène awaits the entrance of a character. It is not the mise-en-scène that coheres around the character, but rather the characters that *complete* the mise-en-scène. After the stepmother's brother and his wife leave, the stepmother suspects that there must be someone in the house. After the father leaves the bedroom to inspect the house, the stepmother is seen facing the red closet doors, which seem to cover the entire wall, with her back to the camera. Her shiny blue nightgown stands in stark contrast to the red background, rendering the space flat. After a cutaway to the father in the kitchen, which is shown in greater depth, we see the stepmother walk from screen left to right, now against a wall of a different color: magenta. It is interesting that before and after she enters the frame, the camera briefly shows only the abstract patterns on the wall, as if it awaits the character's action: stasis is charged with repressed energy (Figures 2.6 and 2.7). Now, the camera cuts to the red closet again, waiting for the stepmother to move into the frame. She paces left and right, punctuated by the empty moment. A similar shot is found when the father comes back home to find Su-mi collapsed in the hallway. He brings medicine for Su-mi, and before he enters the library where he left Su-mi, there is a shot of empty wall, which he slowly enters.

Figure 2.6 Empty moment before stepmother enters, *A Tale of Two Sisters* (Kim Ji-woon, 2003)

Figure 2.7 Character completes mise-en-scène, *A Tale of Two Sisters* (Kim Ji-woon, 2003)

Although the *Whispering Corridors* series and *A Tale of Two Sisters* are set in public and private spaces respectively, in neither case is the protagonist granted a proper place. If the former break downs the boundaries between the public and the private spheres, forcing students to find limited freedom of expression within a public place, in *A Tale of Two Sisters*, characters are absorbed into a "psychological" space, which erases the division between interiority and exteriority, and the separation between subject and object. As school itself is an uncanny space for the characters in the *Whispering Corridors* series — both private and public, or alternating between the two — the home, as the site of inerasable, painful memories and trauma, is not rendered as homogeneous throughout *A Tale of Two Sisters*. Each room is visually marked by different patterns of wallpaper and differing color tones. Although some of the long takes and establishing shots in each room allow the viewer to become familiar with the general layout of the house, space is still fragmented and sometimes confusing due to the withholding of spatial information from the viewer. For instance, in Su-yeon's room new space is disclosed only in accordance with the occupant of the space. In the beginning of the film, only the space in the vicinity of Su-yeon's bed and the closet is activated; it does not show a full view of the room. The same portion of the space is used when the stepmother accuses Su-yeon of killing her bird and locks her in the closet. It is only when the father comes upstairs to confront Su-mi for her neurotic behavior that Su-yeon's room is fully revealed. The two sisters are seated side by side on a bench by the window, a space which has not clearly been established earlier in the film.

Consider also the scene in which Su-mi starts to panic one morning. Su-mi finds her father's note saying that he has gone out to run errands. She finds a white bag smudged with blood. Thinking that Su-yeon is inside the bag, Su-mi runs frantically around the house. The space now turns from the familiar to the unfamiliar, and the house appears as a maze. The bag is dislocated a few times while Su-mi is looking for a pair of scissors. The room with a medicine cabinet is a space that has never been fully established, and its spatial relation to that of the rest of the house remains unclear. This spatial unfamiliarity underscores the psychological confusion of Su-mi, and renders spatial confusion in the viewer.

Su-mi's place within the family, despite her courage to stand up for her younger sister and her aggression to confront her stepmother, is unstable, entering in and out of her subjectivity/interiority. Su-mi's aggression toward her stepmother is, in fact, directed toward herself: her own guilt for being unable to save her younger sister, similar to the Hollywood female protagonist whose apparent agency or gaze in 1940s gothic horror, is often turned against herself.[24] The scene described above is followed by the 360-degree arcing camera, which captures in a single shot both Su-mi pretending to be her stepmother and the visit of the real stepmother. This confrontation dissolves the previously established divides between the aggressor and the victim, and the subject and the object.

The *Whispering Corridors* series and *A Tale of Two Sisters* may register the changing familial relationship in Korean society. The *sonyeo* sensibility in both the *Whispering Corridors* series and *A Tale of Two Sisters* foregrounds the internalized "felt" oppression of both school and family via the mise-en-scène, especially the desire for excessive decoration. The emergence of teen horror might be contingent upon various factors: a changing mediascape in the Korean film industry, the rise of new independent production companies, niche marketing, and the growing numbers of multiplexes. Yet, it provides an outlet for dramatizing some of the conflicts with which Korean female adolescents are familiar and grants a place for representing and expressing adolescent female sensibility, which hitherto has been neglected by many mainstream genres.

3

Inner Senses and the Changing Face of Hong Kong Horror Cinema

Kevin Heffernan

On April 1, 2003, Leslie Cheung Kwok-Wing, for decades one of the most popular movie stars in all of East Asia, leapt to his death from the Mandarin Oriental Hotel in Hong Kong. In the outpouring of grief and bewilderment which followed this loss to the movie world, many tabloid magazines, professional movie critics, and fans could not help but remember Leslie's final film role the year before as the troubled psychiatrist Dr Jim Law in Lo Chi-Leung's *Inner Senses* (*Yee do hung gaan*). The film had concluded with Leslie's character poised to throw himself off of a high-rise building to rid himself of guilt over the suicide of his first love decades before.

Since the breakaway success of *A Better Tomorrow* (*Ying hung boon sik*, John Woo, 1986), Leslie Cheung's name attached to the title of a film was enough to guarantee pre-sales of that film in Hong Kong, Taiwan, Singapore, Malaysia, the Philippines, and Southeast Asia. Often, theater chains in regional markets would put up financing for the movie as long as it starred Cheung, Chow Yun-Fat, Maggie Cheung, or other Hong Kong megastars. But in the lean years leading up to the millennium, Hong Kong movie production plummeted, Hollywood blockbusters showing in gleaming new multiplex theaters were beginning to choke off the production funds from regional theater chains, and many of Cheung's most famous colleagues had emigrated to Hollywood.

Many of the most successful efforts of regional film industries to fight this colonization involved the crafting of self-consciously pan-Asian films in popular genres, with stars, production personnel, and financing coming together from all over Asia in one film or in one distributor's annual release slate. This trend had a huge impact on the way movies were written, cast, financed, shot, and marketed. First, international financing often resulted in films with higher production values and even higher budgets, which in turn required different kinds of film funding and different approaches to writing and preproduction. Second, the cross-pollination of genres between the national cinemas of Asia and the Pacific Rim, which had always been a key component of popular cinema in the region, began to accelerate at breakneck speed. The hugely successful efforts of independent producer Filmko Pictures to produce and release *Inner Senses* is an illustrative example of some of these currents in East Asian cinema in the early years of the twenty-first century.

For a while, Hong Kong filmmakers seemed to have reason to fear the new millennium. Faced with the onslaught of Hollywood films such as *Jurassic Park* (Steven Spielberg, 1993) and *The Matrix* (Wachowski Brothers, 1999), political and economic uncertainties over Hong Kong's return to China as a Special Administrative Region, the loss of overseas markets in the wake of the Asian economic crisis, and ballooning salaries for the biggest stars and directors, film production drastically declined in the late 1990s in Hong Kong, from 140 titles in 1995, 109 in 1996, 82 in 1997, and 60 titles in 1998, and in 1997 "non- Hong Kong films outgrossed local product . . . for the first time since 1980."[1]

Some of the slack in production financing was taken up by the Internet and new media companies such as Star East, who financed movies in order to provide a backlog of product for the video-on-demand Internet download boom seemingly on the horizon. But the main trend was for companies to seek co-production financing from abroad. When Edko Films teamed up with Columbia Asia, Good Machine, and Taiwan's Zoom Hunt International to produce the runaway hit *Crouching Tiger Hidden Dragon* (*Wo hu cang long*, Ang Lee, 2000), the Hong Kong industry had a new model to follow, namely, the prestige regional blockbuster with major stars, international financing, and a star director and/or pan-Asian approach to a popular genre.

However, this required a different approach to filmmaking than had been the norm in Hong Kong. David Bordwell describes the traditional process: "Hong Kong films [were] typically bankrolled by individual investors and distribution/exhibition firms . . . The director [could] get funding and start production with only a synopsis, a budget, and a cast list . . . The typical film was shot according to a rough story outline, with little indication of dialog. Many directors . . . simply asked their players to recite numbers during takes and dubbed in lines later."[2] By 2000–2001, digital special effects, location work in more than one country, and the careful calibration of screen time for performers on whose name the picture would be sold in different territories all required more extensive and detailed pre-planning. Since few investors outside of the film industry were willing to put up production financing on the basis of a script outline, the production and financing process in Hong Kong became closer to the Hollywood model of a detailed screenplay, shooting schedule, and budget forming the basis of a film's investment core.

One of the surest signs that this process was taking place was the opening in 2001 of Hong Kong's first completion bond firm, the Film Financing and Completion Bond Consultants (FFCBC).[3] A completion bond is a form of insurance which guards against overbudget expenses and guarantees that "the film will not have to cease production because of lack of funds."[4] FFCBC director Gilbert Shing told *Screen Daily,* "Hong Kong audiences are demanding films with bigger budgets and better special effects, and *Crouching Tiger's* success had made more international financiers interested in Asian films. If Hong Kong filmmakers want some of that money, they have to have a completion bond. A bonded film shows to financiers that it's been well-planned."[5]

One company that was successful in navigating this new landscape of large scale international productions was Filmko Pictures. The company was formed in 2000 by producer Alex Wong and directors Derek Yee and Jacob Cheung with the explicit aim of enhancing the prestige and economic success of the Hong Kong film industry through "global themed productions and co-productions." The company's first production was Cheung's own *Midnight Fly* (*Huang xin jia qi*, 2002) a romantic thriller starring Anita Mui and Japanese star Junna Risa which featured extensive location work in France and Morocco. Later that year, the company began production on *July Rhapsody* (*Laam yan sei sap*, Ann Hui, 2002) starring Jacky Cheung, Anita Mui, and newcomer Karena Lam, whose role earned her the best actress prize at Taiwan's Golden Horse Awards.[6] Also at Filmko that year, producer Stanley Kwan made Carol Lai's *Floating Landscape* (*Lian zhi feng jing*, 2003) with co-financing from Hong Kong's Si-Metropole, France's Rosem Films and Japan's NHK,[7] and in December, the company announced a co-production deal with mega-distributor Media Asia Group for four films over two years.[8] In addition to a second Jacob Cheung production, *Summer I Love You* (*Hiu sam seung oi*, Banny Lo, 2002), the company produced a psychological thriller, *Inner Senses*, which would turn out to be Leslie Cheung's final film role.[9]

Inner Senses tells the story of Cheung Yan (Karena Lam), a young woman who has attempted suicide and who claims to see ghosts. She rents an apartment from the gregarious but manic Mr Chu and comes to believe she is seeing the ghosts of Mr Chu's deceased wife and daughter. Her cousin's husband, Dr Wilson Chan (Lee Chi-Hing), recommends that she consult with Dr Jim Law (Leslie Cheung), a skeptical psychiatrist who specializes in cases of ghostly hallucinations. In that curious brand of professional ethics known only to Hong Kong movie psychiatrists, Jim and Yan date and begin to fall in love. As Jim prods deeper into Yan's history, he begins to have his own eruptions of repressed memories. He begins to sleepwalk and frantically search his apartment for something while in a trance. Finally, he uncovers the memory of the suicide of Yue, his first love as a teenager and becomes convinced that her ghost is haunting him and wants him to jump to his death from a downtown building as she had done. In complete despair, he stands on the ledge and begins to jump. Yue's ghost appears to him and gently kisses him as he abjectly begs for her forgiveness. She disappears at the moment Yan comes up to the roof at dawn.

Even casual filmgoers will immediately detect more than a passing resemblance between the plot of *Inner Senses* and Buena Vista's *The Sixth Sense* (M. Night Shamalan, 1999). Both films center on the relationship between a repressed, emotionally damaged psychiatrist and his mediumistic, possibly schizophrenic patient. This premise, or key elements of it, also characterized *The Eye* (*Gin Gwei*, Pang Brothers, 2002), in which a blind woman receives a cornea transplant which appears to plague her with visions of death and disembodied spirits. Hong Kong films have a long tradition of working localized variations on Hollywood hits. This is readily apparent in the horror genre, from the cycle of splatter-heavy supernatural films inspired by *The Exorcist* (William Friedkin, 1973) such as *Black Magic* (*Gong Tau*, Ho Meng Hua, 1975), the misanthropic *Killer Snakes* (*She sha shou*, Kwei Chih-Hung, 1975), based on *Willard* (Daniel Mann, 1971), to *Biozombie* (*Sun faa sau si*, Wilson Yip, 1998), which transposes the zombies-in-a-mall apocalyptic vision of *Dawn of the Dead* (George Romero, 1978) to one of Hong Kong's overbuilt shopping complexes, virtually abandoned in the wake of the economic crisis.

But there is more going on *Inner Senses* than the economic process of import substitution, in which an outcapitalized local industry competes with a more powerful rival by imitating that rival's products. *Inner Senses* is another Filmko release tailored for international distribution and carefully reworks many commercially successful motifs of Asian supernatural and horror cinema of the previous decade, particularly those from Japan, as I will soon show. More broadly, *Inner Senses* displays great self-awareness of its place within popular genre cinema. Near the beginning of the film, Dr Law is lecturing an auditorium of students and professors on the power of suggestion to create ghosts in our minds and uses as examples three widely circulated images of the supernatural. The first is a drawing of a *jiangshi* or hopping vampire, which evokes the supernatural martial arts horror comedies of the 1980s one of which, *Chinese Ghost Story* (*Sinnui yauwan*, Ching Siu-Tung, 1987) starred Leslie Cheung. Next, he shows them a picture of the Headless Horseman, whose appearance in *Sleepy Hollow* (Tim Burton, 1999) serves as an example of modern high-tech Hollywood special effects-driven horror cinema. Finally, he shows them an image of Dracula, its evocation of horror films of Hollywood's studio era and their post-studio refinement by Hammer Films seen as quaint by his audience (and presumably, the film audience as well). And, of course, the final hour of the film in which the surviving Leslie Cheung character is pursued and haunted by the ghost of his suicidal lover is a deliberate evocation of *Rouge* (*Yin ji kau*, Stanley Kwan, 1987), in which Anita Mui's lovelorn ghost makes the trip from the underworld to modern Hong Kong in an attempt to find her lost love.[10]

Ringu (Nakata Hideo, 1999), the story of a haunted videotape and the enraged young girl using it as the instrument of her revenge, provides many of *Inner Senses*' most interesting motifs. The Japanese import was the top-grossing film in Hong Kong in 1999, bringing in HK$ 4 million at the local box office.[11] At the 2002 Hong Kong International Film Festival, interviewer Benny Lee pointed out to *Inner Senses*' director Lo Chi-Leung that "scenes in the second half are reminiscent of Japanese female ghosts in [*Ringu*]." Lo gave the somewhat evasive reply, "[i]t never occurred to me if they were Japanese or foreign ghosts."[12] It is impossible not to see the influence of *Ringu* in the white-garbed ghost Yue, and the moment at which the dead Mrs Chu and her son attempt to reach out from Yan's computer monitor to touch her is almost identical in composition to the scenes of Sadako materializing out of the television set in *Ringu*. The final appearance of the shattered corpse of Yue underwater in Jim's penthouse swimming pool, blood flowing into the water from her sheared wrist, recalls in costume, posture, and monochromatic mise-en-scène the appearance of Sadako in *Ringu*'s haunted videotape. Further, the final pursuit of Jim through the apartment building by multiple incarnations of Yue seems to anticipate the multiple images of the dead ghost child in *Ju-on* (Shimizu Takashi, 2003) as Rika (Akina Megumi) rides the elevator to the top of another abandoned high-rise building.

Were director Lo Chi-Leung and producer Derek Yee themselves clairvoyant, then? The skeptic's answer is provided by the wide availability of Japanese horror to Hong Kong fans in a wide range of media such as cable television, import and bootleg VCDs, manga comic books, and translated novels. The made-for-television version of *Ju-on* from 2000, also directed by Shimizu, would have been easy for fans and filmmakers to see well before *Inner Senses* was in pre-production. This also helps explain the presence in

Inner Senses of many situations and motifs which characterize *Dark Water* (*Honogurai mizu no soko kara*, Nakata Hideo, 2003), released just weeks before *Inner Senses* made its Hong Kong theatrical debut. The books in novelist Suzuki Koji's *Ring* cycle, as well as his thematically linked short story collection *Honogurai mizu no soko kara* had been in print for years in Chinese translations in both Hong Kong and Taiwan. "Floating Water" ("Fuyu suru mizu"), the story from *Honogurai mizu no soko kara* upon which the movie was largely based, features a female protagonist Yoshimi who works alone as a reader of manuscripts,[13] anticipating *Inner Senses'* Yan, who translates movie screenplays. Yoshimi moves into a high-rise apartment overseen by the widowed live-in superintendent Kamiya,[14] who provides the model for the manic Mr Chu (Tsui Siu-Keung), the landlord in *Inner Senses* who awaits the return of his dead wife and son, leaving their shoes in the emotionally fragile Yan's rented apartment. The apartment building in *Dark Water* was also the former dwelling of the unhappy dead, namely the child Mitsuko, who vanished under mysterious circumstances and whose corpse Yoshimi becomes convinced is putrefying in the rooftop cistern, polluting the water her family is using to drink and bathe.[15] The first horror set piece of *Inner Senses*, the appearance of the dead, mud-covered ghosts of Mr Chu's wife and son in Yan's bathroom cabinet, appears modeled on the climactic appearance of Mitsuko's decomposed corpse in Yoshimi's bathtub in "Floating Water," and both stories feature a frightening trip up to the roof of a high-rise building to unravel the enigma of a long-dead child.

These efforts to craft a popular horror film from a range of international popular cinema conventions result in a film with some fascinating ruptures, contradictions, and discontinuities. For decades, Hong Kong cinema has displayed, to Western eyes at least, a more disruptive approach to narrative unity than is often found in Hollywood films. A major protagonist may die or be de-emphasized in the second half of a film. Dangling causes and narrative enigmas, carefully set up in the first hour of a film, may never be addressed by the final scenes. The reason for many of these distinctive features is Hong Kong filmmakers' unique set of norms for constructing a film's narrative, regulating and moderating its pacing, and parceling out important moments of exposition. David Bordwell argues that by the 1970s,

> Hong Kong filmmakers standardized film length at 90 to 100 minutes, or nine to ten reels. This maximized theater turnover, allowing audiences to be hustled in and out at two-hour intervals across a day[16] . . . [F]ilmmakers began to structure the action reel by reel[17]. . . . [T]he first reel would grab the audience's interest, the fourth reel would start a

significant line of action, the sixth or seventh reel would provide another major turning point, and the last two or three reels would yield a protracted climax and conclusion, leaving the audience with a strong final impression.[18]

Within these reels could occur numerous digressions, gags, eccentric minor characters, or seemingly unmotivated musical interludes which neither advanced the narrative nor provided exposition or backstory.

The move to a more rigidly controlled budgeting and preproduction led filmmakers away from this model of narrative construction and closer toward, but not wholly consonant with, the more measured, tightly unified model exemplified by Hollywood's approach for the reasons I have outlined earlier namely, higher budgets and greater accountability, sync-sound dialogue, and more intricate special effects and sound design. The norms of narrative unity at work in many American films are outlined by Kristin Thompson in *Storytelling in the New Hollywood: Understanding Classical Narrative Technique*. Although it is probably impossible to find the definitive set of conventions governing classical narrative, *Storytelling in the New Hollywood* outlines a broad set of norms that seem to prevail in many popular and widely praised films from post-studio Hollywood. Among the many characteristics of the self-effacing virtuosity with which Hollywood often tells its stories is the four-part structure, in which two or more narrative lines, each representing one of the protagonists' goals, are interwoven and serve to both retard and advance one another. Each scene represents both a cause and an effect in the linear chain of narrative events. One plot line appears to be near resolution, then a dangling cause from another scene emerges to spin the plot into another direction. The four parts of a thusly defined classical narrative are the Set-Up, the Complicating Action, the Development, and the Climax. Many Hollywood narratives move from each part to the next at remarkably consistent intervals, and the four-part structure can accommodate an extraordinary range of narrative and stylistic figures and sets of generic norms.[19]

In many respects, *Inner Senses* seems to follow this four-part structure to a noticeable degree. The Set-Up takes up approximately the first thirty-one minutes of the film and introduces us to Yan as she arrives at the new apartment and is shown around by Mr Chu. He leads her (and the viewer) through the space in which the action in the first half of the film will unfold. Soon after she moves in, she sees her first "ghost," an apparition near the window of her apartment. The water pipes groan like a tormented soul, and this sound eventually mutates into the howls of anguish of a ghost which she sees through her bathroom mirror. Just under eight minutes into the film, we meet the character of Jim Law giving a lecture in a symposium on "Critical Thinking" in which he disavows belief in the supernatural and posits that so-called ghosts are the result of the brain releasing stored information during times of stress. Jim's friend Wilson suggests that he take on Yan as a patient, and her initial session with Jim at 13:00 provides important backstory information about her long periods of depression and insomnia and her deep distrust of doctors. He is very gentle and supportive to her, and at the end of the session he gives her a "prescription," which turns out to be a box of candies, a sign of both of the two developing plotlines, his therapeutic goal of curing her of her "hallucinations" and the plotline of courtship and romance between the two characters. Twenty minutes into the Set Up, Yan has dinner with Mr Chu. Dinner scenes are often used in horror films to both provide exposition and to underscore the contrast between the normal rituals of everyday life and threatening forces of chaos and monstrosity, and here, Mr Chu tells of his wife and daughter, who were killed in a mudslide while he was at work. Suddenly, he begins to talk about them as if they had just stepped out for a moment and weeps when he tells Yan that they should be back any time. She flees the room, and later she sulks in her apartment, having covered all reflective surfaces with newspapers. At exactly twenty-five minutes into the movie (a "sweet spot" in almost every Hollywood film — studio script readers are often encouraged to reject screenplays which do not feature a plot point at this juncture), she begins to hear dripping water, screeching pipes, and howls coming from the bathroom. When she opens the bathroom cabinet, a torrent of mud pours out and the grimacing, screaming, decomposed remains of Mrs Chu and her son try to dig themselves out into her sink.

Jim comes to her apartment, helps her tidy up, gives her tranquilizers, and while she is asleep, reads her diaries and scrapbooks. This action, right on schedule at thirty-one minutes into the film, begins the second part of the movie, the Complicating Action. In this section, the terms of the Set-Up are often reversed, with characters being forced to alter their goals. As Jim reads, we see short analytic flash cuts of a school-age girl chasing a boy up stairs at school, tearing up a stuffed animal, and crying on a ledge. Jim's internal voice-over asks therapeutic questions including "Have you seen the face of a dead person at a funeral parlor?" These tiny flashback fragments, we will later learn, are eruptions of his own repressed memories surrounding the suicide of Yue. Next, Jim sets up the camcorders in her apartment to help dispel her fears that ghosts are visiting her. The camcorders will later be used to prove that Jim himself is sleepwalking and searching his apartment in a trance. As she sleeps, he again reads her diaries and we see more flashback cuts of the school girl. Troubled at the end of a long night, he takes a sleeping pill and stares at his own face in the mirror. The next day, about thirty-nine minutes into the film, Jim meets with Wilson to discuss Yan's case, and their meeting provides important backstory information such as her parents' divorce, breakups with boyfriends, and suicide attempts, all of which motivate her fear of abandonment, an aspect of her character that will become more important as the film develops. Jim takes her swimming in his backyard pool, and when she scrapes her knee, he bandages the wound and then tells her that a doctor and patient cannot become too close. She leaves in cold fury, and the following scene intercuts Yan and Jim each at their computer that night. Again we see the school girl crying on the roof, and Yan, loses control of her computer, seeing the dead Chu wife and son creeping up behind her as if the monitor were a mirror. She screams, and the movie cuts to Jim rising from bed in a start. He looks out of his window and sees the school girl, whom we have always assumed to be Yan, dangling her legs off a high ledge. He looks again, and she is gone. He is called to the hospital, where he discovers that Yan has attempted suicide. After he discovers that Mr Chu has been using Yan's apartment as an altar to his dead family and that the moaning pipes are from her upstairs neighbor masturbating in the tub, Jim confronts her about her past and arranges for a meeting with her estranged parents. When Yan tearfully confronts them as Jim and Wilson look on, the goal of therapeutic cure for Yan appears to be achieved. Fifty-four minutes into the film, *Inner Senses* appears to already have a happy ending except, of course, for the dangling cause of Jim's vision outside his window.

Jim ignores calls to meet Wilson, his wife, and Yan socially, and then, at precisely fifty-nine minutes into the film, he sees the corpse of Yue in the back seat of his car, riding in the car next to him, and later, floating toward him underwater in the pool, blood billowing from her arms. This onrush of ghostly apparitions signals the beginning of the next part of the film, the Development phase. As with the transition from the Set-Up to the Complicating Action, the movie is spun into a different direction by a genre-set piece, the appearance of a ghost. The Development will reverse the narrative situation and create new goals while ultimately revealing the final bit of backstory needed for the story to reach its conclusion. For the next twenty-three minutes, it will be Jim who is in need of therapeutic intervention and Yan who confronts him with the consequences of his actions. Also, the parallels between Yan, Jim, Yue, and Yan's former boyfriend Mike will be fully elaborated as Jim remembers his rejection of Yue and Yan transcends her learned role as suicidal and abandoned.

As romance blooms between Jim and Yan, his professional life begins to unravel. He sneaks into the hospital and self administers a dose of electroconvulsive therapy. He is placed on paid administrative leave. Just after his brain scans all come back negative, he is attacked in a café by an elderly couple who break a glass bottle over his head. In a dream that night, they scream at him, "Give my daughter back to me!" When Yan tries to confront him about his bizarre behavior, he tells her she is relapsing into mental illness. Yan discovers him sleepwalking, going through all of his papers and carefully replacing them just before dawn. When she videotapes him sleepwalking and uses the video in an intervention with Wilson, he flies into a rage, and she tells him she is moving out. At an hour and nineteen minutes into the movie, all of the terms from the Set-Up have been completely reversed: Jim is sleepwalking and hallucinating, Yan is leaving her boyfriend, and light reflected from the swimming pool outside casts shimmering shadows on the walls of the apartment like those in Mr Chu's rainswept high-rise. When she wakes up, he is weeping, standing over her, moaning, "Why are you still following me after death?" Here, he replays the breakdown of Mr Chu at the dinner table in the Set-Up. Then, he speaks in Yue's voice, hissing, "You can never escape from me."

With this image of the schizophrenic male speaking in a woman's voice, another set piece, even cliché, of the horror genre, the Development ends, and when Jim finds the collection of memorabilia from his romance with Yue, the Climax begins, an hour and twenty-two minutes into the film. Yan wakes him up with an alarm clock, and now we see all of the images from the flashbacks in order, recounting the brief but intense school-age affair between Jim and Yue, her jealous tantrum, his rejection of her, her suicide, and her parents' attack of him at the funeral parlor in front of her casket. The vengeful spirit of Yue appears, and Jim attempts to flee her, but her shattered, creaking body is everywhere he turns. Finally, he goes to the room from which she jumped to her death years before. He walks to the ledge, and Yue walks to him, arms outstretched as if to push him to his death. She embraces him instead, and we see one final flashback as she weeps in his arms, and Jim realizes it was Yan's similarity to Yue that drew him to her. She steps back from him and says, "I don't love you any more. I don't need you now." She embraces him again, and as the camera arcs around them, she is no longer livid and scarred but young, beautiful, and intact. The camera arcs around Jim once more, and we see Yan standing in front of him. In the briefest of epilogues, characteristic of Hong Kong cinema, we see two lovebirds on the ground, and the camera cranes up to reveal Jim and Yan together on the roof at dawn.

So is *Inner Senses* merely a grafting of Japanese motifs onto a Hollywood narrative structure which is then enacted by engaging and attractive Hong Kong movie stars? One of the movie's most striking features, its switch to an emphasis on the tormented Jim Law in the second half, seems to suggest otherwise. An often-seen technique of Hong Kong popular narrative is just such a noticeable shift in emphasis from one major character to another over the course of a movie's running time. One of the most celebrated of all Hong Kong films, Shaw Brothers' *Come Drink with Me* (*Da zui sha*, King Hu, 1966), establishes the female knight Golden Swallow (Cheng Pei-Pei) as its central heroine and most accomplished martial adept, whose brother has been kidnapped by bandit warlord Jade-Faced Tiger (Chen Hung Lieh). After Golden Swallow is struck with a poison dart in a furious battle with the Tiger's minions, the movie shifts emphasis in the second half to focus on the false beggar Drunken Cat (Yueh Hua) and his efforts to avenge the murder of his teacher by Jade-Faced Tiger. That same year, Shaw's color and widescreen updating of the perennial tragic melodrama *Vermillion Door* (*Hong ling lei*, Luo Zhen) reached its midpoint and switched focus from one tragic lover, opera singer Luo Xiangyi (Li Li-Hua), to her doomed paramour, fellow performer Chiu Hai-Tang (Kwan Shan).

One possible explanation for these earlier examples can be found in the vagaries of the star system as Shaw Brothers was undergoing a transition from its early 1960s focus on female stars in *huang mei diao* operas, *gong wei* palace chamber dramas, romantic melodramas, and musicals to the male-centered martial arts movies under its New Action Century production policy. A similar shift was occurring in the horror genre in the late 1990s as horror movies, particularly those from Japan, became increasingly focused on the female protagonist. *Inner Senses*, carefully crafted for pan-Asian appeal with its incorporation of Japanesque horror motifs, was also a calculated attempt by Filmko to increase the star profile of successful newcomer Karena Lam, who had been praised for her lead role in the company's *July Rhapsody*. But her co-star, Leslie Cheung, another lynchpin in the film's commercial appeal, could not be reduced to a mere supporting character, so the filmmakers were able to use a longstanding pattern of narrative construction characteristic of Hong Kong cinema to balance some of the conflicting demands of *Inner Senses'* various commercial elements while maintaining adherence to at least some features of contemporary Hollywood narrative.

This balancing act seemed to work. *Inner Senses* was a very successful release for Filmko, not just in Hong Kong but in Europe as well. In fact, the sales agent who sold the film in Europe for Filmko was Horizon Entertainment, the same company that had successfully handled the *Ring* pictures in Europe for Japanese distributor Asmik Ace.[20] Still, director Lo was not being disingenuous when downplaying the influence of *Ringu* on his movie. *Inner Senses* is a deliberate hybrid between many species of Asian supernatural cinema, from *The Eye* to *Ringu* (and its *kaidan eiga* ghost story predecessors) to *Rouge*, *Chinese Ghost Story*, and *The Bride with White Hair* (*Bai fa mo nu zhuan*, Ronnie Yu, 1993). The first decade of the twenty-first century promises to bring even more vital interaction between the popular genre cinemas of East Asia and the Pacific Rim, and the changing currents of film distribution in the wake of media conglomeration will continue to accelerate this process. A thorough history of this exciting period will trace out these relationships in greater detail.

4

The Pan-Asian Outlook of *The Eye*

Adam Knee

The Eye (*Gin Gwai*, Danny Pang and Oxide Pang, 2002) stands as a particularly fruitful text to examine in terms of the increasingly pan-Asian (as well as more broadly transnational) nature of Asian horror production, inasmuch as it embodies contemporary regionalism and globalization at a range of intra-, inter-, and extra-textual levels. Indeed, the film's substantial success across Asia, as well as subsequent global distribution and an adaptation by Hollywood, suggest that in some way it managed to tap into themes with strong resonances both regionally and internationally. This chapter will be interested in contributing to current discussions about the varied dimensions of the increasingly transnational nature of Asian cinema, centrally through an exploration of some of *The Eye*'s textual resonances. Moving from an overview of the film's production context, this chapter will make claims for a number of key tropes of regional relevance in the film — in particular those concerning the nature of contemporary economic and cultural flows within the region and the status of gender with regard to these — then close with a brief look at a number of other Asian productions that appear to pick up on *The Eye*'s preoccupations.

    The Eye's positioning as a distinctly pan-Asian text was hardly accidental, the film being the creation of a Hong-Kong based production company, Applause, established in 2000 with the specific aim of developing pan-Asian projects. As producer Peter Chan describes it, given the relatively moribund state of the Hong Kong industry in the late 1990s, the idea was not only to expand market base with films appealing to audiences beyond Hong Kong, but also to expand creative personnel to include those from other Asian countries.¹ In following just such strategies, *The Eye* in particular "exemplifies the pan-Asian cinema model," as Bliss Cua Lim has noted.² The film indeed embodies such a model even in its funding, as Hong Kong's Applause Pictures co-financed the film with Singapore's Mediacorp Raintree Pictures, another Asian production firm interested in exploring strategies for reaching a pan-Asian audience.³ In terms of personnel, the film's main producer, Chan, himself comes from a pan-Asian (indeed transnational) background, born in Hong Kong, raised largely in Thailand, educated in the U.S., and having spread his career between all three places. The directors, twin brothers Oxide Pang and Danny Pang, are also Hong Kong-born Chinese, but had achieved their greatest success and visibility in the Thai commercial and film industries, where they had worked for some time before making *The Eye*, while also still working on Hong Kong projects. The film's list of production and post-production personnel, moreover, includes a thorough mix of Chinese and Thai names, with sound mixing and film processing work handled by Thailand's Kantana Laboratories. The cast features a Malaysian-born pop music star and television personality, at the time best known in Taiwan (Lee Sin-je as Mun), and a Hong Kong pop star (Lawrence Chou as Wah), and also includes a range of lesser-known Thai actors.

In generic terms, various commentators have described *The Eye* — with its plot concerning a young Hong Kong woman who can see dead people after receiving a cornea transplant — as alternatively Asian influenced and Western influenced. The most notable exponent of the former position, Tony Rayns, argues that:

> Like earlier Pang Brothers films, *The Eye* owes very little to Hollywood models; it's unapologetically Asian in everything from its supernatural backstory to its characterisations. Its immediate inspiration was local: Ann Hui's *Visible Secret* (*Youling Ren Jian*, 2001) revived the Chinese traditions of "ghost-seeing eyes," Taoist exorcisms and so forth.⁴

Even accepting *The Eye*'s clear immersion in local cultural traditions, as well as its likely inspiration in *Visible Secret* (in which the protagonist's strange new girlfriend believes she can see ghosts), it is hard not to also see the influence of the phenomenally successful American blockbuster *The Sixth Sense* (M. Night Shyamalan, 1999), which concerns a boy who can "see dead people" and which prefigures a wave of Hong Kong films featuring characters who can do likewise, *Visible Secret, The Eye, Inner Senses* (*Yee Do Hung Gaan*, Law Chi-Leung, 2002), and *My Left Eye Sees Ghosts* (*Ngo Joh Aan Gin Diy*

Gwai, Johnny To and Wai Ka-Fai, 2002) among them. (This is even more the case given that Hui, Chan, and the Pang brothers are all cosmopolitan figures who have lived and worked abroad and who are naturally fully conversant in the international film scene.) This is not, moreover, to suggest that any of these films are necessarily in some way unoriginal or derivative of (or "tainted" by) Western culture. Rather, they all partake of the common practice in Hong Kong cinema of borrowing, reworking, parodying, and or commenting upon motifs from successful Hollywood and non-Hollywood films in such a way that they speak directly to a Hong Kong audience.[5] What makes this particular instance of cinematic borrowing so distinctive, however, is that the source text in question seems to have generated such a singular fascination, and its resonance for the Asian context is therefore something that calls for examination in further detail.

The Eye perhaps owes some of its success to its canny tapping in to both local (Hong Kong) and Hollywood horror intertexts, but it also succeeds by partaking of an ascendant contemporary pan-Asian discourse of horror which most of the other Hong Kong films cited here do not link with to the same degree. I speak here of an evolving regional movement in horror film production occurring in the wake of the exceptional success of the Japanese horror film *Ringu* (Nakata Hideo, 1998) — a trend toward glossy, highly stylized, intertextually self-conscious horror films which often feature (among other elements) the vengeful ghost of a young woman and the revelation of grim secrets from the past, in a context emphasizing the technologically mediated unsettling of traditional Asian culture.[6] In addition to achieving a substantial measure of success across Asia, many of these films have also garnered attention among fans in the West, especially owing to their promotion through Tartan Video's Asia Extreme line of releases.[7] It is worth noting, however, that, as Lim has pointed out, the notion of "Asia" understood in discussions of the new Asian horror film are not as broadly inclusive as they might appear, given that the vast majority of horror films linked to this rubric originate in Japan and South Korea (with lesser numbers from Hong Kong and Thailand).[8] Yet, despite the fact that other Asian countries have been largely excluded from both popular and critical understandings of this pan-Asian horror discourse, it is not as though they do not bear a significant relationship to it. Not only do the Asian horror films in question have significant audiences in these countries, in Southeast Asia in particular[9] — these countries are themselves starting to produce numbers of horror films which engage elements of such a pan-Asian discourse.[10]

I would suggest that this absence of much of Asia within the discourse is itself germane to an analysis of *The Eye,* in that the film is in part concerned with working through the ill-defined status of Southeast Asia (as an economically and politically less established Other) within Asia as a whole. One way this is achieved is through specific choices made in *The Eye*'s narrative structure and setting: the film is catapulted from Hong Kong to Thailand at the start of its third act, when, accompanied by her psychotherapist and would-be boyfriend Wah, Mun travels to the rural home of the Thai donor of her corneas to discover the source of her troubling visions. More than simply a device to add "local color" and transnational appeal to a generically allusive Hong Kong horror film, this shift, rather, grows organically out of deeper structures within the text and helps bring into relief some of its fundamental thematic preoccupations — some of which, the following analysis will argue, have to do with the problematics of a larger pan-Asian transnationalism.

Haunted Intertexts

The Eye's most immediately identifiable shared generic element is, of course, the protagonist's ability to see ghosts, which she has in common not only with the young protagonist of *The Sixth Sense*, but with many other horror protagonists. A significant twist here is that she is not at first aware it is ghosts she is seeing; this is narratively made possible in that Mun, now a young woman, has not (until the cornea transplant) been able to see since the age of two, so she is not yet able to clearly distinguish between what are "normal" visions and what are not. This confusion can arguably be seen as having a parallel in Dr Malcolm Crowe's (Bruce Willis) own lack of clarity over who is in fact a ghost in *The Sixth Sense* (in that he is unaware of his own non-living status). It is perhaps more directly similar to Peter's (Eason Chan) misperception of his ghostly girlfriend as living in *Visible Secret*, only his misperception is sustained until that film's surprise climax. Mun, on the other hand, soon figures out most of what it is she is seeing: the newly dead, the dark figures from the afterlife who arrive to guide the newly dead between worlds, and also those who have died with some issues left unresolved (and who are therefore trapped on earth reliving their deaths). (Significantly, the ability to see the arrival of these "grim reapers" also gives Mun some power of prescience — the ability to see when death is going to occur — although, again, at first she does not realize it. In this she is perhaps closer to the character of John Baxter [Donald Sutherland] in *Don't Look Now* [Nicolas Roeg, 1974], whose downfall is caused by his inability to realize his own visions are prescient.)

This theme of unresolved issues from the past is also naturally common to many films with ghostly themes. In the case of *Ringu* and many of the wave of films following it, there is more specifically a vengeful desire for justice on the part of a girl or woman who has been wronged, and it is here that the emotions of both horror and guilt in which these films are often immersed originate. Somewhat in opposition to these vengeful female ghost films, *The Eye*, again, primarily features spirits who just happen to be in transit and those needing to tie up emotional loose ends who just happen to have died in Mun's vicinity. In this, *The Eye* is once more somewhat closer to the spirit of *The Sixth Sense*, wherein the ghosts who seek out the boy Cole Sear (Haley Joel Osment) with particular urgency are those aware of some matters from their lives which still need to be set right, injustices which need to be revealed; they seek him out not because of his relationship to these injustices, but because of expediency, in that he alone has the special power to see dead people. *The Eye*, however, does on one level still significantly evince some of the sense of personal guilt or indebtedness or connection between the haunter and the haunted present in ghost films of the more vengeful variety, in that one of the beings who haunts Mun — the most narratively significant one — is the woman who has donated her corneas to her.

Still another broader thematic repercussion of the narrative device of having the dead visible amongst the living is a heavy emphasis on the co-existence and close interrelationship of the past and the present; as in both *The Sixth Sense* and many (if not most) of the new wave of Asian horror, the past is revealed as still very present, as having direct implications for the now. This idea resonates at numerous levels in *The Eye*, not least in settings themselves. The initial setting of Hong Kong is imaged (much as it is in reality) as at once a city of modern high-rises and highways and of creepy, dingy, disused public spaces, where many a ghost would feel perfectly at home. Hong Kong's architectural variegation is even alluded to in dialogue at one point, when a waitress at an older and indeed haunted roast meat restaurant explains that the proprietor, unlike owners of neighboring shophouses, has not sold to developers (presumably to make way for modern construction) because he hopes to see his late wife and child return. Historical co-existence in setting is inscribed not only within the architecture of Hong Kong itself, but through the eventual shift in locale to Thailand after the film's midpoint. No matter what the actual status of Thailand's development (Bangkok is as modern a metropolis as any), *The Eye* puts the respective settings into a visual opposition which strongly implies that Hong Kong's modern and urban character is in direct contrast to Thailand's underdevelopment and rural profusion. Witness, for example, the counter-positioning of the aseptic corridors of the modern

Hong Kong hospital and the wood construction of the rural Siam Rach hospital, shot in sepia tones, as well as the film's initial elision of any narrative events in Bangkok.[11] We thus have the sense of two historical realms — one more past, the other more present — co-existing within the same narrative time frame, made all the more evident through the characters' apparent ease in transiting from one locale to the other. The two spaces are figured as co-existent within Mun's imagination as well: nightmares she has after her operation in Hong Kong transport her to the setting of the Siam Rach hospital (though she does not know this as yet), and when she awakes from these nightmares, she sees her own bedroom transform into what is eventually revealed to be the (older looking) Thailand bedroom of her cornea donor. These scenes reveal a literal wavering back and forth between the two bedrooms and their national locales, implying a kind of spatial and temporal instability, a vying for predominance among two distinct, but co-existent realms.

This co-existence of past and present, old and new, functions on a more abstract level as well, as a series of oppositions between traditional culture and modern, older regimes of knowledge and systems of belief and newer ones. Most central to the plot may be the interaction of modern, positivist, empirically derived (and largely Western in origin) medical knowledge with traditional, Asian-identified spiritual beliefs, that is, the juxtaposition of the scientific and the supernatural. This is evident, for example, in the Western educated Hong Kong doctors' initial inability to believe Mun's account of her visions of dead people — until she provides solid factual evidence in the form of knowledge about people's deaths. Significant in this respect is that in order to solve the (supernatural) problem of her doubled vision, Mun must travel to Thailand — figured as a nation that is more spiritual, less scientifically minded than Hong Kong — and that once there, the Sino-Thai physician who is informed of her visions accepts the account without hesitation. The Taoist priest whose assistance Mun's grandmother and neighbors seek in ridding their apartment complex of a ghost that Mun has perceived is, along with his particular kind of knowledge and authority, also placed in structural opposition to the Hong Kong doctors and their (more recently developed) belief system. Even the Chinese language (writing in particular) becomes positioned as an element of an older culture persisting into present contexts; as Mun's ageing instructor tells her, "Very few want to learn calligraphy nowadays." It is not incongruous that one of the more fearsome ghosts she encounters appears at her calligraphy lesson.

Significant in relation to the film's contexts of pan-Asian-ness and globalization is that the interaction between differing time frames evinced here is simultaneously an interaction between different national and regional cultures: As the old form of Chinese writing dies away, a new form of language — English, to be specific — ascends. Mun takes note of her apprehension at having to learn English if she is to be taken to Vancouver to live with her father, caught up in modern trends of global mobility. (Her sister too is caught up in this modern mobility, connecting the family to the West, in her work as an international airline attendant which calls her away in the period after Mun's release from the hospital.) The connection of the West with the film's discourses of modernization is also alluded to in Wah's reference to his visiting psychology professor from the U.S. But while such direct references to the West are brief and fleeting, they are more than sufficient to engage most audiences' contextual knowledge of Asian-Western relations (always already inscribed in the post-colonial Hong Kong setting), to thematically link tensions regarding modernization to the film's nexus of transnational flows. In contrast to the West's association with the present and the modern, the film, as already mentioned, uses the setting of Thailand to embody the past and to allow the dramatization of the interaction with the past. This co-existence of realms, time periods, cultures interestingly again takes on a linguistic valence in the scenes of Mun and Wah's arrival at the Siam Rach hospital. They do not understand when informed in Thai of their arrival at their destination, and Wah subsequently addresses the hospital receptionists in the global language of English. When the Sino-Thai doctor whom they are seeking learns that they are from Hong Kong, he begins to address them in Mandarin dialect, and switching between Mandarin, Thai, and Mun and Wah's more accustomed Cantonese continues throughout the Thailand sequence.

This emphasis on multilinguality points to another distinctive and central theme in *The Eye* which links motifs of haunting and transnationalism, that of confusion over identity. Mun's interest in her own identity can be seen from the moment her new vision begins to come into focus: her first request is to be taken to the bathroom so that she can gaze at herself in a mirror. This interest and curiosity turns to mystification and alarm, however, when she realizes that some of her visions may be someone else's, and that the image she has been viewing in the mirror is not her own: "Who the hell are you?" she asks of the formerly misrecognized face (actually that of the dead cornea donor, Ling [Chutcha Rujinanon]) prior to smashing her mirror in frustration. This theme of misrecognition of self — of misapprehension of one's own identity and/or ontological status — interestingly comes up in different forms in quite a few of the films alluded to here. In *The Sixth Sense*, for example, Crowe mistakenly assumes that he is alive and visible to others (until the final climax reveals otherwise), while in *Visible Secret*, Peter erroneously attributes to others actions in fact performed by himself under the influence of a ghost.

It is significant that the figuration of Mun's relationship to Ling (a Thai of Chinese ethnicity) is not typical of horror film images of a predatory or opportunistic spirit possessing an unwilling host; the sense is not one of forced submission, but of natural identity. Part of what is striking about the apparition of Ling's face in the mirror in the above described scene is that that face is communicating *Mun's* emotions, her mouth producing Mun's words and cries. The impression given is that the two young women (who indeed bear some resemblance) are in effect one, sharing the same consciousness and visions as a result of the posthumous transplant. This idea is given further weight with the later implication that it is Ling's volition that leads them to her home in rural Thailand. When Mun enters Ling's bedroom, she tells the deceased, "I know you've wanted me to come here all this time." Mun then learns Ling wanted her to come to Thailand to communicate to her mother on her behalf — to beg forgiveness for having killed herself — and when it comes time for the nightly reenactment of this suicide which Ling must carry out as do all suicide victims who continue to have unresolved issues, the identity slippages between the two continue: Ling is initially seen wearing the same clothing as Mun — and then it is Mun visible going through the motions of hanging herself. Ling's mother at that moment relents and chooses to forgive her daughter, entering the room just in time to cut her down. The girl on the floor, begging forgiveness in Thai, has Ling's face, until the forgiveness is granted and the face subtly morphs into Mun's.

The focus on the mirrored identities of these two young women of Chinese ethnicity, in a text directed by identical twin brothers of Chinese ethnicity, calls up a range of interrelated themes pertaining to interlinked identities, and more specifically to various marked sets of continuities and contrasts among characters. Of the two women, Mun is clearly the one in the position of privilege, having a more economically advantaged life in a richer world, living while her Thai counterpart dies, and ultimately deriving benefits from the quite literal use of that counterpart's body. The relationship thus suggests the senses of guilt, indebtedness, and also closeness or intimacy between haunter and haunted likewise present in many of the vengeful female ghost films. On some level, the relationship as figured here can also be seen as a synecdoche for the Hong Kong-Southeast Asia relationship as a whole, the Special Administrative Region as is well known deriving substantial benefit from the bodily labors of its Southeast Asian workers — primarily female — who can be seen in massive numbers on any given Sunday taking their release time in Hong Kong Island's Central district, but who are otherwise largely invisible in Hong Kong life (just as Ling's presence is also invisible). Taking this a step further, if Hong Kong is understood as a stand-in for East Asia as a whole here, the relationship of intimacy and interdependency on the one hand and structural inequality on the other can also be taken as representative of the larger dynamic between East and Southeast Asia alluded to earlier, their uneasy merging into a larger Asian region.

The women's relationship arguably points as well to the labor division that operates in the production of this film, and to the relations that obtain in the majority of Thai-filmed transnational productions: non-Thai financers make use of the resources of (largely hidden) Thai creativity and labor, along with Thai settings, for the vitality and economy of their films.[12] Still other metaphors related to the production context of the film, other relationships of structural imbalance, also suggest themselves here. One can see a parallel with the relationship between Hollywood and Asian film industries, for example, the more powerful former now making use of Asian creative personnel and creative properties for the production of their own works — including direct remakes intimately linked to, indeed twinning, their Asian inspirations, which in turn run the risk of becoming marginalized in the global film discourse. (This in turn also echoes the former colonial relationship between Britain and Hong Kong, with the East again providing labor and resources for the West — an echo that seems to reverberate as well in *Koma* [*Gau Ming*, Law Chi-Leung, 2004] as argued below.) Yet another parallel exists in the relationship between Hong Kong and Singapore in the filmmaking realms. In a number of high-profile productions (notably, the *Eye* and *Infernal Affairs* [*Mou Gaan Dou*, Andrew Lau Wai-Keung and Alan Mak, 2002] series), Singapore has been an "invisible partner," serving as a source of funding but entirely absented from the text itself.

But again, the exploitative valences of the relationship between Mun and Ling, the historical economic and social imbalances to which it alludes, are undercut by the substantial levels of continuity between the two women. Though separated by class and nation, they are profoundly linked by gender and ethnicity — as well as, arguably, by outsider status within their respective societies. Mun is an outsider by virtue of her (former) blindness, which her grandmother once told her (as she relates in voice-over) makes her an extraordinary person, able to experience what others do not. (Ironically, the restoration of Mun's sight is shown as redoubling her social isolation, in that she now politely invited to leave her former group of peers, an ensemble of blind classical musicians gearing up for a special performance with — most appropriately — the internationally successful Singapore-born Sino-Thai musician Vanessa-Mae.) Ling is also an outsider in part by virtue of perceiving what others do not — specifically, the arrival of spirits who will lead away the newly dead, the facility she eventually shares with Mun. The other members of her rural village blame her for the deaths of which she warns people, assuming she is some kind of witch and therefore ostracizing her; when she sounds an unheeded warning before a disastrous and deadly fire, the animosity turned against her is so strong she is finally driven to suicide.

Ling's outsider status is further reinforced owing to her Chinese ethnicity. While the Chinese in Thailand have not had the same degree of difficulty as Chinese migrants in other Southeast Asian nations, at present holding a largely well respected status in Thai society, her Chinese ethnicity nevertheless makes Ling de facto not part of the dominant social bloc of her own country.[13] In fact, it is that ethnic Chinese connection which appears to help ensure her intimacy with Mun, a diasporic connection that transcends borders, indeed a form of a familial linkage, which eventually becomes literalized when the two women come to share the same flesh and blood. This sense of familial linkage, of great importance in most Asian cultures, is emphasized here in numerous plot references to family. Much of the drama in the Hong Kong sequences, for example, involves Mun's relationship to her grandmother and sister, and Wah's family is also emphasized, given that his uncle (with whom he is sometimes at odds) is also Mun's surgeon. ("Were you reincarnated into wrong body? Why are you so different from rest of the family?" the uncle asks Wah only half-jokingly, incidentally also anticipating the film's sub-themes of reincarnation.) But while Chinese family relations are highlighted as important, they are also figured as under stress, possibly victim to the centrifugal forces of modernization and globalization: Mun and Ling further reflect one another in both living without their respective fathers, Mun's again having moved to Vancouver, and Mun's sister is often abroad with her airline work. The two suicide victims Mun encounters, moreover, have specifically familial disputes to resolve: a young video-gaming boy in her apartment block has committed suicide because his parents do not believe he has genuinely lost his report card, and Ling's present dilemma concerns her lack of forgiveness from her mother.

Subtly underpinning all these other categories of social connection and difference, however, is the category of gender, and plainly their shared femininity provides one of the most significant linkages between Mun and Ling. This deeper preoccupation with the status of the feminine in a changing Asia, moreover, ultimately links *The Eye* more closely to the concerns of other new Asian horrors, with their unruly female ghosts insisting they be recognized, than might first appear to be the case. Both Mun and Ling are at a disadvantage in their respective patriarchal societies. Both women pose problems for the consistently male medical authority figures with whom they interact, both in that their bodies require care (the one with vision problems, the other a suicide) and in that their supernatural abilities pose a conundrum for Western-based, masculinist medical regimes of knowledge; even the aforementioned (male) Thai doctor who is more open to the claims of supernatural phenomena than his Hong Kong counterparts tells the visiting Hong Kongers, "I don't understand any of this spiritual stuff; I just know [Ling] was a kind girl who had a hard life." This affront to masculine notions of order and reason also emerges in the problems which Wah's romantic (emotional, corporeal) attraction to his psychotherapy patient Mun pose for him. The attraction threatens the non-emotional, rational codes of professional behavior which he is supposed to follow and creates a rift with his surgeon uncle — his superior in the rigid patriarchal orders of medical establishment and family. Even the women's ability to see not only present, but past and, to an extent, future as well undermines Western scientific notions of linear time and teleology, suggesting a perspective more akin to an (Eastern) holistic view of time instead.

Thus, while Mun's dramatic resolution of her problems with Ling to some extent bridges certain referenced pan-Asian divides of class and nation, the subsequent merging of the two women points to still more profound structural oppositions that cannot be readily resolved. Whereas women become linked with the spiritual, the emotional, the bodily (labor), the traditional, the Asian, and, more specifically, the Southeast Asian; men become aligned, in opposition, with the positivist, the rational, the intellectual, the modern, and the Western. And whereas women become associated with a fluid, holistic view of reality, which enables them to readily transgress literal borders and conceptual frameworks (viz, Mun and Ling's ability to merge into one), men are associated by contrast with rigid, linear thinking, which requires them to occupy clearly defined and delimited territories.

Given these implicit oppositions, while on the surface the film appears to reach an initial dramatic resolution, with Mun now understanding of Ling and Ling now reconciled with her mother (and hence ready to proceed on to a peaceful afterlife), substantial irresolution still remains at a deeper level, and literally explodes into a surprise coda after this earlier resolution. In this, *The Eye* bears another significant structural similarity to *Ringu*, which likewise makes use of a false initial resolution. In that case, the main protagonists uncover the mystery of the vengeful female spirit, Sadako, and comfort her — but to their (and the audience's) horror, it becomes clear that this is not enough to defuse Sadako's deadly curse, as, presumably, the deeper (structural, social) conditions which have precipitated that curse (evidently those arising from

Japan's paternalistic social and familial systems) still remain. In both films, while the (classical, masculine) rules of causal, linear plot development and resolution would suggest the film is about to conclude, an assertion of female agency in some form prevents this from happening.

In *The Eye*'s final plot twist Mun again witnesses the arrival of guides to the afterlife, this time in large numbers, thanks to powers inherited from Ling, as she and Wah sit dozing off in a bus in a Bangkok traffic jam. Realizing a deadly disaster of some sort is about to occur, Mun dashes off the bus and runs to warn people, to no avail, and her frustrated efforts are intercut with the past parallel efforts of Ling to warn people of the fire to come to her town. In the present time frame there is again a major conflagration, owing to the ignition of fuel from an overturned tanker truck followed by a series of chain reaction explosions, and many deaths inevitably result, with cross-cutting making clear the correspondence to Ling's own earlier traumatic experience with fire. Mun stands transfixed as the explosions occur, and Wah manages to pull her down to the ground before the fireball can reach them, but not before shards of glass enter her eyes.

The overwhelming emphasis on parallels between the two conflagrations suggests, again, a challenge to modern linear temporality, evoking instead a Taoist cyclicality or Buddhist karmic inevitability: In keeping with Eastern modes of thought, past deeds cannot be erased, but rather always make their return.[14] In these terms the event can be seen as the result of Mun's own karmic debt, or perhaps also as the inheritance of Ling's bad karma — as Mun is indeed, on some levels, a reincarnation of Ling, embodying her spirit after her death. Mun's loss of sight as a result of the event, her return to her pre-operative condition, would appear to validate this reading. Yet the sequence also seems to want to do more than evoke these ideas, given the stunning nature of its imagery, its depiction of a sudden and apocalyptic firestorm which catches nonchalant Bangkokians completely unaware, incinerating them in the midst of their actions. There is indeed an *excess* in this imagery which prompts one to look for other meanings.

In a most literal sense, the imagery (especially in an Asian viewing context) recalls that of various Western military attacks upon Asia, in particular the American nuclear attacks on Japan in the Second World War (with their mass incinerations of bodies), but also (more to the Southeast Asian context) the firebombing that occurred in the Indochinese conflicts of the 1960s and 1970s. Given the insouciance of those sitting in the traffic prior to the explosion, one might read this event as a reminder or return of inadequately acknowledged or hidden suffering, of the labor and sacrifices of various socially marginalized or disempowered people, which has allowed modern Asia to develop with the breakneck rapidity it has. And at the same time, considering the film's cyclical temporal register, the event might appear a portent of the future, a warning (for those so comfortably unaware) of a trauma potentially yet to come in the course of Asian history, a function of ongoing polar oppositions (for example, between regions, ethnicities, classes, genders) that cannot readily be reconciled. Indeed, within the conceptual framework of the film's various structural oppositions, it is telling that the explosive event occurs in Bangkok, a city that serves as a transitional point between differing realms, the traffic-clogged beacon of modernity in a country that still perceives of itself in largely agrarian terms and (relevant to themes regarding the broader conceptualization of Asia) a gateway to Southeast Asia for those from elsewhere in Asia, as well as from the rest of the world.[15] In modern history, moreover, Bangkokians' lives have been disrupted by political turmoil and "explosive" violence on more than one occasion — notably with military actions against civilian protestors in 1973, 1976, and 1992 — and such instability has in point of fact repeatedly threatened to resurface in the period since *The Eye* was made.[16]

While the film's climactic conflagration and Mun's subsequent return to blindness, which she seems fully prepared to accept, might on one level seem regressive — a flight from the horrors of the world — Mun's final voice-over suggests a more circumspect, holistic view, noting that "aside from pain, I saw beauty." Along the same lines, *The Eye* perceives a yin-yang structure to the universe, a set of dynamic oppositions which, while having immediate, topical resonances, are also part of certain eternal and inevitable conditions.

This analysis has tried to suggest ways that the narrative of *The Eye* points to a range of tensions underneath the relatively stable surface of present-day East and Southeast Asia. These tensions arise in part from the co-existence of Asian traditions and often Western-inspired trends of modernization, of spiritual cosmologies and materialistic worldviews, and from the interactivity of divergent social and economic classes of people from disparate sub-regions; and the tensions are of sufficient magnitude to produce a sense of identity crisis in both regional and personal terms. *The Eye* figures this crisis as being played out in the body of woman, thus alluding to the gendered dimension of the human costs of change: The literally fragmentary constitution of Mun's identity and her efforts to attain wholeness and stability can readily be seen to parallel crises in Asia itself — including, in the film's most immediate context, crises of production and distribution strategies for the region's increasingly transnational entertainment industries. The explosive nature of the film's coda suggests just how contingent any resolution may be under current circumstances, the protagonist's seeming acceptance of them notwithstanding.

Coda: Ghostly Returns

By way of an extended conclusion to this chapter, a brief look at some of the sequels, remakes, and other films that *The Eye* has at least partially inspired will serve to help highlight some of the themes or qualities of the film that seem to have had particular resonance for its Asian context. It is notable, for example, that the authorized "sequel" from the same producers and directors, *The Eye 2* (*Gin Gwai 2*, 2004), neither continues the narrative nor makes use of any of the same characters of the earlier film. What is picked up, rather — what is seemingly of the essence — is a certain ominous, deliberate pacing and an emphasis on themes of hidden lineage and indebtedness, now linked explicitly to Buddhist conceptualizations of reincarnation and karma. Deeper truths about the universe in *The Eye 2* are again gradually apprehended by the young female protagonist, Joey Cheng (Shu Qi), in part because of an ability to see things others cannot (spirits of the dead in particular) which she has acquired owing (the film explains) to her own proximity to death (as an attempted suicide) and her state of pregnancy. Joey is particularly alarmed by the spirits' evident interest in newborn babies, but she eventually learns that these spirits are merely waiting for the bodies in which they are to be reincarnated — and that the spirit hovering around her own as-yet-unborn child is that of the wife of the child's father, whose infidelity with Joey contributed to her suicide. The film concludes, somewhat along the lines of its predecessor, with Joey's greater understanding of the inevitable (if sometimes seemingly also cruel) cycles of life.

While this brief plot outline might suggest that issues of transnational identity are not as fully germane to *The Eye 2* as to its predecessor, the text's transnational conditions are again, in fact, quite relevant. *The Eye 2* is once more a co-production between Hong Kong's Applause Pictures and Singapore's Mediacorp Raintree Pictures and once more makes use of substantial numbers of Thai production and post-production personnel. The main cast is again transnational — yielding the irony that, while this is primarily a Cantonese-dialogue film, none of them are native speakers of Cantonese: Star Shu Qi, though a fixture of recent Hong Kong film, started her career in her native Taiwan; her husband is played by a major Thai star (Jedsaporn Poldee) who needed to have his dialogue dubbed by a Cantonese-speaking actor; and his suicidal wife is played by the California-born actress Eugenia Yuan, who divides her acting career between the US and Asia. And while, again, transnational interactions are not so central to the plot (the vast majority of which is set in Hong Kong), the filmmakers evidently did see a transnational context as essential enough to the *Eye* "formula" to be certain to emphasize such a context. *The Eye 2* opens with Joey shopping in an upscale Bangkok mall, in an evident effort to escape the emotional difficulties of her Hong Kong life. It is while on the Bangkok trip that Joey makes her own suicide attempt and first begins (unbeknownst to her) to experience supernatural visions, so once more (if only briefly) Thailand is initially linked to the mysterious and supernatural forces which then play themselves out in the film's Hong Kong narrative.

Another 2004 Hong Kong film that bears comparison here, *Koma*, might at first appear quite removed from the Asian horror intertexts being discussed in this chapter — in that it is not technically a film involving the supernatural (though this only gradually becomes evident) nor does it centrally focus on motifs of vision. Indeed, from surface indications, the film might seem to owe more to the Korean drama *Sympathy for Mr Vengeance* (*Boksuneun naui geot*, Park Chan-wook, 2002), with which it shares a narrative focus on kidney thefts and transplants in a context of economic disparity. On a deeper level, however, *Koma*, a highly atmospheric thriller which features the main female stars of the vision-themed horror films *The Eye* and *Inner Senses* (Lee Sin-Je and Karena Lam, respectively), taps into and amplifies several key motifs from *The Eye*. Just as in the earlier film, Lee here plays an economically privileged but biologically frail and emotionally unstable young woman (suffering from kidney failure), whose physical health is indebted to the vitality of another woman (played by Lam), who is physically stronger but economically poorer and, in her turn, indebted to the financial generosity of Lee's character. Also as in the earlier film, these two women share a relationship characterized at once by profound intimacy and intense anxiety, heightened in this instance by sexual jealousy over a boyfriend. The sense of discomfort over intimacy with and (bodily) indebtedness to an economic Other is most literally embodied in the film's closing plot twist, where Lee discovers that, unbeknownst to her, she has had implanted within her Lam's kidney, which she will now be unable to live without.

This crucial motif of profound and inescapable debt to the Other — and in particular to the vitality and to the body of this Other — is not in *Koma* given the explicit transnational dimensions that it takes on in *The Eye*, with its scenes of transit between Hong Kong and Thailand. And yet contemporary Hong Kong, the sole setting of *Koma*, is again in itself a transnational space, by virtue of its recent decolonization from Britain and its re-acquisition by China an overdetermined site of transit between Asia and the West, as well between old Asia and new. Indeed, in this context, it is difficult not to see *Koma*'s final image of transplantation and inescapable interdependence and intimacy as redolent of Hong Kong's new relationships with mainland China on the one hand and Britain on the other.

Such implications of *The Eye* as a distinctively post-colonial narrative about interdependencies among disparate nations in economically unequal relationships perhaps become clearest in the film's unacknowledged (but largely scene-for-scene) Indian remake, *Naina* (a.k.a. *Evil Eyes*, Shirpal Morakhia, 2005). *Naina* hews quite closely to its East Asian model, but its few divergences are most instructive. The most obvious shift is in setting, *The Eye*'s transit from Hong Kong to rural Thailand replaced by a like transit from London to rural India, a context, again, much more directly evocative of post-colonial transnational entanglements. The London-raised protagonist Naina's intimate link to Britain's former colony is inscribed a priori in her Indian ethnicity (indeed, so unassimilated is she, it would seem, that she hardly speaks a word of English throughout the film, despite its London setting); and this linkage is redoubled when she learns that the donor of her transplanted corneas is from a remote and impoverished corner of Gujarat, India (which she visits, in the fashion of her cinematic forerunner, to exorcise the other-worldly and sometimes prescient visions she has been having).[17] Thus we have *The Eye*'s oppositions between modernity and tradition, present and history, technology and spirit now projected into the relationship between former imperial power and former colony.

The Eye's intimations/evocations of the inescapability of karma, the inevitability of the return of past deeds, are also substantially amplified in *Naina* in that the final conflagration witnessed by the title character (in which, again, she loses the sight that had been granted by the transplanted corneas) takes place not in India, but in London, after her return; there is thus much more clearly the sense that the event represents some kind of present-day fallout from past history. Naina's sighting of dark figures, harbingers of doom, circulating among the primarily fair-skinned denizens of London without their being noticed, and her inability to get Londoners to take notice and protect themselves, indeed seem to lend themselves to being read as a pessimistic commentary upon the relationship between Anglo-Europeans and those descended from the people of former British colonies living amongst them. Unsettlingly prescient in this regard is that the catastrophe Naina anticipates is a fiery explosion in a London Tube station — this in a film released some months prior to a real-world series of explosions in the London Underground set off by British-residing descendants of subjects of former British colonies.

5

The Art of Branding: Tartan "Asia Extreme" Films

Chi-Yun Shin

"Asia Extreme" is the first label created to specifically distribute East Asian film titles by London-based Tartan Films, which operated as Metro-Tartan Distribution between 1992 and 2003, before reverting back to the name Tartan Films.[1] Launched in 2001 as the first of its kind, Tartan Asia Extreme has successfully released a number of titles which include Japanese films such as *Ringu* (Nakata Hideo, 1998), *Audition* (*Odishon*, Miike Takashi, 1999), and *Battle Royale* (*Batoru rowaiaru*, Fukasaku Kinji, 2000); South Korean films such as *The Isle* (*Seom*, Kim Ki-duk, 2000), *Oldboy* (Park Chan-wook, 2003) and *A Tale of Two Sisters* (*Janghwa, Hongryeon*, Kim Ji-woon, 2003); Hong Kong films from *Hard-Boiled* (*Lat sau san taam*, John Woo, 1992) to the *Infernal Affairs* (*Mou gaan dou*) series (Andy Lau and Alan Mak, 2002–04) as well as the films from Thailand such as *Bangkok Dangerous* (Oxide and Danny Pang, 1999), *The Eye* (*Gin gwai*, Oxide and Danny Pang, 2002), to name just a few. Now with an extensive and ever growing DVD catalogue, which includes the pan-Asian horror omnibus films, *Three . . . Extremes* (Fruit Chan, Miike Takashi and Park Chan-wook, 2004) and *Three Extremes 2* (Peter Chan, Kim Ji-woon and Nimibutr Nonzee, 2002), Tartan Asia Extreme has emerged as the most high-profile label amongst the East Asian film providers, playing an instrumental role in promoting and disseminating East Asian films in the West in recent years.

Hamish McAlpine, who is the founder and owner of Tartan Films, is in fact responsible for the creation of the Asia Extreme label. The story goes that one weekend at the end of 1999, McAlpine watched two Japanese films on video, and he was "totally blown away by them." The two films he watched back to back that weekend were Nakata's *Ringu* and Miike's *Audition*. Soon after, he came across Thai and South Korean titles — *Bangkok Dangerous* and *Nowhere to Hide* (*Injeong sajeong bol geot eobtda*, Lee Myung-Se, 1999), which were also "outrageously shocking" to him. In an interview, McAlpine emphasized the fact that the films came first: "When I realised that these films were not one-offs and there was a constant flow of brilliant films coming out of Asia, I decided to brand it and make Asia Extreme."[2] And, that was how the label was born. Since then, as the Tartan Asia Extreme website boasts, "Asia Extreme has been single-handedly responsible for the groundswell of interest in Asian cinema and the widespread attention that its roster of World class directors, such as Hideo Nakata, Miike Takashi, Kim Ki-duk and Park Chan-wook, have enjoyed."[3] It is important to note here that region-free or multi-region DVD players and the proliferation of international mail-order websites (Internet DVD shops) since the end of the 1990s had enabled Asian film fans to purchase titles from abroad.[4] What the Tartan Asia Extreme has achieved, however, is successfully infiltrating into the minds of mainstream audience and shelves of high street shops (such as HMV in Britain) as well as Internet shops such as Amazon and Play.com.

Starting off as a cult phenomenon, targeting the cult "fan-boys" but soon incorporating the art-house audiences (or world cinema patrons) to its niche, the Tartan Asia Extreme label has established itself as an immediately recognizable brand.[5] Subsequently, as McAlpine himself described, with the Asia Extreme label, Tartan "found the pot of gold at the end of the rainbow [by identifying] 'the next big thing' ahead of your competitors and becoming the early dominant provider."[6] Recent high profile Hollywood remakes of such East Asian titles as *Ringu, Ju-on: The Grudge* (Shimuzu Takashi, 2002), *Dark Water* (*Honogurai mizu no soko kara*, Nakata Hideo, 2002) and *Infernal Affairs* (the remake of which was directed by Martin Scorsese and retitled as *The Departed*, and won the best film award at the Oscars in 2007), as well as Quentin Tarantino's reported support and endorsement of *Oldboy* at the 2004 Cannes Film festival (where the film won the Grand Prix du Jury), only raised the interest in, and the profile of, East Asian cinema and the size of "the pot of gold" McAlpine had discovered.

Establishing its name in the industry where distribution labels do not normally make much impact in the market place, Tartan Asia Extreme has commendably carved a viable East Asian film niche. Questions, however, have been raised as to the reductive nature of Tartan's marketing practices, which repackages the films "as exotic and dangerous cinematic thrills."[7] In addition, the output of the label, and the name of the label itself, invoke and in part rely on the Western audiences' perception of the East as weird and wonderful, sublime and grotesque. Indeed, it seems to be operating within the discourse of Orientalism, outlined by Edward Said as "a political vision of reality whose structure promoted the difference between the familiar (Europe, the West, 'us') and the strange (the Orient, the East, 'them')" as well as "a certain will or intention to understand, in some cases control, manipulate, even to incorporate, what is a manifestly different (or alternative and novel) world."[8] At the same time, Tartan's branding of East Asian titles also qualifies it for what Mike Featherstone describes as cultural intermediaries that are "skilled at packaging and re-presenting the exotica of other cultures and 'amazing places' and different traditions to audiences eager for experience."[9] As such, both as an industry (commercial brand) and as a discursive practice, "Asia Extreme" provides a fascinating site to explore how the West consumes East Asian cinema.

In what follows, I will outline Tartan's marketing strategies for the Asia Extreme brand in order to illustrate how the so-called Asia Extreme films are presented in the West, because, as Mark Jancovich pointed out, "advertising campaigns were designed in part to present a range of possible ways of reading films."[10] My examination will focus on its horror titles, not only because they have become the most prominent and leading examples of the label, but also because the rise of Asia Extreme has coincided with the phenomenal success of "Asian horror" with branches such as "J-horror" and "K-horror," which have been celebrated as the most original and innovative horror movies of the last decade. (The notion of horror or what constitutes horror, however, is not the main concern here; horror films here broadly refer to films that evoke fright, terror, and abjection from viewers.) The chapter will engage with the critical reception of the most "notorious" Asia Extreme titles — *Audition, The Isle,* and *Oldboy* in the U.K. and the U.S. so as to understand the different discourses through which the Asia Extreme films are evaluated and mediated. As mentioned earlier, however, since the purpose of the chapter is to examine how the West appropriates, incorporates, and consumes East Asian cinema (and also considering the fact that the notion of Asia Extreme is conceived in the U.K. and widely used in the West — mainly in the U.K., Ireland and the U.S. — that is, Tartan's territories), it will not provide information on the reception of these films in their domestic markets. Considering the indications of the phenomenal success of the Tartan label, this chapter will also examine the problematic ways in which Tartan canonizes and genrificates the disparate East Asian film titles under the Asia Extreme banner.

Marketing the Affect

The Tartan Asia Extreme label was initially promoted through various "traditional" marketing practices, including radio and television slots, postcards (Figure 5.1), and posters, as well as what the industry calls "teaser campaign" by revealing just enough information about a film (mostly in film and lifestyle magazines) to intrigue potential audiences. Perhaps unsurprisingly for the "extreme" label, what is emphasized and promoted in Tartan's advertising campaigns is the visceral and hyper-violent nature as well as the shocking and unexpected aspect of the films, as its widely used promotional material declares: "If the weird, the wonderful and the dangerous is your thing, then you really don't want to miss this chance to take a walk on the wild side". Similarly, explaining its raison d'être in the introduction to the promotional booklet, *The Tartan Guide to Asia Extreme*, Mark Pilkington contends that "when Nakata Hideo's *Ring* and Miike Takashi's *Audition* were unleashed upon unsuspecting audiences nationwide, it became apparent that the appetite for such outrageous fare was massive and it made sense to let people know where to find it."[11]

Figure 5.1   *Oldboy* postcard (Courtesy of Tartan Films)

In addition to the more traditional methods listed above, Tartan created novelty merchandises such as the syringe-shaped pen created for *Audition* and *Battle Royale* umbrella (Figure 5.2) and T-shirts (Figure 5.3) to entice particularly younger audiences, who are their main target audience. Indeed, McAlpine might well have borrowed the term "extreme" from extreme sports, which is also an "invented" term referring to activities such as skateboarding, snowboarding, and BMX racing that are associated with youth subculture and inducing an adrenaline rush in participants, even though they are not necessarily more inherently dangerous or generate more adrenalin compared to "conventional" sports.[12] From 2003 to 2005, Tartan also organized an annual "Asia Extreme Roadshow," which toured then UGC cinemas (now Cineworld Cinemas) around the U.K. with the programme of films that Tartan considers to be the most daring examples of "extreme cinema" (Figure 5.4). Notably, the roadshows were set in multiplex cinemas, not in art-house cinemas, which have been the traditional outlets for foreign language films in the U.K. Such "mainstream" positioning of the films was clearly aimed to reach out to the younger audiences who frequent multiplex rather than art-house cinemas.

Following the success of the first roadshow in 2003, Tartan obtained sponsorship from the Singaporean beer brand, Tiger Beer, and the Japanese fashion label, Evisu, for the 2004 roadshow. Maintaining the association with the young and cool, for the 2005 roadshow, Tartan teamed up again with Tiger Beer and Cineworld cinemas as well as their new sponsor Sony PSP

Figure 5.2 Umbrella with the *Battle Royale* emblem
(Courtesy of Tartan Films)

Figure 5.3 *Battle Royale* T-shirt design (Courtesy of Tartan Films)

Figure 5.4 The 2003 Asia Extreme festival pass poster
(Courtesy of Tartan Films)

(games console). In line with the roadshows, Tartan also set up competitions
with prizes including a trip to Japan and Singapore in 2004 and 2005
respectively. While the roadshows showcased the selection of films that can
take the audience to "a world of extreme adventure, extreme horror and
extreme thrills," the competitions provided a chance to go on a real
adventure.[13] To win a trip to Singapore, all one needed to do was to visit

one of the bars that were running the promotion and get hold of a Tiger Beer Tartan Asia Extreme scratch card. Again, these promotional competitions, which were linked with their sponsors such as Asia House in London and other tourist boards whose interests were to enhance and educate young people about Asian culture, were high profile events and clearly aimed to attract young people who would frequent the trendy bars (rather than more traditional pubs).

Tartan utilized the roadshow when it expanded its territory by launching a U.S. branch in 2004, which, according to McAlpine, "was very, very logical extension" as "there was a whole niche that was being ignored by [distributors] in America."[14] Tartan USA employed the same marketing campaigns: stand-alone theatrical releases for stronger titles (such as *Oldboy*) and a roadshow/ cinema tie-in across several major cities in the U.S. Again, Tiger Beer was the main sponsor for the roadshow in the U.S. Initial reactions to the theatrical releases were reportedly lukewarm, but the DVD sales of the Asia Extreme titles started to increase, particularly after the DVD release of the South Korean horror film, *A Tale of Two Sisters* (Figure 5.5). McAlpine explained that it took a while to persuade video retailers into believing that Asia Extreme "isn't just some weird niche market . . . but *A Tale of Two Sisters* changed everything, and now retailers are grabbing [the films] with both hands".

Figure 5.5 *A Tale of Two Sisters* poster image (Courtesy of Tartan Films)

Tartan DVD box designs, which utilize striking images from the films, have been very successful in raising the profile of the label in the U.K., and the U.S. box cover designs clearly aim to achieve a similar effect. It is interesting though to note that some of the U.S. DVD box designs retain no resemblance to the U.K. equivalents on the basis that they are operating in a different market. In addition, there are some disparities between the U.K. and U.S. catalogues. For instance, while the so-called Asia Extreme territories have expanded to include horror titles from Singapore — *The Maid* (*Kimyo na sakasu*, Kelvin Tong, 2005) and Taiwan — *The Heirloom* (*Zhaibian*, Leste Chen, 2005), the American arm has not released titles such as *Audition* and *Battle Royale*, which helped to establish the extreme label in the U.K. The disparity is mainly to do with the fact that other distributors had acquired certain titles already, and it is also because American distributors tend to be more cautious about possible legal problems in case of copycat incidents of any violence depicted in these films.[15] This, however, proved to be pertinent to Tartan Films, as I will discuss later.

Having established its brand image and profile through the Asia Extreme roadshows, Tartan is now concentrating on their home entertainment business in the U.K., the revenues from which can be much more lucrative than those from theatrical releases. Moreover, theatrical release in general is getting harder to achieve as more films are competing for the limited number of screens that are reserved for non-Hollywood products. In any case, according to Tartan's Press and PR Manager, Paul Smith, Asia Extreme titles have always been stronger as DVD rather than theatrical releases. In 2006, half of Tartan's top 20 titles in terms of revenue were Asia Extreme titles, with Park Chan-wook's *Vengeance Trilogy* leading the list (Figure 5.6).[16]

Discourses of Extremity

As noted earlier, reflecting their efforts to attract the young (particularly male) audiences, Tartan's publicity material stresses the subversive and explicit aspect of the titles. This is most evident in the Tartan Video's official website, which invariably presents the films as shocking, dark, and disturbing. For instance, *The Isle*, which is described as "Asia Extreme cinema at it[s] best," is "arresting, shocking, visceral and original," while *Battle Royale* "shocked a nation with its violent portrayal of a society in ruins" (Figure 5.7). Similarly, *Audition*, "stylish slice of extreme cinema" and "twisted vision of a hell on earth" takes "a dark and disturbing turn" in the second half, and *A Tale of Two Sisters* is "stylish and shocking," while the introduction to *Ring Trilogy* simply ends with: "watch at your own risk . . ."[17]

Figure 5.6   Vengeance Trilogy Deluxe Box set (Courtesy of Tartan Films)

Figure 5.7   *Battle Royale* poster image (Courtesy of Tartan Films)

To be sure, some of these titles do include a certain heart-stopping, gruesome scenes. *The Isle* (Figure 5.8), for instance, contains the infamous fish mutilation scenes, as well as the scenes described by Tony Rayns as "sexual terrorism" where the male protagonist swallows fishhooks and pulls them back, and the female protagonist inserts fishhooks into her vagina.[18] *Audition* features a man with no feet or tongue kept in a sack and scenes of sadistic torture that involves piano wire and acupuncture needles. Famously inducing mass walkouts, if not fainting and vomiting, at several film festivals (notably in Venice [2000] and Rotterdam [2000]), both films had indeed inspired extreme reactions from audiences and critics alike. In his *Film Comment* article, which is in fact an outright assault on Kim Ki-duk, Tony Rayns argues that the screening of *The Isle* in Venice was "an archetypal success de scandale," while speculating about why Venice even chose the film for competition and suggesting that the director is "an instinctive provocateur . . . gleefully malicious in his punishment of audiences."[19] Similarly, Richard Falcon wrote for *Sight and Sound:* "*The Isle* sees itself as 'defying genre,' but, like Takashi Miike's *Audition*, it's a gross-out movie in arthouse clothing. *The Isle* flaunts its imagery as bold surrealism while making sure it delivers its share of hooks 'n' hookers horror and sex."[20]

Figure 5.8   *The Isle* poster image (Courtesy of Tartan Films)

Both films, however, elicited much admiration in equal measure and subsequently rendered their directors cult status, for what Jeffrey Sconce termed "paracinema" or cult-film aficionados in particular.[21] According to the Internet site, Classic-Horror's review, *The Isle* is "a gem" — "delicate, brooding exploration of the nature of obsessive love and its potentially damaging consequences." The review, however, categorically warns that the film is "not for the squeamish, feminists, the politically correct or animal activists," and claims that "all you horror addicts who get their fixes from your local art-houses will find this extraordinary movie extremely rewarding."[22] From a more reserved position, the *Chicago Sun-Times* film critic, Roger Ebert describes *The Isle* as "the most gruesome and quease-inducing film you are likely to have seen," while encouraging the readers to be more open mind because "to limit ourselves to the familiar is a crime against our minds."[23]

For *Audition* (Figure 5.9), the Classic-Horror review remarks "Miike's enigmatic allegory of a self-tormenting soul leaves its bloody imprint on the viewer's consciousness," before rating it as "a meditative, melancholic masterpiece that is not for the squeamish."[24] Writing for the *Japan Times*, Mark Schilling also praised the film as providing "a jolt of pure, unrefined terror, while reminding us, with skin-crawling starkness, that actions have consequences," while "most Hollywood films about the dark side are little more than effects-driven melodramas without a practice of conviction behind them."[25] Another awestruck Internet review titled "Gore Galore" commented that *Audition* "pushes the gore and grue to a limit rarely seen outside the cheesy cinematic bloodbaths of 1960s schlocksters," by which of course the reviewer is paying compliments to the film.[26]

Figure 5.9 *Audition* poster image (Courtesy of Tartan Films)

Another extreme title that has been the subject of admiration and admonishment, if not sheer astonishment, is Park Chan-Wook's *Oldboy*. For instance, Peter Bradshaw, who seems to be quite shaken up by the film, wrote for the *Guardian* that *Oldboy* "open[ed] up a whole new sicko frontier of exotic horror" and ends the review by declaring "this is cinema that holds an edge of cold steel against your throat."[27] For Harry Knowles of the *Ain't It Cool News*, *Oldboy* is "an engaging, flawless film that successfully pushes all the right buttons," and its director Park is a genius and "the films coming from Korea are exceptional" and "light years better than any contemporary set film in the US this year or . . . for many years."[28] Although not so enthusiastic as Knowles, Michael Atkinson at the *Village Voice* accounts that "whatever its oversteps and excesses . . . *Oldboy* has the bulldozing nerve and full-blooded passion of a classic."[29] Similarly, Carina Chocano of the *Los Angeles Times* claims: "it says something when you came out of a film as weird and fantastic as *Oldboy* and feel that you've experienced something truly authentic."[30]

Oldboy also attracted no less critical condemnation. As Grady Hendrix puts it, the film "became a critical scratching post for even the most timid magazine writers, who fired off all the insults they'd been saving for a rainy day."[31] Most noteworthy came from New York-based newspapers. Introducing the film as "the frenzied Korean thriller," Manohla Dargis commented in the *New York Times*: "The fact that *Oldboy* is embraced by some cinephiles is symptomatic of a bankrupt, reductive postmodernism: one that promotes a spurious aesthetic relativism (it's all good) and finds its crudest expression in the hermetically sealed world of fan boys."[32] Rex Reed at the *New York Observer* asserted that the film is "sewage" and sarcastically questioned: "What else can you expect from a nation weaned on kimchi, a mix of raw garlic and cabbage buried underground until it rots, dug up from the grave and then served in earthenware pots sold at the Seoul airport as souvenirs?" Reed's hostile and rather reductive response sparked many online protests, including those from the AAJA (Asian American Justice Centre) Media Watch group. The review has since been removed from the *New York Observer* website.[33]

Oldboy came under intense debate and controversy when it was suggested that the Virginia Tech killer, Cho Seung-Hui, might have been inspired by the film.[34] In the package of materials, consisting of 28 video-clips, 23-page printout message and 43 self-portrait photos that Cho sent to NBC News, one photo shows Cho wielding a hammer in a pose similar to the film's image (Figure 5.1), which was widely used in its promotional posters. Another photo shows Cho holding a handgun against his head, which is comparable to the way one of the characters from *Oldboy* poses.[35] Although Cho did not reference the film in any of his notes or messages, and no one can confirm that he had actually seen the film, the speculation over the possible link generated extensive media coverage and the film became the target of moral panics and denunciation of movie violence. It subsequently prompted some to call for censorship, while others dismissed the connection as ridiculous and unfounded.[36]

Genrification of East Asian Cinema

As Julian Stringer puts it, it is perhaps "natural for viewers to want to draw conclusions regarding what the films they consume may have to tell them about the society that produced them."[37] However, it seems that the success of Tartan Asia Extreme reveals more about Western perceptions and obsessions about East Asian countries than what people or societies are like in these countries. It is also notable that the language and approach used in Tartan Asia Extreme's promotional campaigns, based on the discourses of difference and excess, fit comfortably into the widespread notion about the East. In this respect, Gary Needham argues that "the promise of danger and of the unexpected is linked with the way in which these films are marketed according to their otherness from Hollywood, and subsequently feeds in to many of the typical fantasies of the 'Orient' characterised by exoticism, mystery and danger."[38] To similar effect, referring to the fishhook moments in *The Isle*, Grady Hendrix comments on how "art collided with exploitation, distributors heard cash registers ringing and in that single, cringe-inducing moment a whole slew of misconceptions about Korean movies and violence were cemented in the minds of western audiences."[39]

More importantly, because the Asia Extreme label became the most prominent and dominant mode of East Asian film canons at least in the U.K. and the U.S., it became an essential indicator for East Asian cinema and came to "represent" the Asian cinema as a whole. This explains why Michael Atkinson of the *Village Voice* confidently proclaims that "more than any single Korean film as yet released stateside, Park Chan-wook's *Oldboy* crystallizes the reigning characteristic of its national new wave."[40] Most Asia Extreme titles, however, did not top the box-office charts in their native countries. Rather, they are quite marginal within the region's overall outputs, which are regularly dominated by melodramas, comedies, and romances. In this respect, it is interesting to note that Tartan's canonization of the so-called extreme cinema as the "best from East Asia" is not so different from the "discovery" of Japanese film in the 1950s, which started with Kurosawa Akira's *Rashomon* (1950) winning the Golden Lion at Venice in 1951, although the film was not highly regarded in Japan at the time. Just as the West "discovered" Japanese masters in the films of Kurosawa, Mizuguchi Kenji, and Ozu Yasujiro, with the Tartan Asia Extreme label, the world of film in the West "discovered" new master directors, notably Kim Ki-duk, Miike Takashi, and Park Chan-wook.

Subsequently, East Asian filmmakers whose works do not easily fit into the "extreme" label have been habitually left out. Two of the most respected

South Korean film directors, Hong Sang-soo and Lee Chang-dong, are interesting cases in point. Hong's works have won numerous awards and are widely admired and available in France (and in Italy to a lesser degree) and Lee was awarded La Legion d'Honneur by the French government in 2006. Yet, both directors are virtually unknown in the U.K. and none of their films have been released theatrically in Britain.[41] (Tartan's Press and PR Manager had never heard of either Hong or Lee.) Similarly, Iwai Shunji, the Japanese filmmaker whose first feature film *Love Letter* (1995) has been highly inspirational to many East Asian filmmakers, has still a relatively obscure status and a limited appreciative fan base in the U.K., whereas his compatriot Miike Takashi is highly celebrated as a wonderfully eccentric Japanese maestro, although his works are often intended for the straight-to-video market in Japan.[42]

What is also interesting and perhaps unique about the way in which Tartan presents Asia Extreme is that it refers to the label as a genre. For instance, Tartan Films' owner McAlpine has referred the label to be a "brand [and] — a genre in itself," and Tartan's promotional booklet claims to provide "the story of the origin and development of the most exciting and unique of all contemporary genres." Congruently, Tartan USA website promotes the 2007 Asia Extreme Film Festival to "bring the up-and-coming genre of extreme Asian films to the United States."[43] This is problematic in the sense that the label in effect lumps together distinct and different genres of horror, action, and thriller films from Japan, South Korea, Hong Kong as well as Thailand under the banner of Asia Extreme. One Internet blogger's rather sarcastic remark that Tartan would "snap up any Asian movie that lingers over a corpse" does pinpoint the extreme label's antics that contrive to include anything from psychological horror to Hong Kong action thrillers, many of which can hardly be regarded as extreme compared to regular Hollywood thriller or horror flicks with a numerous body count (consider recent titles such as *Vacancy*, *Fracture*, and *The Invisible*).[44]

To be fair to Tartan, generic classification is notoriously problematic. As Mark Jancovich points out, "not only can the generic status of an individual film change over time, it can also be the object of intense struggle at a particular moment. A film which, for some, may seem to obviously belong to one genre may, for others, clearly belong to another genre altogether."[45] Moreover, as James Naremore comments, an individual genre has less to do with a group of artefacts than with a discourse — a loose evolving system of arguments and readings, helping to shape commercial strategies and aesthetic ideologies.[46] In this respect, Tartan's classification of Extreme Asia as a genre is neither wrong nor nonsensical. Indeed, as Rick Altman points out, genres are not "the permanent *product* of a singular origin, but the temporary *by-product* of an ongoing process."[47] Interestingly, Tartan seems to employ what Altman points out as typical Hollywood studios practice that strategically avoids specific generic terms.[48] In fact, Tartan's promotional material seldom employs generic vocabulary prevalent in film reviews. Instead, as noted earlier, it evokes shocking and dark nature that "unites" the films. However, such genrification of certain East Asian films should be understood as an integral part of providing illusions of discovery, that is, a way of knowing and classifying East Asian cinema. It should also be regarded as a marketing strategy that fronts certain films to sell all other titles, bearing in mind that no one in East Asia would set out to make an "extreme" film.

In the mean time, other distributors joined in developing their own East Asian film labels. For example, another London-based, foreign language films specialist Optimum Releasing set up the Optimum Asia division through which they released Studio Ghibli animations as well as Hong Kong comedy action films *Shaolin Soccer* (*Siu lam juk kau*, Stephen Chow, 2001) and South Korean monster film *The Host* (*Gwoemul*, Bong Joon-ho, 2006).[49] Columbia Tri-Star Home Entertainment also started a new series of Asian films called Eastern Edge, which focus on action films, while the Weinstein Company created a home entertainment label Dragon Dynasty. The latter, with Genius products, specializes in action films from East Asia. In 2003, Medusa Communications and Marketing launched Premier Asia, a brand dedicated to the cinema of Japan, Korea, and Thailand (as a sister label to the Hong Kong Legends label that Medusa started in 1999). Anchor Bay Entertainment, the subsidiary of Starz Media, also set up the new label, Dark Asia. While these new competitors can be regarded as attempts to cash in on the latest trend and are still catching up with Tartan Asia Extreme in terms of prestige and profile, they do testify the success of the trend set by Tartan.[50]

As in any business, there is a question as to how long Tartan's success can go on. According to Tartan's Press and PR Manager Paul Smith, the number of films being made in East Asia that can be fit into the Asia Extreme category is shrinking. Tartan already had a dilemma with Kim Ki-duk's *Spring, Summer, Autumn, Winter . . . and Spring* (*Bom yeoreum gaeul gyeoul geurigo bom*, 2003), which does not comfortably fit into the extreme category. In the end, the film was put in the more general Tartan Video category rather than in Asia Extreme. In this context, Tartan may have to look into the wider range of titles that are coming out of East Asia. But for now, it is, most of all, the ability to shock that sells East Asian films in the West.

Acknowledgements

My thanks go to Sarah Bemand, Clare Brownlee, and Paul Smith at Tartan for providing the images in this chapter.

II

Contextualizing Horror: Film Movement, National History, and Taboo

6

The Mummy Complex: Kurosawa Kiyoshi's *Loft* and J-horror

Chika Kinoshita

In the fall of 2006, as part of the publicity campaign for his latest feature *Loft* (filmed and completed in 2005 and released in September 2006), the director Kurosawa Kiyoshi spelled out his vision in making this horror film centering on a mummy and a ghost:

> These days, "Japanese horror" [*Japanizu hora*] in which everyday objects like the telephone and videotapes generate terror is in fashion. This film [*Loft*] is a fiction that deconstructs [*sakate ni toru*] this genre. Originally, the horror genre included a number of elements, like love story. Settings also varied; horror films were set in forests and lakeside, too. So I wanted to try them in a contemporary setting.[1]

Kurosawa clearly positioned *Loft* against the constellation of conventions and norms of "J-horror" films like *Ringu* (Nakata Hideo, 1998) and its cycle that capitalize on urban legends and media technologies in everyday life for the effects of fear.[2]

This chapter locates *Loft* — a hauntingly beautiful and yet enigmatically experimental genre film — within the contexts of J-horror's formations and transformations in Japanese film culture. I strategically subject this chapter's framework to the authorial comment by Kurosawa. Thus, it starts by constructing J-horror as a local movement in the late 1990s that comprised films, TV series, and film theory and criticism written by filmmakers, with particular emphasis on everyday life and media. Then, it analyzes *Loft* as a fruit borne out of Kurosawa's dialogical engagement with this movement. The final section reconnects J-horror and this film to issues of globalized film production and consumption, calling into question the framework of identity and difference that tends to underlie both Japanese critical discourse and North American reception.

This chapter also hopes to kindle further critical discussion on the cinema of Kurosawa Kiyoshi. I am not claiming to be discovering or introducing an unknown Japanese director to the Western audience by any means; on the contrary, Kurosawa Kiyoshi has been justly described as a "leading light" of New Japanese Cinema.³ Jerry White's *The Films of Kiyoshi Kurosawa: Master of Fear*, the first book-length criticism of his oeuvre, was published in 2007.⁴ Since his international breakthrough with *Cure* (Kurosawa Kiyoshi, 1997), his films have maintained regular presence at international film festivals, such as Toronto, Rotterdam, Venice, and Cannes, and occasionally played within the art-house film circuit across the world.⁵ Out of his prolific career, at least seven films, including earlier features such as *The Guard from Underground* (Kurosawa Kiyoshi, 1991), have become available on DVD from the Tartan Asia Extreme collection.⁶ *Pulse* (Jim Sonzero, 2006), the Hollywood remake of Kurosawa's *Kairo* (2000) which shares little aesthetic taste and stylistic concern with the original, came out in summer 2006, and has perhaps helped increase the original's visibility. Nevertheless, in English-language film scholarship, Kurosawa's cinema has not received adequate critical attention that its complexity and audacity deserves.⁷

What Is J-horror?

This chapter proposes to take "J-horror" in its narrowest and most precise meaning — what Kurosawa, in his above-quoted comment, called "Japanese horror" (*japanizu hora*), rather than in the broad meaning that covers all the horrific films made in Japanese language and by the Japanese film industry.⁸ J-horror specifically refers to a group of relatively low-budget horror films made in Japan during the late 1990s, such as the *Ringu* cycle. A closely knit network of filmmakers and critics, including Kurosawa, has been involved in the production of those films. Aesthetically, J-horror films concentrate on the low-key production of atmospheric and psychological fear, rather than graphic gore, capitalizing on urban legends proliferated through mass media and popular culture. Furthermore, by calling J-horror a "movement" rather than a genre in a film industry, this chapter takes filmmakers' writings on horror aesthetics as well as film texts into consideration as integral part of the

J-horror discourse.[9] The J-horror discourse revolves around affective relationships among horror films, the spectator (as a textual construct), and actual fans. Thus, filmmakers' writings go beyond the authorial comments on their own films, encompassing three other genres: (1) descriptive and prescriptive theorizations of the horror aesthetics; (2) reviews of horror films from a variety of cinematic traditions across time and space; and (3) autobiographical narratives of their horror fandom/cinephilia. In this sense, the producer and the consumer of the horror genre overlap with each other within the J-horror discourse, following the well-treaded path of Nouvelle Vague, and, at the same time, forming isomorphism with the contemporary otaku movement in Japan.[10]

The J-horror discourse is identified with a handful of filmmakers and cast whose names are recurrently credited across different films. Beside the directors, screenwriters Takahashi Hiroshi and Konaka Chiaki and producer Ichise Takashige are particularly notable. Takahashi Hiroshi wrote Kurosawa's masterpiece *The Serpent's Path* (1998), Nakata's feature debut *Don't Look Up* (1996), *Ringu* and *Ringu 2* (1999), and Tsuruta Norio's *Ringu O: Birthday* (2000). He also participated in Shimizu Takashi's *Ju-on* (2000) as a supervisor (*kanshu*). Konaka Chiaki wrote Kurosawa's *Door 3* (1996), Nakata's *Sleeping Bride* a.k.a. *The Glass Brain* (2000), and Shimizu's *Marebito* (2004). Both screenwriters have been prolific on horror aesthetics and fandom, thus constituting the very core of the J-horror discourse. Ichise Takashige produced almost everything — from the *Ringu* cycle, the *Ju-on* cycle, Nakata's *Dark Water* (2002), to Kurosawa's latest horror *Retribution* (2006). Furthermore, in 2004, Ichise inaugurated the "J-Horror Theater" (J-Horror *shiata*) label to be distributed through Toho, marshalling the six masters of horror, Kurosawa, Nakata, Ochiai Masayuki, Shimizu, Takahashi (as the director), and Tsuruta, with each director contributing one film to the label. Thus, J-horror has self-reflexively consolidated the 1990s' successes into an international brand name.[11]

Most of the J-horror filmmakers belong to the same generation and culture.[12] Born around 1960 (Nakata 1961, Tsuruta 1961, Takahashi 1959, Konaka 1961, and Ichise 1961), they were fostered by a variety of cinematic and mass-cultural traditions. Those traditions include American and European modern horrors like the works of Richard Fleischer, Tobe Hooper, John Carpenter, and Mario Bava, American and Japanese TV horrors, manga, such as horror comics by Koga Shin'ichi (*Ekoeko azaraku*) and Yamagishi Ryoko, and the best of international cinema that became available in art-house theaters within the bubble economy of the 1980s. They were avid cinephiles who started off making films in college cine-clubs and had a keen interest in film history and critical theory. Some took courses with film critics or scholars, such as Hasumi Shigehiko (Kurosawa at Rikkyo University, Nakata at the University of Tokyo) or Asanuma Keiji (Konaka at Seijo University). All of them developed their film aesthetics and techniques through making low-budget made-for-video features (V-Cinema) and/or TV projects, like the *Haunted School* (*Gakko no kaidan*) series. In addition, in terms of the generation, background, and taste, the creators of J-horror have close professional and/ or personal ties with the cutting edge of contemporary Japanese independent cinema, such as Aoyama Shinji and Shinozaki Makoto.

Kurosawa occupies an odd position, as it were, vis-à-vis other J-horror filmmakers. About one generation older (born in 1955), he had made some of the most important horror films such as *Sweet Home* (1989) and *The Guard from Underground* before the J-horror boom materialized and thus enjoys respect from the J-horror filmmakers as the forerunner. As we have seen, he shares staff and crews with J-horror and often participated in the same low-budget, made-for-video, and/or TV projects. At the same time, Kurosawa acknowledges that the J-horror boom abroad has brought him a retrospective international recognition and influenced his career greatly.[13] As I will argue later, the formations and transformations of the J-horror movement and Kurosawa's response to them are woven into the contexts of global film production and consumption.

The J-horror discourse itself is, however, emphatically aesthetic and affective. The following two sections, therefore, contextualize *Loft's* construction and destruction of cinematic time and space vis-à-vis the J-horror aesthetics. At this point, it suffices to simply state that the central aesthetics of the J-horror discourse is best described as the "uncanny," that is, the feeling of dread and horror aroused by what is known of familiar. Remember that Sigmund Freud clearly defines his celebrated essay as an *aesthetic* investigation. Freud locates the uncanny, both in real psychic life and in fiction, in the two sets of phenomena: (1) the indiscernibility of the living and the dead, the animate and the inanimate, and the human and the nonhuman, and (2) repetition.[14] As perhaps most clearly exemplified by the film *Ringu's* use of the telephone, the videotape, and the TV monitor, J-horror films draw on the media saturated environment in contemporary Japan in order to activate the uncanny, making supernatural apparitions through technologies of mechanical reproduction and electronic communications in the living room. As we will see shortly, this "media horror" aspect of the movement hinges upon the J-horror discourse's broader concern with the possibility of representation and visibility of the supernatural. *Loft* addresses this concern through its rendering of two monsters: the mummy and the ghost.

On the other hand, the J-horror discourse lacks discussion of gender, while insights into family and gender in contemporary Japan abound in films themselves. This chapter interrogates J-horror and Kurosawa's aesthetics of space, pushing them toward gender politics. In his ground-setting essays, Robin Wood spells out that the family is a "single unifying master-figure" of different motifs of American horror of the (post-) Vietnam era; the family produces the monsters, be they psychotics, terrible children, or cannibals.[15] In this light, a casual survey of J-horror films is enough to fathom the depth of crisis in the normative family life of the recessionary Japan; single parents, abused, abandoned, and/or murdered children constitute most J-horror narratives. This thematic obsession and the J-horror aesthetics of the uncanny nurture each other in the setting of urban everyday life. In isolated apartments, women, often mothers, are particularly susceptible to contacts with supernatural beings, if she herself is not among them. J-horror films, most notably Nakata's works such as *Dark Water*, capitalize on women's identification with space.

Kurosawa's cinema, again, takes an odd and yet privileged position within the constellation of the J-horror discourse. He has produced perhaps the most radical media horror *Kairo*; yet, as the same film vividly demonstrates, he makes horror films without normative family as an entity to be threatened.[16] While there are remarkably touching and disturbing depictions of married couples in Kurosawa's oeuvre (*Séance*, 1999, and *Cure*), there is virtually no child as a recognizable character. This lack does not suggest his disengagement with this central issue of the horror film. To the contrary, I will argue that *Loft* questions the gendered dichotomy of narrative and space by destabilizing the woman's relationship with everyday life.

Loft as Media Horror

Loft centers on a young woman writer named Haruna Reiko (Nakatani Miki), a former winner of the prestigious Akutagawa Prize. On top of the writer's block she has been struggling with, she starts suffering a strange physical symptom; she throws up black mud. Moving to an old house that her editor Kijima (Nishijima Hidetoshi) has found for her in the countryside seems to promise a good change. Next to the country house, however, stands a run-down building that belongs to Sagami University. She soon finds out that a mysterious archaeology professor named Yoshioka Makoto (Toyokawa Etsushi) keeps the mummy of a noble beauty from a thousand years ago in the building. The large amount of mud in her stomach probably caused her death and at the same time prevented her body from decay. Reiko agrees to hide the mummy in her house during some students' visit to the university facility; trust and love start to develop between Reiko and Yoshioka. While living with the mummy, Reiko plagiarizes a manuscript she found in the house. Supernatural phenomena start to happen; she has been seeing a ghost. It is soon revealed that Kijima murdered the former tenant, an aspiring writer named Aya (Adachi Yumi), with whom he was romantically involved. After Kijima's arrest, the shadow of doubt about Yoshioka's role in the murder case threatens him and Reiko; when he strangled Aya and buried her body, had she already been dead? Did she come to life or appear as a ghost? Does their love survive this challenge?

While *Loft* self-consciously deviates from the J-horror movement's conventions through its setting in a country house, as Kurosawa states in his above-quoted comment, it also crystallizes its central aesthetics of the technological uncanny in the sequence where Reiko watches a found 16 mm footage of the mummy. Art critic Sawaragi Noi, in his essay on the film, argues that this stop-motion 16 mm footage, showing the *immobile* mummy, perhaps produces the most horrific moment of *Loft*, simply due to the film medium's uncanny nature, its inability to tell the inanimate from the animate.[17] A close examination of the sequence, however, sheds new light on the issues of temporality and Kurosawa's relationship with the J-horror movement.

Reiko, fascinated by the mysterious archaeological research that seems ongoing in the run-down building next door, has her friend, the editor Megumi (Suzuki Sawa), arrange the screening of the footage found in a small film company's archive. The man at the archive (Kato Haruhiko who appeared in Kurosawa's *Kairo* and *The Doppelgänger*, 2002) tells Reiko and Megumi that in the 1930s, a research team located and dragged a mummy out of the Green Lake (Midorinuma), and left the film. The 1930s team apparently filmed the mummy for several days in a row, relying on stop motion; the grainy footage shows the mummy lying still on the operating table (see Figure 6.1). It is unknown whether this mummy can be identified with the mummy that occupies Reiko's mind, the one recently discovered by Professor Yoshioka in the same lake. There is no record of what happened to the mummy and the 1930s research team. Thus, three kinds of time layer with each other in this footage within the filmic discourse: the time of the mummy, that of shooting, and that of projection.

The mummy in *Loft* is, needless to say, a function of the passage of time; it literally comes from the past, one thousand years ago. It compels the viewer to mention André Bazin's infamous "ontology" essay. Bazin speaks of the

Figure 6.1   *Loft* (Kurosawa Kiyoshi, 2006)

practice of embalming: "To preserve, artificially, his bodily appearance is to snatch it from the flow of time, to stow it away neatly, so to speak, in the hold of life. It was natural, therefore, to keep up appearances in the face of the reality of death by preserving flesh and bone."[18] The photographic medium, particularly film, came to fulfill this human desire to halt the passage of time: "The film is no longer content to preserve the object, enshrouded as it were in an instant, as the bodies of insects are preserved intact, out of the distant past, in amber. The film delivers baroque art from its convulsive catalepsy. Now, for the first time, the image of things is likewise the image of their duration, change mummified as it were" (15). I am sure Kurosawa had this passage in mind when conceiving this film. Indeed, Kurosawa reveals his Bazininan profile in explaining his preference for long takes: "Regardless of how conscious Louis Lumière was, film is, in principle, completely different from moved photographs [*ugoku shashin*, such as Thomas Alba Edison's Kinetoscope, in Kurosawa's theory]. Film is a medium that records both time and space and thereby conveys the fact that that was certainly there."[19]

Yet, in *Loft*'s case, even if the footage of the motionless mummy is an index and therefore evidence of what was actually there, the terror operates on film's potentiality to manipulate time and duration as "moved photographs." As the Kato character suggests, the intention behind the filming of the mummy by stop motion for the continuous duration of several days intimates the mummy's history or potential of movement. In other words, the time lapse between frames, rather than the Bazinian duration of material reality, creates terror. This aesthetics of almost invisible discontinuity, as it were, resonates with some other segments of *Loft*.[20] There are barely perceptible and yet disconcerting jump cuts at several occasions; one such example would be the scene in which Reiko ascends the staircase in her country house, sensing something supernatural upstairs.

In this light, the mummy footage aligns itself with another brilliant use of found footage in Kurosawa's career, the recording of the hypnotic treatment of a hysteric woman from the turn of the last century in *Cure* (see Figure 6.2). In *Cure*, Detective Takabe (Yakusho Koji) and psychiatrist Sakuma (Ujiki Tsuyoshi) watch a video transfer of the 16 mm footage Sakuma found in his hospital's archive on a home VCR. In the footage, the finger of the invisible hypnotist in the foreground gestures "X." Takabe plays back the video repeatedly for a better view of the gesture; the slow motion of the moving image on the TV screen, *à la* Jean-Luc Godard in his late films, gets on the viewer's nerves. As we find out, the footage hypnotizes its diegetic viewers, Sakuma and Takabe, into self-destructive and murderous acts. Kurosawa's fake found footage, in *Cure* and in *Loft*, operates on manipulation either at the time of filming or at that of viewing in the diegesis, as well as indexicality. While Kurosawa's medium-consciousness and fascination with luminous screens participate in a number of genealogies from Godard to the radiant TV monitor in *The Poltergeist* (Tobe Hooper, 1982), it most closely intersects with the J-horror discourse.

Figure 6.2 *Cure* (Kurosawa Kiyoshi, 1997)

J-horror films stand out in the field of horror through its aspect as media horror. Of course, *Ringu* in which the copying and circulating of the VHS tape itself constitutes horror most vividly illustrates this point. Yet, a number of other films, such as *Kairo*, *Premonition* (Tsuruta Norio, 2004), and *Reincarnation* (Shimizu Takashi, 2004) take media and technologies, such as the Internet, newspapers, and film, as the sources of terror. Matt Hills points out thematic affinities between *Ringu* and what he dubs as media horror in the U.S., such as *The Blair Witch Project* (Daniel Myrick and Eduardo Sánchez, 1999) and *FeardotCom* (William Malone, 2002), suggesting the Japanese film's indebtedness to a contemporary media environment, rather than to indigenous folk traditions.[21] While I think J-horror films, most notably Kurosawa's works like *The Serpent Path* and *Kairo,* directly inspired such recent media horror films in Hollywood as *FeardotCom* and *White Noise* (Geoffrey Sax, 2005),[22] seeking for a common matrix for those films, as Hills does, is of more critical interest than drawing on a language of influence, let alone that of rip-off. In effect, J-horror films as media horror participate in the project of global modernity in the tradition of André de Lorde's Grand Guignol play *Au telephone* (1901) and its film adaptations like G. W. Griffith's *The Lonely Villa* (1909) that play out anxieties brought to bourgeois everyday life by the then-new technology, the telephone.[23]

Indeed, it is possible to read J-horror's engagement with technology and media as a symptom of human alienation caused by technological mediation in contemporary society.[24] Yet, even if the J-horror discourse addresses, articulates, and ultimately exploits contemporary anxieties as any successful horror narrative should, it undermines the nostalgic and reactionary logic of alienation, a logic that presupposes or imagines a lost paradise in which human beings had organic symbiosis with Nature and with each other. Rather, the J-horror discourse's particular emphasis on simulacra and its concomitant denial (or at least suspension) of narrative causality form what I call a non-originary aesthetics.

At the plot level, there is no need to mystify this. The non-originary materializes itself as the film's hesitation to, failure in, or refusal of achieving the complex discovery plot. The complex discovery plot, as Noël Carroll proposes as the basic plot structure of horror, comprises four stages: onset (horrific phenomena), discovery (of the possible cause of the phenomena in question), confirmation (of the hypothesis), and confrontation (with the cause, most typically the monster).[25] Carroll convincingly argues for this formulae's relevance:

> The emotion of art-horror is generated in part by the apprehension of something that defies categorization in virtue of our standing or commonplace ways of conceptualizing the order of things. That this subject matter should be wedded to narrative structures that enact and expatiate upon the discovery of the unknown seems perfectly appropriate. The point of the horror genre . . . is to exhibit, disclose, and manifest that which is, putatively in principle, unknown and unknowable. It can be no accident that the plots that are characteristically mobilized to motivate this moment of unavoidable recognition are concerned to show that, within the fiction, what is unknown is *known*

or has become, as the plotting would have it, undeniable. Rendering the unknown known is, in fact, the point of such plots, as well as the source of their seductiveness.

That is, horror stories are predominantly concerned with knowledge as a theme. (127, the original italics)

The J-horror discourse undermines, sabotages, or at least frustrates this structure of horror premised upon the play of knowledge. In effect, *Ringu* is rather exceptional in this regard as it perfectly embodies this structure. In a number of other J-horror films, the director concentrates on schizophrenic outbursts of terror and screams so much so that the discovery-confirmation plot is extremely thinned out (*Ju-on*), or in some cases, the discovery and confirmation seed the unknown rather than the known, with no proper resolution at the end (*Premonition*).

Kurosawa goes furthest in this direction. While Kurosawa admits his profound lack of interest in causality in plot structure,[26] he is more than capable of filming well-made linear narratives, as testified by his early features made within strict generic and/or commercial constraints, like the quintessential slasher *The Guard from Underground,* or *Dingdong: The Passion of Men* (*Jan: Otokotachi no gekijo*, 1994) which is about a rivalry in professional cycling. His statue has been elevated among the most prominent directors in contemporary Japan, allowing him to produce non-originary plots in such genre-films-gone-wild as *The Doppelgänger* and *Loft*.

The failed or loosened complex discovery plot in J-horror films is neither a sign of incompetence nor a manifestation of traditional Japanese aesthetics or philosophy — zen, *monono aware*, or whatever. It is, rather, the J-horror discourse's theoretical position-taking within the transnational history of horror aesthetics.[27] The screenwriter Konaka Chiaki, one of the masterminds behind the discourse, succinctly states: ". . . [H]orror stories with clear causal explanations (*in'nen banashi*) are not scary at all . . . After all, terror is absurd."[28] Likewise, Kurosawa points out that the part of *Ringu* that struggles to explain Sadako's history is the weakest element of the otherwise excellent film.[29] Furthermore, the motifs of technological reproducibility and mass media, combined with the negligence of causality in the plot structure, literalize and *textualize* the issues of simulacra — their proliferations with neither a cause nor the original.[30] In order to illustrate this point, let us look at a sequence from *Don't Look Up*, Nakata's 1996 theatrical feature debut that gave him an instant cult status. It is in this film that most actors of the J-horror discourse agree to locate one of its origins, an origin of the non-originary aesthetics.[31]

Don't Look Up takes place in a film studio that apparently has a long history. Murai (Yanagi Yurei), having worked as an assistant director there, is now shooting his feature debut. (It is easy to superimpose Nakata himself who started his career as an assistant director at Nikkatsu with this character.) Murai, together with his crew, watches rushes of his film. In the middle of a sequence, the screen suddenly flashes into blank frames, and then a series of shots Murai never filmed start to appear on screen: shots-reverse shots of a woman in kimono and a man with the 1950s matinee idol looks, and a boy ascending a dark staircase. The woman in a medium close-up shows fear and then agony, with her hand clasped on her chest. In the blurred background of her figure, we see a girl with long hair in a white robe, laughing — an icon that would haunt the J-horror screens as its emblem (see Figure 6.3). This footage is intermittently cut to close-ups of Murai with an impassive — puzzled and/or fascinated — look, sitting in the darkness of the studio auditorium. A full shot of a dark, old bathroom follows, and the projection ends when the door in the bathroom is about to open. As soon as the light turns up, Murai and the staff begin mumbling with each other in confusion.

Figure 6.3 *Don't Look Up* (Nakata Hideo, 1996)

This sequence crystallizes J-horror's take on terror, temporality, and archive, at the genre's genesis. The strange segment turns out to be a found footage, whose identity and status in the objective reality of the diegesis remains unclear throughout *Don't Look Up*. In the narrative, an old-timer projectionist (Takahashi Akira) initially rationalizes the creepy images as an old undeveloped footage accidentally mixed up with Murai's film. Yet, Murai insists that he has seen it somewhere, probably on TV, as a child, and undertakes research on this matter. Its outcome suggests that it probably belongs to a TV drama in the 1960s, the production and broadcast of which was halted after the mysterious death of the leading actors. Then, how could Murai possibly have seen a show that was neither completed nor broadcast? Moreover, no one finds out the identity of the ghost — that laughing girl — even after she has presumably taken the young actress Saori (Ishibashi Kei)'s life and eventually Murai's. In this sense, the original Japanese title *Joyûrei* (the Actress Ghost) is erroneous; the film is not about the ghost of an actress. Not a horrible story behind the surface of the celluloid, but the lack thereof and the surface itself, generate terror.

In his book, *Hora eiga no miryoku: fandamentaru hora sengen* (The fascination of horror films: A manifesto of fundamental horror), Konaka reveals what Takahashi and Kurosawa called the Konaka Theory (*Konaka riron*), that is, a set of formulae for the horror film aesthetics. The Konaka Theory and Takahashi's film criticism, read together, take us directly to the heart of J-horror's media-specific concern: how to represent the ghost. Konaka contends that while the horror film genre has monsters, vampires, zombies, and extraterritorial creatures, nothing is as scary as ghosts. Thus, *The Innocents* (Jack Clayton, 1961), *The Haunting* (Robert Wise, 1963), and *Kill, Baby . . . Kill!* (Mario Bava, 1966), are always on top of most filmmakers' favorite film lists in the J-horror discourse. Takahashi clearly links the issue of ghosts to the photographic uncanny:

> Suppose there is an actor. We have a photograph of him. No one can tell whether he is a ghost or a human being just by looking at his photo. In the world of cinema, such a strange situation can emerge. Some time ago, strange rumor about an actress in a TV commercial spread among children. In fact, the actress had been dead, and what we watched on TV was none other than the dead, it said. Of interest is that this rumor saliently indicates the limits of the photographic image; it cannot clearly tell a human being from a ghost.[32]

I am not suggesting that this is a novel idea. Rather, it aligns the J-horror discourse with a long tradition of film theory that shows particular fascination with the photo-based film's ability to render the living and the dead, the human and the ghost, and the animate and the inanimate indiscernible. The horror film, however, has to go beyond this recognition; it has to terrify the viewer by making the ghost ghostly, discernible from the human being. Takahashi and Konaka suggest a number of techniques that activate the uncanny, liberally exploiting the iconography of spirit photographs that proliferates in tabloids, teen magazines, and afternoon TV shows in contemporary Japan. Takahashi offers a list of the six existing techniques for representation of the ghost:

1) Don't show the face.
   Show only a fragment of the body or clothes. Or, put it in a long shot so that the details of its face are blurred.
2) Make the standing position or behavior unnatural.
   Human beings have a specifically human sense of space and distance between themselves. Position someone in such a way to defy this sense subtly. If it glares at us from that position, it would be scary.
3) Make its movement non-human.
   Make its movement unrelated to the natural motility of human muscles. It could look like a zombie if handled poorly, though.
4) Put it [a body part] in an impossible position.
   A well-known spirit photograph shows a hand put on a classmate's shoulder. Also, things like a face looking up from the bottom of a doorway would be creepy.
5) Use an awesome face.
   There is nothing to add, if the actor's face terrifies. It is an ultimate tour-de-force, an ideal of the ghost film.
6) Show nothing.
   Your weapon is premonition and atmosphere in space and the use of sound. Robert Wise' *The Haunting* [1963] is an exemplary case.[33]

For Takahashi, what approximates the experience of seeing a ghost is the sight of a corpse (24). Konaka, agreeing with Takahashi, adds further technical specifications: it is not a good idea to let the ghost speak directly; the ghost's voice is most scary when mediated through technology of mechanical reproduction, such as recording and broadcasting (Konaka, 114–15).

In this context, Shimizu Takashi's *Ju-on* (video, 2000), *Juon: The Grudge* (film, 2003) marked a certain break in the history of J-horror. Some even locate the end of J-horror at its release. As we know, Shimizu has no hesitation in *showing* the monster or the ghost. Takahashi conveys his and his colleague Kurosawa's sense of shock and awe in watching a short video project by Shimizu, then one of their students at Tokyo Bigakko (the Film School of Tokyo). The four-minute clip was what would become the climax of the feature video and film; the woman-monster crawled down the stairs, with absolutely no build-up of narrative or atmospheric fear (48).

The mummy in *Loft*, too, breaks with the J-horror aesthetics when it starts being animated and moving onscreen. Its movement takes place in Yoshioka's laboratory, dimly lit by the flickering florescent light and waving sunlight shed through the curtains. In this sequence, Yoshioka's three women, as it were — Aya, the mummy, and Reiko — visit him.³⁴ While Yoshioka attempts and hesitates to dissect the mummy's stomach in order to "free" her from her eternal life by removing the black mud, Aya's ghost appears to threaten his conscience. Then, having left Aya in the next room, Yoshioka buries his face in his hand, sitting on his bed. The slightly shaky hand-held camera conveys his agony in a medium shot. It cuts to the mummy lying on an operating table in another room; the shot is dark, making her body a silhouette. With eerie music on the soundtrack, she swiftly raises her torso. As she stably sits up, sunlight from screen right mysteriously lights up her hair (see Figure 6.4). A long shot juxtaposes her moving toward the camera in the background with Yoshioka sitting with his face covered by his hands in the foreground. While a series of close-ups show the mummy's face in full view — a fine-featured gray face with no eyes — a brief close-up of the frightened Yoshioka is inserted only a moment before she throws herself on him in a two-shot. As Yoshioka tells her to "solve your problem by yourself," her head falls on the ground all too soon. He removes the mud from her headless body and eventually burns it, accompanied by Reiko.

Figure 6.4 *Loft* (Kurosawa Kiyoshi, 2006)

Thus, the mummy deviates from the uncanny of the photographic medium that conflates the living and the dead, a central concern of the J-horror discourse that has already lost its initial shock value. The mummy transgresses the boundary between the living and the dead, without being mediated by either technology or Yoshioka's gaze. Then, what is the mummy in *Loft*, after all?

It is no accident that the mummy sequence is held between two imageries of the incinerator located in the back of Reiko's house. Reiko burns her manuscript, that is, her plagiarism of Aya's novel, and, together with Yoshioka, burns the mummy. As both Aya and Reiko are under the influence of the mummy for some reason which the film does not explain, the incinerator turns the links between the two women into ashes. Moreover, the mummy and writing encapsulate time in a different manner from technologies of mechanical reproduction. Both attest the woman's desire to survive the passage of time and overcome death, even though her desire has been distorted through either material transformation or plagiarism. By burning the mummy and the manuscript, Reiko pulls them from circulation in media culture: Yoshioka's university colleagues were planning to display the mummy in a much-publicized exhibition; Aya's novel would have gone into press by Reiko's name, if she had not taken it out of Kijima's files. Unlike more conventionally well-crafted horror narratives, however, what motivates Reiko's act of pulling the novel and the mummy from circulation is not prevention of contamination or infection. *Loft* opens with the close-up of Reiko in the mirror with no make-up who fears the sign of aging.[35] Thus, Reiko's burning them is to "free" herself, as well as the other two women, from the desire to overcome the passage of time, or the mummy complex.

Then, is *Loft* Reiko's story? I will pursue this question of possession, ownership, origin, and subjectivity as I examine the issues of space in *Loft* and J-horror in the following section.

Gender and Space in *Loft*

Kurosawa has repeatedly described *Loft*'s focus on the women characters as an exception and therefore a challenge in his career.[36] Yet, he has made at least two other films that have significant female protagonists, *Door 3* and *Séance*, both of which possess strong J-horror elements in terms of production, target audience, subject themes, and motifs. *Door 3* centers on an obsessive romantic relationship between a beautiful and ambitious insurance saleswoman, Miyako (Tanaka Minako), and a seductive young executive, Fujiwara (Nakazawa Akiyasu), who turns out to be possessed by an exotic parasite like those in *Shivers* (David Cronenberg, 1976) (White, 53). It shares the motifs of possession and orality with *Loft*. *Séance*, originally made for TV, focuses on Junko (Fubuki Jun), a middle-aged homemaker gifted with the ability to see things, featuring the emblematic image of J-horror, the evil ghost of a little girl with long hair. The drama in this psychological horror hinges upon the question of whether Junko and her husband Sato (Yakusho Koji) have murdered the little girl who is accidentally trapped in his trunk: Is she still alive when she creeps out of the trunk? Does the ghost play tricks on them, staging a murder of the already dead? The same motif of killing the already dead returns to *Loft*, haunting the relationship between Reiko and Yoshioka. Within Kurosawa's filmography, *Loft* certainly pronounces close affinity with these two films, rather than with his "art-house" productions, such as *Bright Future* (2003).

On the other hand, indeed, the gender of the protagonist functions to question the politics of space in Kurosawa's world. As I have argued elsewhere, the space in Kurosawa's previous films, characterized by the erasure of history and ownership, embodies the non-originary aesthetics.[37] The ruins that have ubiquitous presence in his films — from the basement in *The Guard from Underground* to the run-down building occupied by the child pornographers and murderers in *The Serpent's Path* — are not the site of memory and history. They are abandoned by their proper owners long before the films' diegetic time starts, and therefore appropriated by criminals, yakuza, and ghosts for murky activities. The ruins in Kurosawa's world, however, are not always shadowed by negativity. In his non-horror films, such as *License to Live* (Kurosawa, 1998) and the *Suit Yourself or Shoot Yourself* (*Katte ni shiyagare*) series (Kurosawa, 1995–96), ruins or abandoned dwellings provide the socially marginalized with sites for constructing family-like communities based on the practices of play and negotiation, rather than on "natural" and normative bonds such as blood lineage or the institution of marriage.

Introduction of gender as a perspective offers a different view of this potentially emancipatory practice of space in Kurosawa's films. In a number of his films, women characters are tied to specific spaces often called "home." In *Cure*, the mentally disturbed Fumie (Nakagawa Anna) awaits her husband Takabe in their apartment every day, with the empty dryer continuously running. For Detective Anjo (Aikawa Sho)'s impeccable wife Saeko (Osawa Itsumi) in *Fukushu: unmei no homonsha* (*Revenge: The Fateful Visitor,* Kurosawa, 1996), their apartment is the only safe place. As soon as she leaves it, she is kidnapped by a monstrous family and ends up as a body in a garbage bag. The above-mentioned two films centering on women pronounce the gendered politics of space most saliently. In *Séance*, most sequences take place in Junko and Sato's suburban house; her confinement in the domestic space causes her depression and dissatisfaction. She takes a part-time job as a waitress at a local family restaurant only to quit it after seeing a ghost on the shoulder of a customer. In contrast, *Door 3* presents Miyako as a woman on the go who is always literally moving from one space to another. Yet, her involvement with Fujiwara who is strongly associated with the space of his house eventually compromises her mobility. In other words, Kurosawa's characters are split into two categories in terms of their relationship with space:

the appropriators of space with no name, which do include some young unmarried women (*shojo*) in the *Suit Yourself or Shoot Yourself* series, and the women who belong to specific spaces — or rather, places. In this sense, Kurosawa's previous films generally reproduce the classic gendered dichotomy in space and narrative; women are tied to or identified with a space through the prescribed gender roles.[38]

The instability of and contradictions in the politics of space in *Loft* largely derive themselves from the women's ambiguous relations with space, which indicate, I think, an intriguing departure from the gendered dichotomy. Let us start by considering the narrative device of a woman writer from a big city moving to a country house to finish her novel. This device functions as an intertextual knot, invoking at least two films that draw on the same motif, *I Spit on Your Grave* (Meir Zarchi, 1978) and *Swimming Pool* (François Ozon, 2003). Unlike the rape revenge masterpiece *I Spit on Your Grave*, however, the countryside in which Reiko moves — somewhere within an hour of drive from downtown Tokyo — is completely devoid of the cultural and economic codes of the "rural" that are set in stark opposition to the urban in the American horror imagery.[39] Along with *Charisma* (Kurosawa, 1999), *Loft* suggests that in Kurosawa's world, the evil is not localized in a culturally coded "place" like countryside but ubiquitous in homogenized space. In other words, *Loft*, in line with other Kurosawa films, undermines the stable identity of geographical locations.

With *Swimming Pool*, *Loft* shares the implicitly sexualized relationship between the editor and the writer, and it manifests itself through her moving into the property he controls. Yet, while Sarah (Charlotte Rampling) meets her editor (Charles Dance)'s oversexed daughter (Ludivine Sagnier) and ends up covering her accidental murder, Reiko finds the ghost of Kijima's former lover-victim. Reiko thus joins the ranks of gothic horror heroines, like the Joan Fontaine character in *Rebecca* (Hitchcock, 1940), following Claire (Michelle Pfeiffer) of *What Lies Beneath* (Robert Zemeckis, 2000), the film Kurosawa cites as an immediate source of inspiration.[40] The woman's entrapment in the place filled with a horrible history of murder sets those paranoiac narratives going. *Loft*'s flirtation with this subgenre, however, stops here. Kurosawa's mise-en-scène refuses to establish Reiko's tangible connection with, and sense of belonging to, the house, primarily through the lack of descriptions of everyday life. She writes on her computer, smokes, drinks water, walks inside her house with her shoes on (blatantly defying the Japanese custom), falls asleep in her daytime dress, and never cooks nor eats. In this sense, her life exactly mirrors Yoshioka's with the mummy in his university facility.

Moreover, unlike *Swimming Pool*, *I Spit on Your Grave*, and *What Lies Beneath*, the film's narration vacillates between Reiko's perception and Yoshioka's. In *Loft*, a film obsessed with the acts of seeing and being seen, the introduction of dual perspective has two significant consequences. First, it shatters the film's possibility of belonging to the "fantastic" as Tzvetan Todorov defines it, that is, the genre of fiction where it remains uncertain whether a seemingly supernatural event is what the protagonist imagines or what actually takes place.[41] As Kurosawa himself admits, it is not possible for Reiko to be imagining things like the mummy and Aya's ghost, as it is for Claire in *What Lies Beneath*. Second, Yoshioka's perspective aligns Reiko with the ghost and the mummy, resulting in a fascinating confusion where it is no longer clear who is the monster. While Aya's appearance in the house is conveyed through Reiko's perception (not necessarily optical POV), Reiko's visit to the Sagami University facility is captured from Yoshioka's perspective from the inside, rendering her exactly like the ghost she is afraid of, as a blurred figure that presses her hand onto the frosted glass window (see Figure 6.5).

Figure 6.5   *Loft* (Kurosawa Kiyoshi, 2006)

Of course, there is a long tradition of forging an affinity between woman and monster in terms of the allocated position as a spectacle-image-object within patriarchy.[42] Above all, in *Loft*, the two monsters are female. Nevertheless, I would argue that the value system of Kurosawa's politics of space privileges those who, without belonging to a place, appropriate a space with neither history nor origin, be they monsters, ghosts, criminals, or freeters. Starting with the framework of woman's horror, *Loft* ends up depicting Reiko as an appropriator of space. It is in this sense that Reiko stands alone at the ruins of the J-horror discourse, presenting a possibility of going beyond gendered identity and definition.[43]

J-horror as a Function of Globalization

The J-horror discourse involves the filmmakers' self-reflexive consciousness of globalization and the international film market. Remember that Kurosawa's statement I quoted at the beginning of this chapter transcribes the English words "Japanese horror" in *katakana* (the phonetic script often used for foreign words). Kurosawa participated in the Sundance Festival's month-long workshop in 1992 in Park City, Utah; his autobiographical writings in this century have been filled with impressions of foreign film festivals where he had direct contacts with the international audience. *Loft* is Kurosawa's first co-production with the Korean producer Jason Chae. Above all, Kurosawa, a horror fan who bought the videos of *The Texas Chain Saw Massacre* (Tobe Hooper, 1974) and *The Night of the Living Dead* (George Romero, 1968) on his first paycheck and watched them repeatedly until they were literally worn out,[44] would never determine his or other's genealogy as a filmmaker by the national boundary. While I have called attention to the local network of Japanese filmmakers in a specific place and generation, I am not suggesting that J-horror is a *native* film movement, if there is such a thing. By the same token, it is misleading to immediately label Hollywood remakes of J-horror films as global capital's exploitation of a native culture; a local film culture and global capital are not distinct and autonomous entities. The use of "J," not the neutral "Japanese," let alone "Nippon," helps us spell out this point.

At the close of the twentieth century, the letter "J" emerged with particular significance in Japanese cultural production and consumption. Starting with J-League (the professional succor league that inaugurated in 1993) and J-Pop (popular music), it became prevalent in a number of different spheres, like J-*bungaku* (literature) and J-*hihyo* (critical theory). "J" certainly stands for "Japanese" to both Japanese and international audiences but at the same time announces a break from the putative tradition as self-consciously mass-cultural.

In his oft-cited critique of J-phenomena, particularly J-*kaiki* (Return to "J"), social critic Asada Akira succinctly unpacks the historical connotations of J as an emphatically pop "return" to Japan as a simulacrum on the surface of commodity culture. The "Japan" to which J-artifacts and their producers, fans, and critics seek to return is not the imagined abiding national tradition, as the "Return to Japan" (*Nihon kaiki*) movement in the 1930s cultural production.[45] This time, the return is to an inauthentic Japan of pop and otaku cultures, thoroughly mediated by consumer capitalism. Asada argues, however, that the J-phenomena, nonetheless claiming on certain uniqueness and indigenousness on the very ground of its status as simulacra, prove to be none other than a reactionary response to the cosmopolitanism and multiculturalism conditioned by globalization and late capitalism.[46] Tomiko Yoda justly points out that Asada's critique of J-culture unwittingly reproduces the dichotomy of Japanese parochialism and global postmodernity. Cultural nationalism has always necessitated the international framework for its formation and validation since its inception. Yet, the immediacy with which the local is subsumed into global capital has become unparalleled.[47] In other words, the letter "J" is of use as a reminder that globalization is constitutive of local culture.

While J-horror snugly fits in the constellation of J-cultural artifacts in the late 1990s, a close examination of the discourse, as I have demonstrated, reveals its emphatically *modern* interest in the uncanny, the medium specificity, technologies of mechanical reproducibility, everyday life, and implicitly, the changing gender roles and family. Even Kurosawa's particular concern with the space with no name cannot be reduced to the denial of will to history. Homogenization of space is a historical issue of modernity par excellence. The J-horror discourse operates along with a local paradigm, which includes such aesthetic questions as how to represent a ghost. Innovations and experimentations of J-horror films, like *Loft*, need to be measured vis-à-vis such paradigm, which was, conversely, shaped by the modern media environment, international art cinema, and the field of horror.

Acknowledgements

Kuzuu Satoshi brought the writings of Takahashi Hiroshi and Konaka Chiaki to my attention and discussed J-horror films with me. Without his friendship, this project would not have taken shape. I would like to thank the audiences at the Asian cinema conference at Yonsei University and Kinema Club in Frankfurt for their helpful feedback. I am grateful to Joe Wlodarz and Zoran Maric for sharing their insights into and love for horror films with me.

7

The Good, the Bad, and the South Korean: Violence, Morality, and the South Korean Extreme Film

Robert L. Cagle

Two days after the April 16, 2007 shootings at Virginia Tech University, the focus of news coverage abruptly shifted from details of the tragedy itself to reports of a possible link between the actions of Seung Cho (referred to in news coverage by his full name, rendered Korean style as "Cho Seung-hui"), the young man identified as the lone gunman, and images from Park Chan-wook's 2003 film, *Oldboy*. The decidedly tenuous logic that transformed Park's film into Cho's motivation hinged solely on similarities between two (of more than twenty) photographs sent by Cho to NBC network headquarters and two images from Park's film. This sudden swing was not entirely unexpected, given the lack of other newsworthy events taking place during that time period; the absence of any real developments to report (there was no manhunt, the suspect died at the scene of the crime); and the surplus of individuals ready, willing, and able to get in front of the television cameras and talk about anything even remotely related to the case.

This shift in focus from individual to inspiration opened the floodgates for "experts" to rush into a heated crossfire of debate over violence in the media and its supposed role in desensitizing today's increasingly alienated youth, turning everyone with a Game Boy into a potential Charles Whitman, Eric Harris, or Dylan Klebold.[1] Although the argument that violent entertainment promotes real-life brutality is hardly new, what made this particular instance so noteworthy, judging from the prominence it was given in news reports, was the fact that both Cho and the film from which he arguably drew his inspiration shared a single national origin. Like virtually all coverage of the case, stories linking Cho to Park's film insistently characterized Cho as *Korean*, despite the fact that he had lived in the U.S. for nearly fifteen years — far more than half of his brief life. This Korean connection prompted Korean-American civic leaders and even the South Korean government to issue apology after apology, and provided the basis for claims that, as one online respondent to *New York Times* writer Mike Nizza's April 20, 2007 piece put it, "Koreans make weird and violent movies [that] inspire other Koreans like Cho to fly off the handle."[2]

The rhetorical strategy of identifying the agency behind such tragedies as foreign constitutes a reaction known in psychology as *projection* — a phenomenon by which the subject "attributes tendencies, desires, etc. to others that he refuses to recognize in himself."[3] In a larger cultural context, projection can take more generalized forms as for example in the perpetuation of various stereotypes[4] and in the persecution of ethnic, racial, or other types of social groups.[5] This practice creates an artificial dichotomy of "us" (or in the case of Cho/Park, "U.S.") versus "them," "good" versus "evil," and "sane" versus "sick." As the reader's comments above illustrate, a similar project can be found at work in U.S.-based journalistic criticism of recent South Korean films. In a scathing review of Park Chan-wook's *Oldboy* (2003), for example, Rex Reed unleashes a malicious tirade of racist slurs, conflating Korean, Japanese, and Chinese cultures, and, in a fit of tangible exasperation, asking:

> What else can you expect from a nation weaned on kimchi, a mixture of raw garlic and cabbage buried underground until it rots, dug up from the grave, and then served in earthenware pots sold at the Seoul airport as souvenirs? . . . Part kung fu, part revenge-theme Charlie Chan murder mystery, part metaphysical Oriental mumbo-jumbo, all of it incomprehensible.[6]

Manohla Dargis, in her review for the *New York Times* (March 25, 2005), shares Reed's disdain for the work, opening her critique with a question clearly intended to shock readers into dumbfounded agreement with her assessment of Park's film as "symptomatic of a bankrupt, reductive postmodernism." "What," Dargis asks, "does art have to do with a guy eating a live octopus and then hammering a couple of (human) heads?" Dargis's rabid denunciation of the film for its purported excesses poses, however unintentionally, another question: What is the impetus that has so surely driven American critics to dismiss South Korean films as "extreme" while lauding films from Europe and North America that veer into equally excessive territory as "art"?[7]

Of course, the allegation that South Korean films are any more violent, any more sadistic than American films is as ludicrous as it is unfounded, a fact that crowd-pleasers such as *Hostel* (Eli Roth, 2005) and *Saw* (James Wan, 2004) more than adequately illustrate. Indeed, as one of the editors of the present volume indicated, the same kind of moral ambivalence that marks these works can be found in numerous other films, both past and present. Why, then, have American critics been so quick to voice their disapproval of Korean films, and what role does this disapproval play in American views of Korea, its culture, and its citizens? What drives the censure of these works, and why is it that the slippage from criticism to racial persecution (as evidenced in the comments above) occurs so easily in this specific case? What makes these films so dangerous, so scary that not only they, but also the nation that produced them deserves such utter and complete condemnation?

Perhaps the most obvious reason is that although contemporary South Korean films share a set of common stylistic devices and high production values with Hollywood blockbusters, South Korean films rarely, if ever, conform to the same narrative codes as Hollywood feature films, especially with regard to the role played by violence in the organization and unfolding of the plot. Furthermore, the refusal of these works to identify characters with moral positions drawn along distinct and unwavering lines is clearly critical of the overwhelmingly dominant American model. Thus, although they must conform to Hollywood standards on some level in order to win audiences and become commercially viable products, Korean films still find ways to subvert what are seen from a culturally defined perspective as problematic elements of the classical Hollywood text.

Violence, for example, in the Hollywood film generally fulfills one of two functions: it signals the disruption of order — a violation of the law — that sets the narrative into motion and triggers spectatorial desire for resolution — for the restoration of order. Alternately, it provides the means by which order is restored and the narrative is resolved. Along the way, the film assigns specific moral values to different acts of violence by creating a system of parallelisms that identifies the agents behind the violence as either good or evil, depending upon whether these acts lead to further disruption or work toward resolution.

In his seminal study of Hitchcock's *North by Northwest* (1959) entitled "Symbolic Blockage," Raymond Bellour aligns this process of narrative development with the Oedipal trajectory of the male subject theorized by Freud. Bellour argues that the classical Hollywood narrative develops through a series of repetitions and differences — blockages of sorts — articulated on all levels of the representation, from the film's stylistic basis in the shot/reverse-shot formula to the protagonist's journey from immature subject to

Oedipalized adult. Bellour remarks that "this Oedipal itinerary [coincides] with the hero's trajectory"[8] and goes on to illustrate that resolution rests directly on the restoration of the masculine power and privilege of the lead character; the subordination, usually through marriage or some form of heterosexual coupling, of the female subject; and the reestablishment of the "law," as represented by the family.

In her "Melodrama Revised," Linda Williams analyzes Hollywood narrative form from a slightly different perspective: Although she maintains a focus on the importance of repetition and difference, and on the ultimate goal of restoring order and "innocence," Williams sees these elements not as steps in the path to Oedipalization, but rather, as the defining qualities of melodrama, "the fundamental mode of popular American moving pictures."[9] Furthermore, in a related essay she notes that the melodrama "most often typifies popular American narrative in literature, stage, film, and television when it seeks to engage with moral questions."[10] She characterizes the basic melodramatic structure as "an evolving mode of storytelling crucial to the establishment of moral good"[11] that "begins and wants to end in a 'space of innocence.' "[12] The threat to this innocence propels the narrative forward, prompting the development of a dialectic of pathos and action, and fostering the desire for resolution in the form of retribution, redemption, or some combination of both. Williams cites Peter Brooks in her explanation that the melodrama ultimately concerns itself with the simultaneous projects of uncovering hidden evil and acknowledging virtue that has gone unrecognized. Far more than mere entertainment, then, these works function as object lessons of a sort, reiterating the national ethos and, shoring up "American culture's (often hypocritical) notion of itself as the locus of innocence and virtue."[13] Thus, the closure offered by the standard Hollywood "happy ending" represents a particular kind of realization of the American Dream — a reaffirmation of both dominant cultural ideas about gender and sexuality (as theorized by Bellour), and at the same time, a flattering, if unrealistically idealized view of the United States and its history of expansion and acquisition.

South Korean film, too, exhibits a clear affinity with the mode theorized by Williams, and like its American counterpart, it too reflects its own nation's self-image, but in more decidedly self-reflexive terms. Whereas American films consistently retell stories of success in the face of adversity, South Korean films generally revisit instances of historical, political, and cultural trauma, examining these events from more contemporary perspectives and rarely providing any sort of resolution, but more often than not, offering important insights on these events and their significance to modern-day Korea. As critic Kyung Hyun Kim explains in his book, *The Remasculinization of Korean*

Cinema, contemporary South Korean cinema has "engineered a master narrative that engages with trauma" — the narrativized representations of the seemingly endless suffering that the Korean nation has faced throughout its long history — that is at the same time "intricately tied to the . . . conventions of melodrama."[14] As Kim points out, "[t]he depictions of emasculated and humiliated male subjects set the stage for their remasculinization, and occasioned a revival of images, cultural discourses and popular fictions that fetishized and imagined dominant men and masculinity."[15] The end result of this process, though, is not the establishment of a strong Korean male, but rather, as Kim argues, a simulation "of Hollywood action heroes,"[16] a sign of the national cinema's colonization by U.S.-based images and ideals.[17]

To understand the specific historical and cultural environment that gave shape to these images, we must first review some key events in Korea's recent past. For nearly three decades, South Korea's economy grew at an amazing pace, reaching a peak of sorts in the late 1980s and early 1990s. However, by November of 1997, the economy faced overwhelming obstacles and eventually collapsed when a number of large-scale investments failed to pay off and went into default. Because the companies (*chaebol*) involved in these business ventures enjoyed privileged connections to the government, they were able to absorb an ever-increasing amount of capital investment. Ultimately, though, all of the temporary solutions failed, and South Korea suffered a crippling economic disaster. By 1998, Korea's gross domestic product had fallen by nearly 7 percent, triggering the intervention of the International Monetary Fund, which responded by awarding Korea "an emergency rescue package amounting to fifty-five billion dollars — the largest loan in the IMF's history."[18] Although this move saved Korea's economy, it also opened up opportunities for outside influences to control and shape its economy, and be extension, its political and cultural life.

In the period of time immediately following the IMF crisis, the South Korean film industry underwent a massive transformation. This change represented the realization of a uniquely Korean model of globalization known as *segyehwa*.[19] Proposed in November of 1994 by President Kim Young-sam, *segyehwa* combined strong nationalist sentiments with the implementation of Western methods of production, reclaiming domestic markets while simultaneously pursuing global initiatives — a formula that must have sounded promising in the gloomy days following the IMF's intervention. However, although this formula allowed the South Korean film industry to win back Korean audiences from Hollywood and to trigger the pan-Asian phenomenon known as *Hallyu* (the Korean Wave), it did so by copying the style of

Hollywood productions[20] — a situation that resulted in a kind of representational identity crisis.

One of the most successful productions to emerge from this early renaissance was Kang Je-gyu's *Shiri* (1999), a film that restages the conflict between North and South Korea as a Hollywood action film. *Shiri* takes its name from a freshwater fish that lives only in the Demilitarized Zone, the area that both separates and unites the two Koreas. Like this fish, one of the central characters is trapped, at least symbolically, between the two countries. She has both North Korean and South Korean identities and is romantically involved with agents on both sides of the border. At stake in this film, then, is not the conflict of "good" South Korea and "evil" North Korea, but rather, the negotiation of identity in a world where the political import of one's identity is both formulated and assigned by others, a fact that even has bearing on the form and content of Kang's film, modeled, as it is, upon American action films as a way of guaranteeing its commercial success both at home and in other pan-Asian and international markets.

It is important to remember that South Korea is, after more than half a century, still occupied by American troops. Indeed, the presence of these troops — supposedly deployed in South Korea to defend the Republic of Korea against invasion by the North — seemed for a while to be more threatening than reassuring — especially in light of the George W. Bush administration's initially aggressively negative stance against North Korea and statements following the 9/11 tragedy in which Bush simplistically divided the world into two camps: those "with us" and those "against us." According to recent surveys, "South Koreans are more concerned with the threat posed by the US than by North Korea . . . [fearing] that the US might be bent on invading North Korea."[21]

That the violence in Kang's film takes such an obviously American (read "Hollywood-inspired") form serves to underscore the extent to which the animosity between North and South Korea is — like the Hollywood aesthetic that the film espouses, perhaps not entirely voluntarily — not something natural, but rather is a product of the powerful political and cultural influences imposed upon Korea by the United States.[22] While the violence itself recalls the Hollywood film, the anxieties that lie underneath it — the powerful motivations that prompt the violence — arise as a reaction to the recognition of this undue influence.

In his essay "Detouring through Korean Cinema," Paul Willemen argues that the imposition/acceptance of Western representational conventions on/ by the East creates a disparity between Eastern experience and Western standards, resulting in "a compromise between foreign form and local materials."[23] The inability of Western narrative forms to accommodate Asian realities results in moments of textual disjuncture — disturbances that point toward incongruities arising from the inadequacy of the representational form to express culturally specific desires and anxieties.

Willemen refers to such disturbances as "blockages," echoing Bellour's earlier use of the term, thus shifting the focus away from the psychosexual development of the male subject and toward the cultural, economic, and political subjugation of the nation — from the personal to the political — illustrating, in the process, the disconnect that takes shape at the juncture of Western-style narrative and Eastern experience. Willemen's analysis shows that although both types of story operate along similar structural lines (due in no small part to the adoption of the Western model of storytelling), the negotiation of a political identity (as typified by the South Korean films that he examines) is far more fraught with contradiction, less easily reconciled, than the dissolution of the Oedipus complex (characteristic of the Hollywood feature). Willemen cites the freeze frame, a popular motif for ending films of the 1970s and 1980s, as a key example of this phenomenon. The freeze frame, Willemen explains, functions as metaphor for the impasse in which South Korea found itself at the time, emerging from the painful experience of condensed modernization and lengthy occupation. With "both the way back to tradition and the way forward to modernity . . . blocked" Korea had nowhere to turn. Although modernization was a desirable, indeed, necessary step in asserting economic and political autonomy, the cost of achieving this transformation was the loss of tradition and identity. The imperfect synthesis of Eastern content and Western form has yielded a hybrid that, despite phenomenal international success, has resulted in a crisis of identity that consumes these works.

C. Fred Alford argues that this crisis is the result of globalization, pointing out that although Korea has experienced various forms of imposed Westernization and modernization, from the mid-eighteenth century forward, "globalization," in this particular instance refers to a specifically contemporary phenomenon, that is, a project of Neo-Colonialism with far-reaching economic, cultural, and political consequences. Globalization is a phenomenon with "roots in economic and social developments arising at the end of the Second World War," but only recognized as a "*cultural* process with vast and profound implications . . . in the 1980s."[24] As such, Alford's understanding of globalization is perfectly in line with the prevailing usage of the term in contemporary cultural studies. As historian and cultural critic Charles Armstrong explains in his study of the phenomenon in a specifically Korean context, "globalization is nothing new; such processes have existed since the beginning of human civilization. What is new is the rapid acceleration and intensification of these processes in the last one hundred years, and especially the last fifty."[25]

Alford explains that although Koreans do not possess a concept synonymous with the Western idea of evil, they do see the obligatory acceptance of American cultural norms — the very modes of thought that create such binary divisions as good versus evil — as immoral. Instead of dualities, Alford asserts, "Koreans create relationships among people, relationships that are woven so tightly that the duality on which concepts like evil depend cannot find expression. Conversely, evil depends on a type of separation and division that is so terrifying it cannot be allowed to exist."[26] To call something evil is to bestow upon it the quality, the power, of otherness. But even this process, seemingly simple, is actually quite complicated, as Alford explains, asking at one point:

> What if it is not otherness that one most fears? What if what one fears is the quality of being the other, alienated, isolated, and alone, bereft of attention? Then evil may become unspeakable, too close to home. The experience of evil cannot be projected onto an other because it is the very experience of otherness that is so terrifying.[27]

Globalization demands that Koreans surrender their cultural identity and become "global" citizens, a move that exchanges the security of cultural sovereignty for the promise (not guarantee) of financial gain. The erasure of tradition that results from such an arrangement recalls Korea's traumatic past as occupied and oppressed nation, and its current political situation, too, "experienced largely in terms of division and in terms of the national security state that necessitates oppressive laws and makes south [*sic*] Koreans depend, to some extent, on U.S. military assistance." This experience, in turn, creates *han*, "a consciousness of ongoing trauma and a lack of resolution . . . a path for the movement from the present into the past, and for a fresh and creative movement from the past and present into the future."[28]

Since throughout its history Korea has been invaded, occupied, and oppressed by foreign powers, *han* has been widely theorized as a national trait unique to Korea, arising from years of internalizing anger rather than resorting to violence. An excess of *han* results in what is known as *hwabyeong* or "anger illness." This condition, recognized by the *Diagnostic and Statistical Manual of Mental Disorders* (DSM-IV) as a "culture-bound illness . . . attributed to the suppression of anger,"[29] significantly resembles, both in form and etiology, what in the West is referred to as conversion hysteria[30] in that in both of these phenomena anxieties find expression through outward physical symptoms. Like hysteria, then, which has successfully been used as a model for interpreting Hollywood melodramas, *hwabyeong* may provide a key for interpreting the psychic and cultural motivations behind the unique dynamics of South Korean film. Of interest to the current study, then, is not the status of *han* as a psychological disturbance, as a clinical phenomenon, but rather, as Nancy Abelmann has characterized it, as an "idiomatic convention . . . [that] connotes both the collective and individual genealogical senses of the hardship of historical experience [that] relaxes the temporal and geographic patchwork of passive and active, resistance and nonresistance — by not forcing the distinction."[31]

Roy Richard Grinker situates *han* similarly when he writes:

> . . . Korean tragedies do not "speak for themselves" but are always distilled, filtered, converted into something else; *han* is a culturally distinctive manner of conceptualizing and experiencing misfortune, but it is also a method for thinking about the relationship between historical experience and the future. It provides for sufferers a means of converting their tragedy into a dynamic and active process — whether externally through revenge or internally by self-reflection and the development of a new identity or art. This might also be explicated by saying that *han* expresses a continuous tension between enduring one's misfortunes and doing something about the misfortunes and the personal hardships and resentments that result from them.[32]

Thus, for Grinker, *han* represents not only the ongoing suffering of the Korean people, but also *the means by which they may express this grief*, much in the same way that the symptom that allows the expression of the neurosis has its parallel in artistic creation.

Geoffrey Nowell-Smith uses the model of conversion hysteria to explain how, in seeking to represent the psychic and social determinants that influence its form and content, the melodrama often makes use of a discourse of symptoms. Since the melodrama is a work of representational art, these psychic and cultural factors cannot merely be reflected or described, but rather, must be *signified* — that is, they must be expressed through standard representational conventions. As Nowell-Smith explains, because of the limitations of this process — for example, the overpowering imperative of such narrative conventions as resolution — any troubling contradictions must be repressed. This inevitably generates what Nowell-Smith refers to as "excess" — emotionally charged material that the narrative cannot accommodate.[33] Thus, the question is not so much that there exists no means for representing this material, but rather, that this material resists representation.

"The 'return of the repressed' takes place, not in the conscious discourse, but displaced onto the body of the patient," writes Nowell-Smith. In the case of the film, "where there is always material which cannot be expressed . . . a conversion can take place into the body of the text."[34] These messages find representation through conversion into visual or acoustic glitches and excesses or what the author refers to as "hysterical moments" — breakdowns articulated through excesses in music, performance, and mise-en-scène, moments that shift the burden of representation from the narrative to the detail. This movement from realism to a more symbolic mode allows the work to, as Christine Gledhill notes, "[deal] with what cannot be said in the available codes of social discourse; [to operate] in the field of the known and familiar, but also . . . to short-circuit language to allow the 'beneath' or 'behind' — the unthinkable and repressed — to achieve material presence."[35] In the films of Douglas Sirk, for example, the excesses that mark the *mise-en-scène*, the performances, and the musical accompaniment, all point toward an overpowering "unconscious" unrepresentable by other means.

Similarly, the violent outbursts that characterize some South Korean films, and in turn, lead to their marginalization as "extreme" in the U.S.,[36] can be read much in the same way as the moments of textual rupture or excess discussed by Nowell-Smith and Gledhill, as symptoms, as instances of material once repressed (in the case of South Korean cinema, a culturally identified resentment) seeking expression in the body of the text. However, unlike violence in Hollywood films, the interruptions in these works are not associated with agents of "good" or "evil," but rather, arise at moments of crisis in which, as Alford theorizes, the protagonist recognizes that he/she has become an Other to him/herself.

The startling climax of *Oldboy*, singled out for its supposed role as cinematic *agent provocateur* in the Virginia Tech shootings, provides an example of this phenomenon. Near the end of the film protagonist Oh Dae-su (Choi Min-sik) and Lee Woo-jin (Yoo Ji-tae), the man who has orchestrated Oh's kidnapping and fifteen-year imprisonment finally confront one another. Their exchange, repeatedly delayed and thus highly anticipated, is not direct, but mediated by various objects. Lee does not address Oh face to face, but first showers and then, while dressing, directs his comments to Oh's reflection.

The sequence graphically positions Lee in glowing close-up on the left, with Oh, in half-shadowed long shot on the right. Although Oh has the power of evidence and recollection on his side (he stands in front of a wall of photos of Lee's deceased sister, the focus of their exchange), the asymmetry of the shot reveals that these are no match for the class-related privilege signified by Lee's clothes, demeanor, and home. In addition, the composition of the shot suggests that Lee (who is visible as both subject and reflection) has reduced Oh (who is visible only in the mirror) to an image — like the photos, a representation, an element of the mise-en-scène (see Figure 7.1).

Figure 7.1 Oh Dae-su (Choi Min-sik) confronts Lee Woo-jin (Yoo Ji-tae) in the mirror in Park Chan-wook's *Oldboy* (2003)

This all changes when Oh remarks that, given the presence of a photo taken at the reservoir, Lee must have been present the day of his sister's suicide. His words transform the photos on the wall from mere decorations and memorabilia to evidence. Suddenly the perspective changes: Oh is no longer shown as reflection, but in medium close-up. Lee, momentarily annoyed, is no longer shown on the left of the screen, but on the right, Oh on the left, and as reflections (i.e., Lee's body is no longer visible in front of the mirror) (see Figure 7.2). Lee then sneers, "This is no fun," regaining narrative authority by describing how he arranged for Oh to be hypnotized and coerced into a sexual relationship with a woman who is, unbeknownst to Oh, his own daughter.

Figure 7.2 Oh and Lee switch positions in Park Chan-wook's *Oldboy* (2003)

Oh reacts with a look of horror as the visuals shift away from the present: Lee continues to speak as abstract techniques — flashbacks, split screens, and superimpositions — create the cinematic equivalent of condensation, equating

Oh (who is now guilty of the very act for which he earlier condemned Lee) with Lee, visually completing Lee's project of reducing Oh to what Oh, through his actions, once made Lee. Even Oh's clothes and accessories, all provided by Lee, create the illusion that he no longer exists as an autonomous subject — the visual symbol of which takes the form of a split screen and partial superimposition uniting both Oh's and Lee's faces.

Reeling from the shock of the revelation, Oh begs Lee not to disclose this secret to his daughter. In an effort to atone for having revealed the secret of Lee and his sister's relationship, an act that resulted in the sister's hysterical pregnancy, Oh cuts off his own tongue. Through this act of Oedipal significance — an action tantamount to castration, given Lee's earlier comment that "it wasn't Lee Woo-jin's dick, but Oh Dae-su's tongue" that made his sister pregnant — Oh both confesses his own guilt and administers his own punishment, collapsing the binary structure that has developed between them and between the past and present of the narrative, thereby signaling Oh's "passionate submission" to Lee.[37]

Lee later exits, dropping a small, pen-like device that he has earlier told Oh controls his artificial heart. As Lee pushes the button for the elevator, Oh presses the button on the remote device, believing that his actions will kill his tormentor. He is horrified to discover that instead of stopping Lee's heart, the remote control activates a reel-to-reel tape player that broadcasts the sounds of Oh's sexual encounter with his daughter. The recorded sounds and voices parallel Oh's earlier revelation of the indiscretion between Lee and his sister, an act that leads to both the suicide of Lee's sister and, after Lee's revenge is complete, the end of Lee's own life.

It is only after the cathartic completion of this highly perverse equivalent of analysis that the origin of all of this excess can finally find expression. As Lee boards the elevator the film flashes back to the reservoir again. Lee reaches out and grabs onto an arm that appears to reach up from the space in front of him (see Figure 7.3).

Figure 7.3   Lee (Yoo Ji-tae) hallucinates in the elevator in Park Chan-wook's *Oldboy* (2003)

At once all dualisms collapse — past and present, fantasy and reality come together as the film re-enacts the tragic suicide of Lee's sister at the reservoir. As Lee watches his sister fall into the abyss (he is, at this point, shown alternately as both his younger self and present self), he slowly pulls back his hand, forming the shape of a gun with his index finger (see Figure 7.4).

Figure 7.4 Lee's hand/gun. Park Chan-wook, *Oldboy* (2003).

With his thumb he cocks an imaginary hammer (the sound of which appears on the track) and as the visual register cuts back to the present, Lee, obscured by the elevator door, fires the gun into his own temple and falls dead onto the elevator floor. The transformation of Lee's hand into a gun (a hand/gun) echoes the analogy at the heart of the joke he made earlier, equating Oh's tongue and his own penis. It also provides yet another example of the functional collapse of signifier into signified that characterizes this sequence.

Far from being an example of purloined Tarantinian style (as Dargis suggests), this representational excess pulls the spectator into a vortex of sights and sounds that undercuts — in fact, effectively obliterates — the artificial distinction between good and evil, desire and representation. Indeed, the spectacular finale of the film suggests that the characters who, up to that point have been (mis)understood as the hero and villain of the film are, in fact, both victims. Moreover, because the violence found in Park's film (and in other films as well) takes a form clearly reminiscent of the American action film, it redirects the very cinematic techniques by which, in Hollywood films, the distinction between good and evil is solidified, and conflicts between these terms resolved, to, in effect, reject such divisions as invalid. Furthermore, it radically reconfigures a trope common to many mystery and serial-killer films, by which the desire for the solution of the crime becomes, through a series of narrative shifts, the desire for the successful union of a heterosexual couple. The romantic/sexual pairing of the father and daughter refuses to be repressed, shut down, and flies in the face of the Oedipal formula that dictates the design and form of the classical Hollywood film. And although the end of the film does, at least technically, respond to the beginning (father and daughter are reunited), it does so only in the most radically subversive of ways.

Like *Oldboy*, Lee Jeong-hyeok's *H* (2002) makes explicit use of the mirror as a symbol of the loss of agency and wreaks havoc on the Oedipal narrative model. *H* details the investigation of a series of murders that exactly replicate those committed by an already incarcerated psychopath, Shin Hyeon (Cho Seung-woo). Although the police identify and arrest a suspect responsible for two of the murders, the killings continue. The film eventually reveals that the murderer is not single person, but a series of individuals, all acting under the influence of post-hypnotic suggestion. This group includes the two police officers assigned to the case: Detective Kang Tae-hyeon (Ji Jin-hee) and Detective Kim Mi-yoon (Yeom Jeong-ah).

The film comes to a violent conclusion as Kang, prompted by the cues of music and sunlight, kills his own mother, thus mirroring the only unexplained link in Shin's killing spree (Shin's dying words, "I killed my mother," finally put the case to rest). Thus, like Oh in *Oldboy*, he becomes the object of his own hate — the Other that he has relentlessly pursued. Upon arriving at the scene, Detective Kim first lights a cigarette (an action she does habitually throughout the film) and after passing the cigarette to Kang, fires a fatal shot into his temple. Kim's action, also motivated by a post-hypnotic suggestion (triggered by the lighter), represents the completion of an action started and stalled earlier in the film.

The scene takes on greater significance when considered in the context of the earlier scene in which Kang and Kim interview Shin in a visiting cell. Shin examines Kim's lighter and notes that it once belonged to Kim's deceased fiancé, who, as another victim of Shin's murderous hypnosis, killed himself while investigating the first set of crimes. Enraged by Shin's arrogant cruelty, Kim, who has remained almost pathologically calm throughout the entire investigation, stands and points her gun at Shin's head, cocking it and preparing to shoot (see Figure 7.5).

Figure 7.5 Detective Kim (Yeom Jeong-ah) takes aim at
Shin (Cho Seung-woo) as Detective Kang (Ji Jin-hee) watches, in shock,
in Lee Jeong-hyeok's *H* (2002)

Instead of directly stopping her, Kang stands and hits Shin across the face, knocking him to the floor and temporarily defusing the tension. Kim's killing of Kang, who has, in a sense, become Shin, brings to a conclusion both Kim's earlier suspended action, and the investigation itself, and perhaps most important of all, destroys any possibility for the formation of what Barbara L. Miller refers to as the "investigative couple" — the establishment of which stands as a guarantee of narrative resolution and successful Oedipalization — in her exhaustive study of the serial killer film.

The film's use of repetition (the copycat nature of the crimes) and doubling underscores its ostensible debt to the Hollywood thriller. Marketed in the U.S. as "*Se7en* meets *Silence of the Lambs*," the manner in which the film clearly plays with these intertextual references gives an impression of self-aware, self-reflexive critique. In other words, by so obviously playing with Hollywood conventions and references in a film about the investigation of copycat crimes carried out by characters operating in a post-hypnotic trance — carrying out actions scripted by someone else — the film links its own representational strategies with the action of the narrative. Viewed in this light, the film's focus on copycat crimes and hypnotic control both parallels and comments on its status as created under the controlling influence of American culture.

Figure 7.6 Actor Ji Jin-hee as Detective Kang in Lee Jeong-hyeok's *H* (2002)

The poster for the film features a stark black and white photograph of Detective Kang staring wide-eyed into a water-splattered bathroom mirror — a scene that notably does not occur, at least in this particular set-up, in the film (see Figure 7.6). A cigarette hangs limply from his lips. With his right hand he rests a handgun (aimed listlessly, almost unintentionally, at his own reflection) against the mirror; in his left hand he holds the gun's magazine, evidently preparing to lock it into place.

Of course, the use of the *doppelgänger* is not specific to South Korean films. Otto Rank wrote a psychoanalytic investigation of some of the first instances of mirroring in early German cinema, *The Double: A Psychoanalytic Study*, in 1914, and in 1919 Freud dealt extensively with the subject as an enduring theme in art and literature in his study, "The Uncanny," which itself was clearly influenced by an even earlier work (1906) by Ernst Jentsch. However, the appearance of doubling in a South Korean context underscores the extent to which the distinction between "good" and "evil" in these works is, like the motif of the double, something foreign, something borrowed, and as such, the source of disturbance, of splitting in a specifically South Korean context. In a sense, the two images of Detective Kang not only represent two opposing moral positions (his potential to act in the name of the law and against the law), but also the dual identity of the film itself (Korean/American).

Both Kang and his mirror reflection are visible in the photo, shot from behind and to the left of Kang's shoulder. Under the film's title (the ambiguous letter "H") appears the line "The name that summons murder — [H]." A second inscription, written vertically, reads, "I thought this would end after I caught him." Both the "him" in the second inscription and the "H" of the first can be read as references to Shin (*H*yeon), the serial killer already incarcerated at the start of the film, as it is he whose agency Kang hopes to destroy, and also he whose control (through *h*ypnosis, the real referent of the film's ambiguous title) transforms Kang into the "him" implicated in the second inscription. The success of Kang's mission, then, hinges upon his own capture and execution. The poster takes this final psychodrama and restages it, distilling it into a single image frozen at the moment of greatest narrative conflict: Kang stares into the mirror and sees in his own reflection the face of the murderer.

The title of the film plays with the ambiguity suggested by this single letter — a signifier that, freed from its association with other signifiers, becomes loaded with possible associations and potential significance. Instead of "The End," the film closes with the mysterious letter "H," once again, this time revealing its symbolic value as the initial letter of the word "Hypnosis." It is interesting to note that despite the fact that there does exist a term for "hypnosis" in Korean — 최면술 — "Hypnosis" is rendered in English, while the definitions are presented in Korean. In other words, the title, or the means of identification of the film, is a letter from the Western alphabet, while its interpretation comes in the form of a Korean dictionary. In making this narrative play, the film both explains the motivations behind the events that have preceded it, and, more important, serves to reinforce the interpretation of the mind control that leads to violence with the English language, and arguably, by extension, with the influence of American culture on Korea. In this respect, *H* represents a uniquely Korean reinterpretation of a characteristically American sub-genre, the serial killer film.

A similar confrontation between self and image occurs just before the bloody gunfight that brings Kim Ji-woon's *A Bittersweet Life* (*Dalkomhan insaeng*, 2005) to its conclusion. As protagonist Sun-woo (Lee Byung-hun) washes his face and bandages a deep knife wound in his abdomen, he pauses for a moment and looks into the mirror. Sun-woo, a hit man, has recently fallen out of grace by refusing to kill the unfaithful (and much younger) girlfriend, Hee-soo (Shin Min-ah), of his boss, Mr Kang (Kim Young-cheol). As punishment he has been shot, stabbed, and buried alive (twice). He now stands in the men's room of the club La Dolce Vita,[38] loading a variety of semi-automatic firearms that he has stolen from an arms dealer, and steeling himself for what will most certainly be a final confrontation. His face, seen only as a reflection, is shown in close up — his eyes are bloodshot, his face filled with despair. "Why did it turn out like this?" he sighs, "It's ok . . . it's ok." As he turns, the camera cuts away to a medium shot of him from behind (a shot similar to that used in the poster for *H*). Both Sun-woo and his reflection are visible again for an instant before once again, as he stands, the camera refocuses on his reflection. As he exits the bathroom his reflection is eclipsed momentarily by his own figure, thus creating a visual disturbance that motivates a cut to the space of the next scene, and also reiterating the character's own mortality by privileging corporeal presence over specular image.[39]

The exchange in the mirror represents the final phase of Sun-woo's reclamation of his own agency from not only his boss, but also the oppressive system in which he has accepted a position. Sun-woo has effectively surrendered his own desires, his very identity, to the gang in which he is a member, a fact illustrated by his lack of a personal life — we know nothing of his parents, his family, or even his tastes. Even his clothes — the stylish black suit, starched white shirt, and impeccably knotted tie — although very chic, provide Sun-woo with the means to suppress his identity, to manipulate his own self-image in such a way that allows him masquerade as cold, uncaring — something that the film ultimately reveals, he is not (see Figure 7.7).

Figure 7.7   Sun-woo (Lee Byung-hun) faces his reflection in the mirror in Kim Ji-woon's *A Bittersweet Life* (2005)

The intensity and magnitude of the violence as Sun-woo engages in an extended gunfight with an army of gangsters gives some indication of just how profound this repression is. However, as he dispatches each successive opponent with an ever-decreasing arsenal of weapons, Sun-woo himself loses strength and suffers additional injuries, the implication being, as is commonly the case in narratives that involve doubling, that in killing off these opponents — the people who represent his choices in life, his experience — Sun-woo is also killing himself.[40] Violence is not, therefore, seen as liberating or positive, but rather, as wholly destructive.

As Sun-woo sits dying amidst the shattered ruins of the club, he opens his cell phone and dials Hee-soo, the woman whose life he spared, and in so doing, triggered this catastrophic tragedy. As Hee-soo speaks into the phone, the film switches modes as the image track slows and Hee-soo's voice echoes on the soundtrack. Sun-woo stares into space, thinking back to a moment from his past — a seemingly insignificant event — when he spent an afternoon listening to Hee-soo play the cello in a recording session. As "Romance" by Yuhki Kuramoto plays on the soundtrack the film reveals information that it withheld before: Sun-woo sits listening to Hee-woo and her companions play, closes his eyes, and smiles.

Although some reviewers have cited this sequence as evidence that Sun-woo is secretly in love with Hee-soo, it seems far more likely that this fleeting instant of happiness represents Sun-woo's experience of not only a shared act of kindness (something that, as the film reveals, does not occur in his other life) but also of his own (temporary) autonomy, freed from Mr Kang's grip and the criminal life into which he has fallen. Indeed, when viewed from the perspective offered by Bellour in his reading of classical Hollywood film, this scene can be read as an unmistakable refusal of psychosexual and cultural forms of Oedipalization — revealing that the promise of power and privilege associated with accession to the Father is an empty one, only serving to further distance the subject from the possibility of realizing his/her desires. The image track cuts back to the present, and Sun-woo is shown from the left, rather than straight on, as tears roll down his face. Sun-woo's sudden experience of emotion signifies not the regret of lost *romance*, but rather, like the "behind" and "beneath" theorized by Gledhill, "something that cannot be put into words," [41] because it exceeds language, defies representation.

This reverie is cut short, as the image track quickly shifts to a long shot, filmed from Sun-woo's right, as he is shot point-blank by the brother (Eric Moon) of the gun dealer he has earlier murdered. It is worth noting here that, as in *Oldboy*, the startling sound of a gunshot merges with a jarring edit and brings to a sudden and unexpected close a highly emotional musical accompaniment that signals a recollection — a memory of loss and despair. In one respect, the gunshot that kills Sun-woo is, like the gunshot that kills Lee in *Oldboy*, self-inflicted. In his haste to leave the hideout where he has murdered the gun dealer and his companions, Sun-woo, who has been meticulous throughout the film, leaves behind his business card. Sun-woo thus becomes the agent of his own death — the double from whom he cannot escape — an interpretation that is underscored by the fact that the gun dealer's brother tosses the lost business card onto Sun-woo's lifeless body, thus delivering Sun-woo's message to its proper final destination. Like the violent acts that conclude *Oldboy* and *H*, this final gesture both brings to a close a circle of deception and double-crossing, while at the same time, by providing formerly withheld information, redirects the spectator back to the narrative again, encouraging reconsideration and reinterpretation.

This reading is further supported by the fact that following a brief spoken epilogue the image track dissolves to an earlier unseen shot of Sun-woo, shown only as a reflection in a window, sipping a cup of espresso and staring out into the night. After he finishes his coffee, he looks up, adjusts his tie, and suddenly begins boxing with his reflection. The camera cuts to a medium shot from outside — from the other side of the mirror/window — as Sun-woo continues to throw punches at himself, stopping occasionally to laugh and readjust his tie. This final shot, like the earlier reverse shot that reveals Sun-woo smiling while listening to the musical performance, reveals a perspective that has, up to this point, remained unconsidered, unrepresented — Sun-woo as playful, almost childlike. In introducing these images, the film performatively directs spectators to reconsider what they have just seen. It points toward its own inability to represent characters or events with the complexity necessary to make them "real." In other words, like the melodramatic mode theorized by Gledhill, it indicates a level of narrative that remains beyond or behind the images that have just passed. Unlike the illusory resolutions that conclude Hollywood films, the endings of *A Bittersweet Life*, *H*, and *Oldboy*, not to mention those of numerous other South Korean "extreme" films, do not impose closure on the stories they have presented, but rather, in the spirit of *han*, push the viewer from the present into the past, suggesting that it is only by way of such contemplation that the true meaning of the film can be understood.

Ultimately, it is this refusal to espouse the most conservative elements of the Hollywood film — the binary opposition of good against evil, the insistence upon closure — and the resulting exposure of this system — the basis, as Williams has argued, of the Hollywood film — as false that makes these works so horrifying to American critics. Although South Korean films emulate Hollywood films, they undercut the basic belief system at work in the Hollywood film, illustrating that the violence glamorized in the Hollywood picture is not in any way productive. They likewise reject the moralistic distinctions between individuals or groups that structure the Hollywood picture and American popular culture since they do not use it to scapegoat or vilify a convenient other, suited to fit the current political or social climate. To Western audiences raised on the Hollywood film, these works must seem dangerously irresponsible. Ultimately it is not that the violence in these works is more graphic or explicit, it is not that the characters are somehow more pathological, and it is not even, as some have argued, that violence is more personalized in South Korean film, instead of being glamorized or abstracted in Hollywood film. Rather, these works illustrate the invalidity of the simplistic view of the world as divided into camps of good and evil as was the monolithic rhetoric that characterized the Virginia Tech reports, soullessly transforming a tragically disturbed young man into the personification of evil. Moreover, as Williams has illustrated in her work on melodrama, such a view is a defining characteristic of the American ethos. This simple fact is what renders them scary and dangerous — it is what makes them *extreme*.

Acknowledgements

This project was made possible in part by a generous grant from the Korean Film Council. The author wished to thank KOFIC, the editors of the present volume, and the anonymous readers who provided helpful critiques of earlier versions of this work, and to recognize Margaret Montalbano, Lalitha Gopalan, Cynthia Childs, Frances Gateward, David Desser, Aaron Han Joon Magnan-Park, and Mac Kang for their thoughtful suggestions, continued support, and valued friendship.

8

Magic, Medicine, Cannibalism:
The China Demon in Hong Kong Horror

Emilie Yueh-yu Yeh and Neda Hei-tung Ng

Horror, or ghost film, has a long standing in Hong Kong cinema. Since the 1970s, the film industry in Hong Kong has steadily churned out horror/ghost films for audiences in the region and horror has become a staple in Hong Kong cinema.[1] We can identify at least two narrative prototypes in Hong Kong horror. The first is called the ghost erotica, referring to romances between female spirits and male scholars. Based on the well-known Chinese classic *Strange Stories from a Chinese Studio* (Liaozhai zhiyi) written by Pu Songling in the seventeenth century, this type of story delineates the return of female spirits to repay their debts to men who have lent a helping hand. It touches on the liminality between the spiritual and the human world and the ambiguity between life and afterlife. Because of its classical setting and humanist treatment of the interplay between the libidinal and the moral, Pu Songling's ghost erotica has inspired such film classics as *The Enchanting Shadow* (Li Hanxiang, 1960), *A Touch of Zen* (King Hu, 1972) and *A Chinese Ghost Story I, II, III* (Ching Sui-tung et al., 1987–1991).

Vampire takes center stage in the second prototype of Hong Kong horror/ghost films. Based on folklores from the provinces, this type of narrative is characterized by religious rituals and customs. It features spirits as lethal vampires or *jiangzhi* (literally stiff corpses), whose long-lasting grudge has turned them into monsters. To suppress them, one must use either martial arts or kung fu, or evoke supernatural force such as exorcism. Religious mysticism and martial arts are hence added to enrich the dramatic effects and action of the horror pictures. As noted by Stephen Teo, "[f]or a genre so rooted in traditional motifs, indeed in ethnological matter, the kung fu horror movie depends on surface glitz, action and slapstick humour to succeed."[2] With these additional ingredients, the vampire pictures became immensely popular during the boom days of Hong Kong cinema. For example, *Mr Vampire* (Ricky Lau, 1985) was ranked the fifth in the Hong Kong top-ten list and topped Taiwan's list.[3] "The kung fu horror" nexus shows the cross-fertilization and free mixing of two distinct genres, further exemplifying the malleability of Hong Kong popular genres.

The number of horror films drastically declined in the late 1990s, but the genre did not entirely vanish. Video film was a new shell for the genre to extend its life. Between 1997 and 2003, nineteen installments of a horror series called *Troublesome Night* were released when the Hong Kong film industry was in rapid decline. Shot on video, the series proliferated due to their low budgets. Nevertheless, the industry's overall interest in horror was not significantly advanced until local filmmakers began to remake horror based on J-horror — a new Japanese horror genre characterized by its urban milieu, familial relations and communication technology. In early 2000, with the independent Applause Pictures taking the lead to capitalize on the phenomenal success of J-horror, horror/ghost re-emerged as a marketable genre. Following Applause, renowned directors produced *My Left Eye Sees the Ghost* (Johnnie To, 2002), *Visible Secret,* and *Visible Secret II* (Ann Hui, 2001, 2002). With these various inputs, it appeared that horror regained its popularity in the local cinema. However, this resurrection has less to do with either recycling previous narrative or copying Japanese stylistic formula. Rather, the new Hong Kong horror is distinct in its impulse to render a deep political anxiety and identity crisis.

What is this anxiety and crisis then? Identity politics has occupied the center of Hong Kong film studies since the 1990s.[4] It peaked around 1997 when Hong Kong's sovereignty returned to China. The return in this context meant repatriation, "going home." While officials from both sides celebrated the return in grand style, critics within and outside of Hong Kong expressed different views toward the 1997 event. With respect to Hong Kong's new identity, Rey Chow remarks that the new era could bring more intense cultural struggle as "Hong Kong's cultural productions are often characterized by a particular kind of negotiation. This is a negotiation in which it must play two aggressors, Britain and China, against each other."[5] Ackbar Abbas suggested that the return might carry Hong Kong's second colonization: "When sovereignty reverts to China, we may expect to find another colonial situation, but with an important historical twist."[6] The two critics implied that resistance or ambivalence toward a new "Chinese" identity might underlie Hong Kong's cultural production before and after her formal entry into its postcolonial stage. For instance, Hong Kong action classics *A Better Tomorrow* and its sequel (John Woo, 1986, 1987) deal with the reunion with China in subtle ironies. As Tony Williams suggests, "Woo's spectacular violent confrontations depict the end of history for this former colony. But within the very nature of the struggles, he contrasts desolate worlds of present and future with visions of China's heroic past as a means for survival."[7] The uncertainty intensified as 1997 approached, and the independent *Made in Hong Kong* (Fruit Chan, 1997) was praised for its allegorical response to China's takeover. The film illustrates the urban angst of working class youth to insinuate the political impotence felt by Hong Kong's majorities, as they had no role to play in the making of the historical decision.[8]

While pessimism reigned in the general views toward Hong Kong's "going home," there was another, different voice. Some pointed out that Hong Kong's historical role as an intermediary would find her a new place in China's rise as an economic superpower. With China's shift from planned to market economy, Hong Kong's return, as some argued, would not necessarily lead to China's colonization, but allows the former British colony to profit from the many assets China could provide. Kung Ho-fung and Law Wing-sang described this reversal as "northbound colonization," referring to Hong Kong's taking advantage of the Mainland's rich resources, cheap labor and lack of knowledge. This "northbound colonization" was best exemplified in the weekend exodus of Hong Kong residents to the Mainland for cheap consumption. Kung also added that apart from consumption, Hong Kong businessmen regularly paid visits to China for new opportunities and resources not available at home.[9]

These contrary views indicate two important symptoms of Hong Kong's return: Hong Kong's ambivalence and uncertainty of going home, and her difficulty in coming to terms with the idea of "home." To return to a home that is 150 years old is to re-encounter an alien "origin," both strange and familiar, powerful yet vulnerable. Films made in postcolonial Hong Kong were preoccupied with this concern. Fruit Chan's so-called "China Trilogy" — *Little Cheung* (1999), *Durian, Durian* (2000) and *Hollywood Hong Kong* (2001) — are notable examples. The trilogy features Chinese sex migrants as enigmatic, yet nourishing, goddesses for deprived men living at the margins of the Hong Kong society. By doing so, Chan "attempts to bring the Other to the forefront, giving her a voice and enabling her to construct her subjectivity and to challenge stereotypes."[10] Chan's treatment of the Chinese women adds a twist to the "northbound colonization" idea: that the north may well be at home instead of some anonymous Chinese geographies afar. When one looks closely at the underground economy of sex and menial labor, the boundary between China and Hong Kong may not be as distinct as perceived. *Durian, Durian* and *Hollywood Hong Kong* present confident Chinese sex workers traveling across various borders of neighborhoods, cities, and regions. Their mobility and penetration deep inside Hong Kong locality indicates that they too obtain similar cosmopolitan attributes that are flexible and savvy, much like most permanent Hong Kong residents.

While Chan's films envisage Chinese women within the Madonna/ Whore prototype, other films, including Chan's recent *Dumplings*, take the same imagery into a deeper, darker terrain of the political psychosis. By the interpellation of the "motherland," Hong Kong's return has also been framed as a long lost child's homecoming, a "natural" and emotional reflex, adding complexities to an already entangled political integration. Some even argue that the "mother-child" relations could be seen as "the sources and origins of horror." When a child creates boundaries between himself and his mother, "the mother is 'horrific' in the sense of being all-engulfing, primitive . . ."[11] As the integration between capitalist Hong Kong and socialist China has deepened and accelerated in the past decade, Hong Kong's identity crisis seems to acquire a more insidious, twisted expression with respect to its relations to the "mother." This is especially evident in the changing imageries of China in horror that extends political and cultural anxieties outside the usual bounds. This chapter focuses on two signature horror films from Applause Pictures, *Three: Going Home* (Peter Chan Ho-sun, 2002) and *Three Extremes: Dumplings* (Fruit Chan, 2004), and analyzes their new treatments of the transgressive ghosts and ghostly bodies. By employing the literature on Hong Kong identity and its changing relations with China, we argue that these new treatments are latent representations of Hong Kong's increasing desire for a "home" and "mother" previously feared.

Going Home and *Dumplings*

Applause Pictures was established in 2000 by director-producer Peter Chan Ho-sun, writer-director Teddy Chan and distributor Allen Fung. At that time the Hong Kong film industry was experiencing a steady decline in production and its market share in Southeast Asian markets was abruptly shrinking. The company's plan was to initiate flexible production packages in order to recover markets lost to Hollywood pictures. According to Davis and Yeh in their recent studies on East Asian screen industries, the initial strategy was to invest in local Asian movies and directors capable of making low-budget films that are commercially competitive. Areas such as Korea, China, and Thailand were carefully researched and underwritten by Applause.[12] Another strategy was to repackage genre pictures to stimulate new interest in popular forms. In the first slate of Applause's pan-Asian projects, these two strategies were integrated.

The horror genre stood out in the Applause slate, as a response to J-horror's huge success. Low-budget J-horror was a gem in the sleepy Japanese film market in the late 1990s and spawned an international horror trend.[13] Seeing the surprising payoffs of Japanese horror, Applause seized the chance to rework traditional Chinese materials into a new form of "C-horror" for Chinese-speaking audiences. The result was *The Eye* (Oxide and Danny Pang, 2002, Hong Kong/Singapore/Thai co-production) and the omnibus *Three* (Nonzee Nimibutr, Kim Kee-woon, Peter Chan, 2002, Thai/South Korea/Hong Kong co-production) and its sequel *Three . . . Extremes* (Miike Takashi, Park Chan-wook, Fruit Chan, 2004). *The Eye* remains by far Applause's most commercially successful film while *Three* and *Three . . . Extremes* were critically acclaimed.[14] *Going Home* is the Chinese segment from *Three* and *Dumplings* is from *Three . . . Extremes*. Both were spun off into feature-length horror films of their own and received several film awards from Hong Kong and Taiwan for their new treatments of horror.

Three's Chinese title, *San geng* (three bells, 11:00 pm), is a specific time of night. As a stock phrase in many Chinese ghost films, "three bells" conjures supernatural visitations, nocturnal chills, and the uncanny. *Going Home* tells a horror story about bodily resurrection and Chinese herbal medicine. The plot revolves around two families living in an abandoned public housing estate — a policeman Wai (Eric Tsang) with his son and a mysterious medicine doctor from China named Yu (Leon Lai). After breaking into Yu's home to search for his missing son, Wai discovers Yu's secret that he has been living with the corpse of his dead wife (Eugenia Yuan). Yu is awaiting his wife's resurrection so that they can go home together. But the policeman's unexpected visit ruins Yu's plan.

Dumplings is a gruesome story about a rich, former TV idol named Ching (Miriam Yeung) desperately seeking remedies in order to save her failing marriage. Ching's wealthy husband Lee (Tony Leung Ka-fei) has an insatiable appetite for youth, so she needs a quick fix for her aging looks. Ching seeks help from a woman from China, Auntie Mei (Bai Ling), known among the local socialites for her dumplings that have an unbelievable regenerating power. The sixty-year-old Mei has a body and looks that are thirty years younger than her age. And her fitness secret is kept inside her 'magical' dumplings. Thoughts of cannibalism do not prevent Ching from tasting Mei's dumplings, whose ingredients prove to be miraculous. Gradually Ching becomes addicted to the dumplings, and believing that beauty is the only solution to her unhappy life, she turns herself into a cannibal.

Human or Demon? Chinese Medicine Doctors in Hong Kong

Chinese medicine doctors are featured prominently in both *Going Home* and *Dumplings*. Yu is a trained, certified Chinese herbalist and Mei was formerly a gynecologist known for her surgical dexterity and precision. Their professional credentials become invalid once they cross the border to Hong Kong — a Chinese city predominantly organized by capitalist, Western institutions, including its medicine. As their professional identity is denied, Chinese medicine doctors make a pitiful living out of their former training. To remain in Hong Kong they have to descend from the "legitimate" medical sphere to the underworld of ancient Chinese medicine. This world is depicted by two devices: the doctors' exterior traits and their surroundings.

Going Home introduces Yu, the mainland doctor, as a mysterious and menacing immigrant. His first encounter with his new neighbors occurs when he is seen dragging garbage out from his apartment. With the scene's background being completely opaque, Yu seems to have just stepped out from the underworld. His simple, grey jacket — recalling the old communist days — adds to the otherworldliness of his presence and his impassive expression portrays him as a lingering soul in a forsaken land.

Yu is not alone. He has a family living with him — the ghost of his aborted baby girl and the diseased body of his wife Hai'er. Dressed in red, the girl's uncanny presence is clearly depicted as the supernatural other. She never speaks a word and is invisible to most human beings except Wai's little boy, who then follows her and disappears from the intelligible human world. But the visual contrast between her red dress and the greyish, icy surroundings of the empty housing estate loudly announces her existence, pointing to the feeble threshold between life and death, and consciousness and unconscious. Yu's wife Hai'er appears in an even more grotesque aspect. Hai'er "lives" inside a bathtub full of water and herbs. Although she has been dead for three years, she is hibernating into recovery from a fatal disease. In order to prepare for her awakening, Yu bathes Hai'er daily, talking to her and preparing meals for her (Figure 8.1). One wonders whether Yu is human at all? Could he too be a ghost, or a zombie awakening to complete unfinished business?

Figure 8.1 Awaiting his wife's resurrection, Yu hugs and talks to the corpse everyday (Source: horror-fanatics.com)

While Yu keeps Wai under house arrest to protect his private undertaking, Yu behaves nothing like his frigid and ghostly appearance when he is first introduced. He treats Wai kindly, and acts like a caring nurse toward a handicapped patient. To Wai, if Yu is a demon, he is of a most unlikely kind. Wai almost wants to identify with Yu's (in)sanity, but he does not quite believe Yu's explanation. Yu was diagnosed with cancer years ago and was told by a Hong Kong (Western) doctor that his days were numbered. So the couple decided to use their Chinese training to save his life. It requires a total change of the constitution to rid the disease. So Yu killed himself and under Hai'er's care, he came to life again. Soon after that, Hai'er was struck down with the same disease.

But just when Hai'er is about to wake up, Wai's police colleagues break into Yu's apartment, arresting Yu and confiscating Hai'er's body. When an ambulance is taking Hai'er and her nascent new life away, Yu runs after her, only to be hit by a car. Finally, the coroner confirms that Hai'er's life is indeed continuing even after her death. The testimony from the doctor who treated the couple years ago supports Yu's story. At this point Wai realizes the truth of Yu's story. This understanding further calls the initial perception of the Chinese doctors into question. Are they human or demon? Or something in between?

Compared to the subdued images of Yu and Hai'er that are overshadowed by reason and science, Auntie Mei represents a captivating, sexualized demon from China, destabilizing the affluent,instrumental Hong Kong way of life. Contrary to the grey, cool undertone of the ghost world inhibited by Yu and his family, Auntie Mei's lair is enchanting and mesmerising, like an antique emporium attended by a voluptuous shaman.

Dumplings opens as Mei crosses the China/Hong Kong border to return to her home in Hong Kong. Mei, like many mainland immigrants, crosses the border daily to make a living (northbound colonization). She is a good-looking woman. With trendy attire revealing her curvaceous body, heavy makeup, high heel shoes, Mei's image fits the stereotype of Chinese sex workers as depicted in Fruit Chan's "China Trilogy." But she is not. She tells the customs officer that she is delivering lunch to her children studying at Hong Kong schools. She is right; there are homemade eggs and ham inside her old-fashioned lunch box. The old red Chinese lunch box helps dissolve the usual suspicion for a woman with her appearance. But the ordinary lunch is just a decoy; underneath it is the precious raw material for her flourishing health management business in Hong Kong (Figure 8.2).

Figure 8.2 The opening shot of *Dumplings*: Auntie Mei and her lunch box at the customs between Hong Kong and the Mainland
(Source: http://www.ejumpcut.orgcurrentissues/Dumplings.com)

Indeed, Mei is not into the typical trade to which most young Chinese women are resorted when they cross the border to Hong Kong, even though her appearance might have hinted that. As Barbara Creed suggests, "[t]he concept of border is central to the construction of the monstrous in the horror film; that which crosses or threatens to cross the "border" is abject."[15] And "abject," according to Julia Kristeva in her book on the powers of horror, is "what disturbs identity, system, order. What does not respect borders, positions, rules."[16] Although Mei does not sell her own body, she purveys those of anonymous Chinese peasant women who are forced to abort their baby girls under the one-child policy and the persistent patriarchal ideology that writes off female newborns. Instead of casting Mei as a compassionate goddess like the previous mainland characters in his films, Fruit Chan portrays

Mei as a vamp, a go-between who exploits the vulnerability of women from both sides of the border. Mei knows that to survive in Hong Kong, she must do something out of the ordinary, something disturbing to the order and class system of an advanced society like Hong Kong. She ingeniously makes use of the "waste" of the Communist Party's population control policy and turns it into an antidote for Hong Kong women's body management. In order to obtain the so-called "top quality" infantile flesh, she performs an abortion for a local teenage girl who has been raped by her father. While Mei is happily showing off her product to the customer, the girl is dying from excessive bleeding. By manipulating other women's bodies that "bear the inscription of social, political, economic, cultural and legal pressures,"[17] Mei embarks on a demonic enterprise. Is this beautiful vamp from China less than human? Can she be a modern demon in a globalized culture worshipping excessive, insatiable consumption?

China as the Haunted Past

Mei's body management business is tucked away inside a small flat located in a decrepit public housing estate. Mei's flat is the key space where the major action takes place, including dumpling offerings, singing revolutionary songs, fornicating with her patron in the post-cannibalistic climax, and operating on a sixteen-year-old schoolgirl. In all of these deeds, Mei performs and perseveres, from a dubious chef and a throwback of the 1960s to a calm midwife and an irresistible nymph.

The interior décor in Mei's tiny "office" adds to the eeriness of her routines. In the center of her office sits a shrine stuffed with startlingly promiscuous kitsch, ranging from Mao figurine, Daoist goddess of nativity and mercy, revolutionary peasants, *maneki neko* (Japanese lucky beckoning cat), Virgin Mary sitting alongside Hello Kitty (Figure 8.3). Inside her emporium of kitsch are two old black and white photos of herself taken in the old country. When were these pictures taken? The answer is nowhere to be found until a point of view shot from Ching's husband Lee reveals their (and Mei's) age. As Lee is fornicating with Mei on her table after eating her dumplings, a photo on the shrine catches his attention. When he looks at it closely, he sees that the photo showing Mei in her twenties was taken in 1960. Mei is in fact in her sixties. Lee stops, wondering with whom he is having sex — the irresistible Chinese nymph, or an old hag in a fake body. Knowing his fear, Mei convinces him that age is just a number and her body, though an unbelievable one, is what matters. Then they continue with their unfinished business. But the revelation brings a chill. Next to a photo from the past exposes a different truth: Mei is a ghost in a gorgeous shell.

Figure 8.3   Auntie Mei and her emporium of kitsch
(Source: eyeswidescreen.wordpress.com)

Photos, in print or electronic format, are images of the past. They are used in *Going Home* and *Dumplings* as crucial narrative links to the past (in China). For Chinese immigrants who are treated as ghosts in Hong Kong, photos from the past help maintain their present lives in the affluent but alienated Hong Kong. Inside Yu's home, a TV monitor constantly plays a home video of Hai'er talking as if Yu was listening behind the camera. Here, memories of the past turn into moving pictures, bringing the ambiguity of Hai'er's living death to the fore. Mei proudly displays her decades-old photos on her emporium of international kitsch, showing little difference between the look of her past and present, and the "magic" of her everlasting youth, much like those "immortal" statutes.

Going Home begins and ends with an old-fashioned studio where a photographer is seen taking a formal family photograph. The studio here is the locus of the uncanny, a memory bank of the repressed and aborted, where dead family members unite to take a picture. Being together is a wish denied to Yu and his family while they are alive. Now they are dead they are able to be together as a family. At the beginning of *Going Home* when Wai and his son are taken to their apartment by a grumpy guard, they go through one empty room after another. The abandoned family photos on the walls communicate the previous lives and histories of these forsaken spaces. Forever hidden, old lives and histories must rely on photos and images to show the proof of life. The liminality between the past and the present thus forms the narrative of the haunted, channeled by chilling mise-en-scène and unsettling sound effects.

If Chinese from the Mainland are portrayed as ghosts from the past, Chinese in Hong Kong are depicted as the Mainlanders' evil twins in their disavowal of the past. To Wai, Yu's obsession with the past is pathetic and futile, if not insane. In a capitalist society that emphasizes efficiency and pragmatism, it is the future that leads the way, not the past. Unlike Yu, Wai tries to bury his past. He is reluctant to talk about the loss of his wife and his descent from a comfortable middle-class life to a semi-homeless state. Moreover, like many Chinese in Hong Kong, Wai believes little in traditional Chinese medicine, not to mention Yu's radical experiment. Only when a local doctor presents him with evidence about the Mainland couple is Wai willing to accept a different reality from his own experience. Perhaps for the first time in his life, he sees the present in a different light, by way of the prism of the past. As if to echo Wai's new insight on life, the film closes with the same antiquated photo studio introduced at the very beginning. Inside the studio, Yu takes his little red girl to join her mother and together, they have their family portrait taken. The camera tracks into their family photograph and remains there, until the film fades to black. This closure suggests the final reunion of the ghost family, a dream impossible to realize in the human world. Meanwhile, Wai is still waiting for his son to come "home" in the abject public housing estate. The Chinese demon and his cohorts have gone home, but the Hong Kong character remains dejected and alone.

Cannibalism: Magic Horror

Contrary to the abandoned public housing estate and its dejected residents, *Dumplings* presents an affluent Hong Kong of comfort, confidence and wealth. A former TV idol and the wife of a real estate tycoon, Ching has all the money she needs to buy happiness. But she is miserable because her husband has long lost interest in her. Time has taken Ching's beauty away and the last thing Ching would like to be reminded of is her past. Nevertheless, it does not prevent Auntie Mei, the inscrutable doctor from the past, to taunt Ching when they first meet: "Ah, Mrs. Lee, I remember you, from those old TV drama series, you were very popular, very pretty." Despite Mei's sarcasm, Mei has to rely on the doctor from the Mainland to reverse the hereditary predestination of lifelong aging.

Consuming a fetus, the unborn human flesh, is the narrative highlight, and horror, of *Dumplings*. To illustrate the horrific cannibalism — an inhuman act — visually arresting shots are presented to show the ingredients of the magical dumplings — close-ups of the little curly human in bright orange shade and the juicy orange delicacy nicely laced inside each dumpling. As if these visual details were inadequate to demonstrate the characters' appetite for human flesh, the film goes on to show Mei slurping down a fresh fetus like a piece of sashimi. Her unbridled excitement toward a five-month-old male fetus is illustrated in her sales pitch to Ching: "It is covered by a layer of creamy fat. The colors are defined and you can even see the cranium.

Figure 8.4   Hong Kong rich woman Ching is about to taste the dumplings
(Source: wikipedia.Dumplings)

The tiny limbs will still be moving around. It is so cute, like a kitten." Mesmerized by this euphoric image of cannibalism, Ching cannot wait, "Don't you waste any more time, get it done quickly!" (Figure 8.4)

In *Three Essays on the Theory of Sexuality*, Freud claims that cannibalistic urges prevail at the oral stage because "sexual activity has not yet been separated from the ingestion of food." Although aiming at the incorporation of the object, this urge is not simply destructive in nature. It is also an attempt to incorporate the maternal figure as part of self in order to gain possession and control over the external world and to make up for the inevitable loss of the comforting object.[18] The act of eating/consuming embodies an intrisic contradiction, a dialectic of the subject and the other. It is a way not only to contain the other but also to destroy it. Caleb Crain suggests that love and cannibalism can be confused because "cannibals and lovers both pay exceptional attention to the body of the desired."[19] Orality hence is both affectionate and hostile. As Melanie Klein remarks, " [i]n the very first months of the baby's existence it has sadistic impulses directed not only against its mother's breasts, but also against the inside of her body: scooping it out, devouring the contents, destroying it by every means which sadism can suggest."[20] The infant indulges in the fantasy of total sadistic control when it fails to master its love object.

The ambivalent feeling of love and hatred behind the cannibalistic urge mirrors Hong Kong's difficult return to China. As China's long lost child, Hong Kong has mixed feelings toward the putative mother. By consuming human flesh (fetus) as a symbolic act of integrating with the maternal object, the child rejuvenates herself, prolonging her youthfulness. Furthermore, cannibalism can be seen as a syndrome of late capitalist, postmodern consumer society—a perpetual pursuit and craving of new stimuli. In seeking these stimuli, the long-dead past must be evoked to fill the gap where sophisticated technologies fail. The past also must return with a new face, in new packaging. Once linked with medicinal therapy, cannibalism no longer horrifies, or seems inhuman. Instead, it re-emerges as alternative, magical treatment for those who are desperate, and for those who can pay. As Mei proclaims, her cannibal dumplings are a "legacy" of Chinese culture, "treasure" from the ancestors. She even quotes from a classical Chinese medical dictionary to lend authority to her argument. She astutely recounts the long history of cannibalism in China to reassure her clients that eating human flesh is but an observance of tradition, just like the practice of Chinese medicine in modern times. Here, the undesirable and primitive China turns out to be the savior of privileged Hong Kong women defeated by age and patriarchal control.

Conclusion: United in Horror

Going Home and *Dumplings* both employ class difference to define Hong Kong and China as two distinct entities. "Primitive China/Mother" is the other that keeps the modern, Westernized Hong Kong intact. However, as both films demonstrate, Hong Kong and China might not be as separate as perceived at the time of the handover. According to Ackbar Abbas, "[t]he colonized state, while politically subordinate, is in many crucial respects not in a dependent subaltern position, but is in fact more advanced — in terms of education, technology, access to international networks and so forth — than the colonizing state."[21] This statement needs to be re-examined with regard to the rapidly changing relationship between Hong Kong and China. Each day, 150 immigrants from China are allowed to enter Hong Kong as permanent residents. The number is dwarfed by the number of Hong Kong people traveling to China for work, affordable housing and cheap leisure. Knowingly or unknowingly, Hong Kong is integrating into a rising China, a process that is happening much faster than anyone expected. The heavy traffic between China and Hong Kong implies that the border might only be "administrative" in nature.

The relationship between mother and child and the distinction between "subject" and "object" blur as they become mutually dependent on each other. In a new relationship formed by consumption, both parties engage in empathetic subjectivity.[22] The fetus colonizes the maternal body, which in turn nourishes her colonizer. "Horror is fundamentally about boundaries — about the threat of transgressing them, and about the need to do so," says Freeland.[23] Precisely because of such need, horror/cannibalism is both repulsive and attractive. This dialectical relationship of mother and fetus is analogous to Hong Kong's postcolonial ambivalence toward China. The grand design of "one country, two systems" has proved to be only an administrative device. Hong Kong and China are getting closer and more like one another as no separate, self-contained self can be found in their mutual affinity. To rejuvenate, Hong Kong scavenges on the unwanted lives from China. Yet the rejuvenation in turn takes over the scavenger and colonizes her body. Like a venomous antidote, dumplings made of human flesh rejuvenate the aging Hong Kong woman but they are also capable of turning her beauty into disease. Ching uses her economic power to consume and possess resources from China but in the end, her addiction turns her into a cannibal. Desperately in need of a male fetus to rejuvenate, Ching pays her husband's Chinese mistress for an abortion. In turn, Ching gets to keep the aborted "treasure." A scene toward the end depicts Ching wiping her shiny knife, getting ready to cut open a small, orange human being. A low-angle medium close-up shows her close examination of her trophy; meanwhile, the soundtrack begins to play Mei's old revolutionary song. Enchanted by the familiar tune, Ching cuts downward and blood splashes onto her face. Cut to black. With this closing shot, a new vamp is born.

Both *Going Home* and *Dumplings* represent the past (China) with an eerie nostalgia. *Going Home* concludes with a regretful Hong Kong policeman who is moved by an old-fashioned love entwined with Chinese medicine. In *Dumplings*, the borders between China and Hong Kong prove to be elusive, administrative barriers only. As Mei is chased out of Hong Kong for causing the young girl's death, Ching assumes Mei's role as the new agent of cannibalism in the city of profane consumption. In this switch, Hong Kong and China are united in horror by their mutual affinity with cannibalism.

III

Iconography of Horror:
Personal Belongings,
Bodies, and Violence

9

That Unobscure Object of Desire and Horror: On Some Uncanny Things in Recent Korean Horror Films

Hyun-suk Seo

The list of recent Korean films that made the industry more visible includes titles that ought to sound familiar to any movie-goer: *Zero for Conduct*, *Public Enemy*, *Vengeance Is Mine*, *La Dolce Vita*, *The Scarlet Letter*, *Mean Streets*, *The Red Shoes*, and so on.[1] The young consumers that make up the majority of the domestic marketing targets today are not likely to have seen Jean Vigo's legendary boarding school comedy or Warner Brothers' landmark crime drama, which is precisely why this fashionable mimicry can work as an effective marketing scheme. Bordering on remembrance and oblivion of the mass, the ghostly aura of the fading signifiers could have very well affected the box office. The complimentary remark upon the heroine's shoes that her ungallant lover affords in *The Red Shoes* reflects with ironic accuracy the young viewers' initial reception of these vaguely familiar titles: "Oddly enough, they don't seem unfamiliar. I bet I have seen them somewhere before."[2] The need for the mass attention that created the rather strange lives of these signifiers may account for or reduplicate the inner workings of the cinematic pleasure and fantasy in the psychoanalytic sense. These uncanny signifying doubles may even reveal bits of truth about the ways memory, desire, loss, and repetition function in the Korean popular culture. This proposition can at least be a useful entering point to illuminate the psychological dynamic of a film that precisely deals with memory, desire, loss, and repetition. *The Red Shoes* (*Bunhongsin*, Kim Yong-gyun, 2005) is in fact about the obscure memories of the past embodied in the "new but familiar" sign.

Remarking upon the oddly ambiguous familiarity of "the red shoes" in the film, the heroine's boyfriend is quite accurate in reminding the informed movie fans that the red shoes in the 1948 British fantasy by Michael Powell and Emeric Pressburger served female desire, but nevertheless were used to both transpose and conceal the male desire to control the female body. In the Korean take-off, the fatal lure becomes the object of excessive female greed and reconfigures the ways through which desire is renegotiated in cinematic representations. This chapter examines how the fetishistic system of signification regenerates horror and desire in *The Red Shoes* and other recent Korean horror films that recycle the motif of female greed.

In addressing the oblique fraudulence of the above-mentioned semantic replicas, I need to clarify that the fatal lure in *The Red Shoes* is not exactly red but *pink*. The exact word-to-word English translation of the Korean title, *Bunhongsin,* would have to be "*The Pink Shoes,*" which accords with the old Korean-translated title of the British production and the originating Hans Andersen tale. The British film *The Red Shoes* as well as the Danish fairy-tale has always been "*The Pink Shoes*" in Korean books, movie theaters, and television for decades. And so is the official English title of Kim's contemporary horror. What we see on screen is effectively a pair of unmistakably *pink* pumps, as the Korean title "correctly" announces. In this bizarre case of *misrecognition*, the erratic (English) signifier slips from the screen and hovers like a ghost in the semantic rift. Caught between the underlying semantic constancy that they attempt at weaving and the inevitable paradigmatic shift that they perform, the vacillating signifiers evoke the impossible object, the true terror of the unconscious.

This semantic slippage or false color-blindness, of course, hardly surfaces in the story itself. The impossible object evoked in the ghostly signs, however, nearly symbolizes the system of metonymic displacements that recirculates desire and anxiety throughout the narrative. The Korean title of the film, *The Pink Shoes,* simultaneously recalls and resists the memory associated with the "original" signifiers, while the English title, *The Red Shoes,* deviates from the present and reveals the fragility of (dramatic) reality as a historical artifice. Incidentally, though not thought out by the makers of the dual signs, this is precisely what happens to the heroine of the story, Sun-jae (Kim Hye-su). The past beyond her consciousness is simultaneously repressed and conjured up by the sign she carries; her everyday reality is disintegrated by the hidden, unconscious memories embodied in the sign. The horror lies in the irreducible rift between the present and the past, between the text and the pretext, between the uniqueness of the signifier and its historical doubles. We ought to recall after all, in our quest toward the "origin" of the horror, the Lacanian proposition that "the Truth itself is constituted *through* the illusion proper to transference — 'the Truth arises from misrecognition'."³ Error is not only "part of the Truth itself," as Slavoj Žižek elaborates, but also a necessary constituent, without which the truth cannot be conceived. It is perhaps from this simple misrecognition that a "truth" about the horror evoked by the named object will arise for us.

The impossible signification of the English title *The Red Shoes*, to begin with, precisely reverberates the Lacanian notion of language, according to which, language never fully points to what it means to convey. In the Freudian/Lacanian context, loss is always comprised as an integral condition of signification; the signifier is necessarily a self-referential index of its own semantic failure. The reason why I go on with the questions of signification is that the horror rendered in recent Korean films involves larger networks of cinematic signs beyond each diegetic world. *The Red Shoes* as a signifier produced by an error precisely evokes this paradoxical semantic representation of the lack. What it slips to is its fragility and duplicity that it wants to elude. The erroneous sign, in other words, is a symptomatic indicator that reveals what the horror film in general always intends to flirt with — the symbolic wound. To unveil this "unconscious" layer of the text, it might be useful to first focus on what the Korean title demands us to gaze at with firm yet failing plainness: the pink shoes.

Wild Things

The pair of pink high heels functions as the unequivocal central motif in the film imposing their material presence in every key sequence and vociferously demanding all human attention, the characters' as well as the audiences'. Not unlike the ramen noodle soup in *Tampopo* (Itami Juzo, 1985) but devoid of the delicacy of self-mockery, a mere object unwittingly becomes the governing symbol and source for all forms of desire and anxiety in and out of the screen. Indicting a piece of prop for misfortune is not an unfamiliar gesture in recent Korean cinema, calling for another uncommon list of common names. I am referring (while keeping in mind the semantic impossibility in the Lacanian sense) to such films as *Phone* (*Pon*, Ahn Byeong-ki, 2002), *Acacia* (Park Ki-hyeong, 2003), *The Wig* (*Gabal*, Won Shin-yeon, 2005), *Cello* (*Chello Hongmijoo Ilga Salinsagan*, Lee Woo-cheol, 2005), and *Apartment* (*APT.*, Ahn Byeong-ki, 2006). Each of these films spotlights and thoroughly exploits the material presence of none other than the named object. What does it mean when all of a sudden the utterances of absolute horror begin amounting to some petty household inventory or yellow pages index?

This list of object-titles alone begins to unravel the very nature of horror rendered in these films already if we remind ourselves that the horror genre in history had not necessarily nourished objects as the source of fear. In contrast, the two major sources of the Korean horror genre, Korean folktales and Hollywood genre cinema, rely on representations of various forms of monsters and ghosts. Even though recent Korean horror films are quick to rely on the Hollywood conventions and motifs to generate shock or revulsion, the wide range of Hollywood *monsters*, the diverse origins of which are deeply rooted in history from ancient mythology and Christianity to the Enlightenment,[4] have hardly translated themselves into the Korean stories; Korean screens are not populated by aliens, vampires, zombies, mummies, reptiles, automata, deformed creatures, paranormal psychopaths, and other forms of the cast "other."[5] The variety of the Korean folk ghosts is not readily visible in the cinematic world, either.[6] Most Korean horror films rely heavily on one dominant supernatural prototype: the virgin ghost, or *cheonyeo-gwisin*. It is indeed this femme fatale *par excellence* that motivates the horror in the above-listed object-oriented films. In these "virgin ghost" variations, each of the named objects embodies the deceased damsel's memories of distress and affects the living, whom she seeks her revenge upon (*Phone, Acacia, Cello, The Wig, The Red Shoes*) or communicates her resentment to (*Apartment*). Added elements of animism, however, shift the focal point from the haunting to the haunted; if Rebecca's power captivated the second Mrs. De Winter precisely through her sheer absence in Hitchcock's rendering of horror and mystery, the belongings of the dead have much more say in the recent Korean popular imaginations. It is often the thingness of the thing itself, both material and symbolic, not some illusory images of the ghost/owner, that enthralls the spectators inside and outside the screen. The innately not-so-scary everyday thing attains its terrorizing status through a kind of Pavlovian stimuli staged by the cinematic means that associates it to blood-shedding supernatural events. The title, the plot, and the mise-en-scène of each film conspire to fetishize its appearance as the distinctive embodiment of the deceased's undischarged libido. The virgin ghosts get to appeal to the audience, if ever, only when the repressed memory is spoken toward the end (*Phone, The Wig, Apartment*).[7] Otherwise, they remain silent or absent (*Acacia, Cello, The Red Shoes*).

"The thing film" also departs from the usual virgin ghost tales by introducing the thematic elements of mobility, ownership, surplus value, and competition, the defining characteristics of modern consumerism.

Reminiscent of the murderous VHS tape in *Ring* (*Ringu*, Nakata Hideo, 1998), a likely precedent of the Korean object-driven fantasies, these articles thus can be found, lost, transferred, exchanged, and circulated, entailing any possible effects of uncertainty and insecurity. Through the object erupts the *symptom*, an indicator of the systematic breakdown in the psychoanalytic sense. This eruption occasions dual effects. On the one hand, not unlike the Lacanian notion of "das Ding," it encircles what he calls "the real," or what resists the symbolic register of the world.[8] In Lacan's view, "das Ding," or "the Thing," is the immaterial absence that constitutes the subject as desiring.[9] On the other, the named thing in these films initiates the goal-oriented narrative structure as a makeshift by demanding interpretation and understanding of the symbolic wound; the narrative attempts at eradicating the elusive aspect of "das Ding" by furnishing causal relations to replace the ununderstandable void. A symptom in the Lacanian sense is that which signifies something even though it can be nothing in different registers. Symptoms open the fissure in the symbolic order and demand knowledge with which one can situate their meanings within the symbolic order.

Remembrance of "Things" Past

The named object constitutes the characters as sexually desiring subjects. The exchanges among female characters surrounding the object take various forms of competition, and the thing becomes the means to measure as well as conceal the excess of female sexuality. Even though the sexual level of the female characters' actions is not rendered manifest, it is always an integral part of the entire network of jealousy, concealment, betrayal, and murder, in which every character participates actively or secretly. Sexuality even underlies such films as *Phone* or *Apartment*, in which the heroine is depicted as an ascetic, unmarried workaholic. In *Phone*, Ji-won (Ha Ji-won), the heroine who seemingly has nothing to do with the family harassed by the virgin ghost, turns out to have donated her ovum to the wife and unconsciously participates in the network of kinship with other competitors including the wife, the infant daughter, and the dead, who all share the desire for the man of the family. The gender specificity of this circulating desire is made clear when naïve young girls suddenly mature sexually when they learn to desire the thing (*Phone, The Red Shoes, Cello*).

The sexual level of the exchanges of the thing is most blatant in *The Red Shoes*. Sun-jae's obsessive attachment to shoes is conveniently rationalized within the plot structure when she accidentally witnesses her husband's extramarital affair taking place in their own bedroom. The only visual depiction of the affair available for the audience is the very detail that seems to mesmerize and traumatize Sun-jae: a pump dangling on the erect foot of the orgasmic woman lying underneath the husband. This vision (which is rendered from a disembodied point of view that belongs to no one before Sun-jae sees it from her own point of view, a point that I shall come back to later) serves as a kind of "primal scene" in the Freudian sense within the sequential context of the plot, giving an essential piece of clue to account for Sun-jae's excessive obsession with high heels. Not surprisingly, the very first act she displays for the audience after this traumatic incident happens to be putting on her own pair of black pumps (Figure 9.1). It is "in her own shoes" that she decides to take her own direction; far from the magic that Dorothy's famous shoes activate in *The Wizard of Oz* (Victor Fleming, 1939), Sun-jae's take her further away from "home." A few shots later, we find her in her own newly rented apartment adorned with large glass shelves for a carefully displayed and theatrically lit collection of pumps, sandals, and mules, to which the fatal pink pumps are to be added.

Figure 9.1 Sun-jae's feet sliding into shoes
(*The Red Shoes*, Kim Yong-gyun, 2005)

What is exactly the lure of the shoes? Against the Korean custom that strictly forbids shoe-wearing inside a house, the dangling shoe may indicate the husband's (or his partner's) sexual fancy in particular, affirming the most common use of the term *fetish*. In the male psyche explicated by Lacan, to elaborate further the symbolic aspect of the Freudian fetishism, the misrecognized female lack of the symbolic phallus, which can but does not necessarily take the form of a penis, leads the man to devalue the woman whom he had thought possessed the phallus, accounting for his infidelity.[10] According to the rather murky causal leap in *The Red Shoes*, *his* lack prompts *her* invention of makeshifts. As Freud noted, fetishism renders desire reciprocal, fulfillment impossible; the "thing" films fetishize the named objects to the extent that the excess of desire fruitlessly amounts to impossibility, expressed as anxiety and horror in effect.

As if demonstrating the classical Freudian notion of fetishism as a male symptom, these objects also establish their symbolic presence through close contacts with various female body parts. In the most palpable cases of fetishism, the objects are worn as the protruding extension of the body (*The Wig, The Red Shoes*); in others, they make symbolic exchanges with female organs or orifices in intimate proximity (*Phone, Cello*). The victim who pricks her own eyes and ears to block herself from the piercing auditory omnipresence of the phone ring in *Phone*, the "voice" of the big Other in Lacan's topology of desire, suggests that the symbolic lack is readily materialized and sexualized in the female body. Even the least likely symbol of sexuality in our inventory is associated with female sexuality; for the very first object of obsessive desire that the mentally challenged daughter secures after her first, premature menstruation in *Cello* is naturally none other than the bulky, grave musical instrument that spreads her legs.

What is important is that the mechanism of fetishism that demands the female body to signify the lack involves male subjects not only as spectators but also as other bearers of the lack. It is as if the male characters, minimized and marginalized in the thing films to begin with, demonstrate the Lacanian explication of fetishism, in which the Name of the father has failed to release the child from the disquieting arrest of the imaginary lack; the male subjects project *their* own symbolic lack onto the female body. In this sense, Carol J. Clover's point about the "reversed transvestism" in American slasher film[11] is even more widespread in the object-driven stories as the fetishistic desire becomes the common ground for diverse subject positions to participate through shared signs and gaze. The cross-gender intersubjective substitution even functions as a device for plot twists. In *The Wig*, the utmost "femininity" that the female user finds in the soft, thin, and long hair of the wig turns out to have belonged to her sister's boyfriend's dead male lover. Embodied in the uncanniness of the thing is the repressed femininity of a man. The homosexual man is not simplistically depicted as a threat to society as in the English-language horror culture observed by Harry M. Benshoff,[12] but initially contextualized as a victim of social pressure and hegemony, serving as the source of grudge and motivation for the afterlife revenge. As the instigator of the thing, the virgin ghost has taken a male body. Ambiguously split into voyeuristic exploitation of the fetishized body on the one hand and immersion in the feminized position on the other, male subjects in the thing films oscillate around the alluring possibilities of castration. The cross-gender exchanges of gaze and desire extend to include the viewers as well. In *The Red Shoes*, the recurrent shots of Sun-jae's feet sliding into shoes (Figure 9.2) are likely to entertain the invisible, classical Mulveyian male fetishist-voyeur. By simulating a mirror reflection from *her* point of view, however, these shots also equate *his* position with *hers*. The voyeuristic/narcissistic camera, in short, circulates the lack as it registers the imaginary onto the symbolic; the disquieting imaginary lack emerges out of the overlapping subject positions.

Figure 9.2 Sun-jae's feet sliding into shoes again
(*The Red Shoes*, Kim Yong-gyun, 2005)

One True Things

The thing in these films appears at a glance markedly different from the classical Freudian fetish in one important account. It is not metonymically multiplied as a classical fetish would (collecting habits, for instance, being the most common form of multiplication); rather, it assures its presence within the diegesis as *the one and only thing in the world*. The pair of pink shoes that Sun-jae discovers outshines all others in her collection and becomes the supreme object of adoration. Unlike the bewitching videotape in *Ring*, which can extend its power precisely through duplication, the wig, the pink shoes, the apartment, the cello, the acacia tree, and the phone number in these films strive to stand out as the irreplaceable, *one-of-a-kind* thing in a world populated by mass-produced, identical replicas. It is as if the horror that they evoke is designed to serve the primary purpose of upholding their material and semantic singularity. The thing assumes the status of the *art object par excellence* in the age of mechanical reproduction, so to speak, faithfully transposing the heroines' desire to be the very best (*Cello, Apartment*) or the chosen girl (*The Red Shoes, The Wig*) in the world where aesthetic beauty is a means of competition. In these moral fables, ironically, the horror of the singular objects surfaces precisely when the original owner or the heroine herself fails to retain or take the position of the best or the chosen one in the highly competitive social environment. The uniqueness, or resistance against metonymic repetition, is that which valorizes the system of exchanges. The good news then is that the bewitching cell phone, the cello, the wig, the tree, and the pink shoes are not likely to bewitch the same household. It is precisely because there is only one phone number, wig, tree, cello, or pair of pink shoes that it can symbolically connect and bond the characters, who are then reduced to recurrent types according to their patterned (re)actions.

The horrifying irony is precisely that the human subjects who surround the unique object often participate in the exchanges as mental doubles even when, or especially when, they strive to be the best or chosen one. The desire for the singular object is duplicated by multiple characters, who identify with one another or take one another's position. The mirror effects are prompted as repetition or misrecognition: Sun-jae, the schizophrenic murderer in *The Red Shoes*, is the reincarnated double of the deceased dancer who adored the same shoes; the female voyeur (Ko So-young) in *Apartment* eventually assumes the position of the watched and follows the same suicidal path of the deceased girl; Su-hyeon, the wig-wearer, takes the appearance of the dead male owner of the hair, while the distressed daughter of the wig-maker is mistaken by the heroine for Su-hyeon in *The Wig*; the housemaid (Lee Ju-na) is misrecognized by the heroine (Seong Hyeon-a) as the deceased friend in *Cello;* the heroine (Shim Hye-jin) strives to take the place of the mother while the boy thinks his real mother is dead and stood in by a tree in *Acacia;* and so on. The aura of the elusive, unique object amounts to repetition.

The film that illuminates the nature of the horror embedded in the interchangeability of subjects most explicitly is *Cello,* in which repetition itself becomes the horrific motif. It is as if the heroine is trapped in the chain of events that repeat themselves, the most repulsive repetition being the sounding of the tape music recorded by her and her dead friend; the heroine dreads *repetition* itself, not just the music. In another occasion, the originating trauma of the car accident, during which the heroine willfully withdrew her helping hand to let her best friend and superior competitor fall to death, is repeated by the heroine's two daughters at the balcony of the house. This Hitchcockian motif of a hand that suspends another does not necessarily pertain to any specific meanings but nevertheless repeats itself. As Žižek notes, these repetitive motifs inscribe certain enjoyment, or *sinthoms*, operating in the Freudian account of "compulsion to repeat."[13] Compulsive indeed, the repetition of sinthoms does not necessarily unveil the fissures in the symbolic order like symptoms do, but they nevertheless "fixes a certain core of enjoyment, like mannerisms in painting."[14]

All the more in *Cello*, the entire plot structure is built in near symmetry with two mirroring sequences that depict the same birthday party differentiated by the heroine's split states of mind, marking the blindly euphoric beginning and the ominous closure. The unfamiliar dread, as Freud observed in his uncannily layered essay "Das Unheimliche,"[15] precisely dwells in the sheer familiarity of its components. When the event is repeated, the complacency of the first occasion falls apart, signaling the fractures in the reality of the nuclear family. Trauma is not simply repeated, as Hitchcock has shown in *Vertigo* (1958); it is repetition itself that renders the past traumatic. In the thing films, the disquieting effects of *doubles* and *déjà vu*, two discernible instances of the uncanny in the Freudian sense, indicate the disruption in the link between the imaginary and the symbolic. As Freud acknowledged, the uncanny is a "semiotic" problem;[16] it activates the metalinguistic trap.

The plagiaristic mimicry or semantic exorcism exercised in the titles of *The Red Shoes* is then a part of the entire system of duplicity run by replicas. Not unlike the bewitched found objects in these films, the motifs and signs in individual texts extend their meanings beyond its diegetic parameters through intertextual repetition. Even though the thing is materially irreplaceable within its own discrete diegetic world, it forms a chain of metonymic displacements beyond its limit, symbolizing the impossibility of desire or the falsity of the ego's imaginary unity. Although the "thing film" as a sub-genre may not prevail for its repetition precisely betrays the very premise of its power of horror constituted by its singularity, it illustrates the nature of the horror rendered in recent Korean cinema overall, that is, the disruption in the link between the imaginary and the symbolic. The doomed male aide in *Ring* had offered an insight on its repetition when he declared: "This kind of thing . . . it doesn't start by one person telling a story. It's more like everyone's fear just takes on a life of its own. Perhaps that's what everyone wants."[17]

When the uncanny thingness of the (intertextual) chain of metonymic repetition is materialized in a single signifier, say a pair of pink shoes, the placement of the signifier among the patterned subject positions determines how their shifts take place; it is the signifier that instigates intersubjective substitution. This pattern in the thing film corresponds to the Lacanian account of compulsion to repeat.[18] The semiotic function of the thing is in its repetition, from which emerges the subject of unconsciousness, the true specter of the cinematic fantasy whose compulsive repetition produces the uncanny. The thing film, in other words, reduplicates the necessary process through which, according to Lacan, the imaginary is registered onto the symbolic. This process entails anxiety and affirmation, neurotic or compulsive, when it is represented in horror films in general. The defining characteristic of the horror genre is in its failure in valorizing the effects of intersubjective substitution.

Family Plot

Tracing the origins of these uncanny objects beyond the memories of the deceased characters, our search reaches as far as the Hitchcockian objects, of which the relation to the surrounding characters is particularly illuminating. Žižek identifies three different types of the Hitchcockian objects, which not only correspond to three different periods in the director's career but also accord with three distinct forms of desire. Among them is what Žižek describes as the index of the lack of the father to refer to some objects in Hitchcock's films of the Selznick period (1940s). As Mladen Dolar elaborates, such objects can be differentiated from the McGuffin, the empty space that sets the plot in motion.[19] Whereas the Hitchcockian McGuffin, immaterial in essence, functions precisely through its pure absence ("It means nothing at all."), the index of the lack occupies material presence and enables symbolic exchanges among characters. Unlike the "pure semblance" that McGuffin represents, the symbolic object of exchange is usually a "unique and non-specular" material, playing a crucial role in the world constructed by doubles or mirror-relations. Symbolized as S(A̶) to follow the well-known Lacanian formula, that which circulates among subjects serve as "a kind of guarantee, pawn, on their symbolic relationship."[20] The "barred A" refers to the big Other to whom the subject owes its formation but cannot get access. As the signifier of the denied access to the mother, Žižek notes, the S(A̶) registers the "impossibility around which the symbolic order is structured." Žižek's list of such key objects includes the key in *Notorious* and *Dial M for Murder*, the wedding ring in *Shadow of a Doubt* and *Rear Window*, and the lighter in *Strangers on a Train*. Žižek continues, if the McGuffin signifies and functions as the gap in the symbolic order or what Lacan calls the *objet petit a* and sets the hero on the track of the Oedipal journey, S(A̶) signifies the lack in the mother on the one hand and the impotence of the father on the other. In the narratives governed by S(A̶), "the father cannot live up to his Name, to his symbolic Mandate, in so far as he is caught in an obscene enjoyment."[21]

The domestic objects in the thing film extends what Žižek introduces as the function of S(A̶) in Hitchcock's films beyond postwar America and elucidates for us the role of the impotent father in the Korean horror. These moral tales largely evolve around the absent place of the dead or fallen father, from which the supernatural law instigates itself as the alternative family order. The fallen Name of the father is not necessarily acted out by the supreme male subject immersed in the "obscene enjoyment" as in *Shadow of a Doubt, Dial M for Murder,* or *Notorious*; rather, it is symbolized by the uncanny material object that is fought over, possessed, "played" (in various masturbatory fashions), and lost by the female subjects. It is the female subjects, in other words, who dominate the "obscene enjoyment," twisting the exclusivity of the father rite in the Hitchcockian world. The trans–gender intersubjectivity is the form that both conceals and actualizes the absent father's involvement in the narrative.

The world in which women dominate the father's awry playthings is initiated by the absent father and works to keep him out. This absence precisely characterizes the nature of the obscene pleasure in the thing films. The entire originating trauma in *Apartment* was initiated because the suicidal girl's father was killed in an accident; in *The Wig*, the absence of the dead father is constantly reminded through the heroine's flashbacks; and *The Red Shoes* eventually reveals that Sun-jae has punished the unfaithful husband with death, the father whom her daughter (Park Yeon-ah) claims is still visiting her. It is the structural negativity of the father's authority, the domestic interior deprived of the Name of the father, that nurtures the female greed; it is within the "darkness" of the shattered patriarchy that the thing becomes the object of symbolic exchanges among the greedy female characters. The female greed that replaces the father's enjoyment turns the world into a kind of nightmarish dog-eat-dog hell propelled by the hunger for possession, the immorality of which serves to edify the Name of the father in effect. The fallen Name of the father is an integral part of the entire network of meanings generated by the lack that the objects signify.

The absent father renders the daughters' enjoyments trivial, vulgar, and hysterical; the degradation is an integral part of the absent father's enjoyment. In *The Wig*, the fatally ill and fatherless adolescent receives the wig from her older sister to initiate the barrage of schizophrenic symbolic exchanges between them. In *Phone*, the cellular number given to the heroine reveals that all four key primary characters — the heroine, her female friend Ho-jeong (Kim Yu-mi), Ho-jeong's infant daughter, and the former owner of the number — are linked to Ho-jeong's husband in one frantically sexual way or another. In *Apartment*, the apartment building next to the heroine's ultimately becomes a sort of twisted mirror reflection onto which she projects her own guilt and fear that nourished in the fatherless family.

In *The Red Shoes*, the mise-en-scène renders the fatherless shelter occupied by Sun-jae and her little girl dark and sinister, sharply differentiated from the brightly lit paternal family home that they abandoned. In this darkness, the mother and the daughter literally wrestle against each other over the trivial and yet desirable thing, providing a kind of misogynic spectacle that once characterized the American women-in-prison film of the 1970s. The coven-like atmosphere, devalued as an effect of the patriarchal ideology, also recollects Hollywood's postwar women's films, or the period and sentiment that the slippage of the English title refers back to. If the daughter in *Mildred Pierce* (Michael Curtiz, 1945) functioned as "a part of the [mother's] body, the extension of herself, the phallus she will not relinquish"[22] as Pam Cook has suggested in her famous essay on the film, the daughter in *The Red Shoes* is the one who wants to turn the phallic mother back to what she is supposed to be, namely the lacking subject. The pair of pink shoes as the object of symbolic exchanges, in other words, becomes the means of symbolic (re-) castration, reinstating and displaying the effects of the fallen Name of the father; the process of symbolic exchanges among women accords with the act of castration.

If the thingness of the thing dwells in the demise of the patriarchal system of meanings, the narratives reduplicate one of the oldest themes that have haunted Korean cinema: the fall of the father. The Korean cinema under the military dictatorship from the 1960s to the 1980s was preoccupied with the dilemma of manhood caught between the demand of traditional value and the threat of the changing family relations.[23] The prototypical modern father in *The Aimless Bullet* (*Obaltan*, Yoo Hyun-mok, 1960), castrated and self-pitying, still captivates today's screen as a spectral semblance precisely through its symbolic absence. In this sense, the thing film recirculates the theme of male crisis deeply felt in the deteriorating patriarchal order. The impossible name that "*The Red Shoes*" is doomed to slip to and be reciprocally displaced by is the lost Name of the father. The fallen father cannot make his symbolic presence in the world operating through women's desire; he can only exercise his spell negatively, or through his absence. The alluring deadly object not only replaces but also *is* the dangerous plaything of the fallen father secretly immersed in obscene enjoyment. Self-degrading in essence, the absent father not only adores the fetish but also desires the lack. The "aimless" father takes the place of the lack.

It is no coincidence then that this mechanism involves another Hitchcockian sinthom, the sacrifice of "the third woman," or a female character who makes futile attempts to overcome the lack. In *The Wig* and *The Red Shoes*, the heroine's female friends who borrow or steal the attractive article have to pay for their greed with agonizing death. Although Sun-jae's "official" motivation is jealousy inherited from her former life, the psychoanalytic content of the spectacle serves the need to turn women back to the castrated state; Sun-jae, around whom the network of exchanges centers, is both the castrator and the castrated. In both films, the sight of the castrated state of the third women is presented in photographic images within the diegesis. The reportage that renders the (undesirable) female body as an evidential representation of criminology is a part of the mechanism that responds to the misogynic demands of the ghostly patriarchy and its obscene desire for the repulsive lack.

Presumed Innocent

To solve a mystery, according to the Lacanian account of transference, one has to rely on the necessary illusion that someone has the knowledge. The goal-oriented narrative structure in the thing film produces the *presumption* that someone within the diegetic world has the knowledge about the symptoms. In line with this presumption, I have so far scrutinized the absent place behind the alluring object in the thing films, narrowing the search to the absent Name of the fallen father as the likely subject produced as an effect analogous to that of a psychoanalytic procedure.

Before narrowing the search, it is useful to examine one usual but misleading suspect who in actuality does possess the knowledge about the meanings of the symptoms within the plot. This character type that cooperates with the overriding theme of male crisis is also a Hitchcockian type, acceding to its famous nickname, "the woman who knows too much." These are the female characters who hold crucial information to help unravel the mystery. The deceased girl's close friend in *Phone*, the daughter of the wig-maker in *The Wig*, and the old housemaid who has witnessed the tragic death of the original owner of the shoes in *The Red Shoes* all possess the missing piece of the puzzle, without which neither the heroine nor her male aide can complete the journey toward coherent knowledge. The possession of important information, however, does not necessarily grant authority or power; they cannot undo the spell of the dead themselves. The woman who knows "too much" about the uncanny thing is horrified precisely by her excessive knowledge. Despite the knowledge that she has, she is depicted as the bearer of the lack, subject to the enjoyment of the absent obscene father. In excess that she is, the knowing but lacking woman is indeed a stand-in of the absent father immersed in ambiguous enjoyment; she is a mere effect of the entire system of substitution propelled by the castration fantasy. In the world of shifting desires around the fundamental lack, knowledge is always a harmful charm.

This said, it is time to return to the array of the invisible subjects that I have passed through: the nameless narrator who recollects the ghost's trauma, the invisible male subject whose lack is substituted by a woman's fetishes, the invisible spectator who identifies with the mirror image of the castrated female body, the subject of the unbinding gaze who witnesses the dangling fetish before Sun-jae sees it, and the historically lost translator whose semantic slippage allowed the unconscious life of *The Red Shoes* to slip out. These spectral subjects are consistent with the Lacanian "subject," who precisely dwells on the place of the lack. This is the subject whose representation of itself fails, in the paradoxical sense that "the failure of representation is the only way to represent it adequately,"[24] as Žižek puts it. The subject is the effect of the failed signifier ("*The Red Shoes*"). The leftover of this semantic failure does not necessarily take the center stage but nevertheless haunts the screen.

In a popular riddle, four friends indulge themselves in a dark empty room with what they call "the corner game." Each of the four corners of the room is occupied by a player, one of whom approaches in darkness and takes over the adjacent corner to start the game; the one who is pushed out must substitute for the next adjacent subject and so on. The relays keep replacing another, and the game cycles on happily, until someone comes to a chilling realization that logically the game should not have been made possible beyond the first cycle without the element that was not present in the onset of the game: the absent fifth player. The lesson of this revelation is that what produces horror is a byproduct of a semantic system that constitutes itself precisely through its structural impossibility.

Each of the "thing films" tells its own story about a woman and an object, but the leap from the "official" content afforded by a Freudian reading points to a paramount tale that features the absent subject. Its power nourishes and simultaneously overrides all that threatens the patriarchal order: the greed of the female searcher, the terror of the virgin ghost, the logical flaw in the deaths of the third women in regard to *their* own grudge, and the cryptic supremacy of the women who know too much. There is, of course, a demand not to pinpoint any concrete character type so as to poetically embrace the ominous residue that suggests the open-ended continuation of the evil spell at the end of the story. We cannot say *too much* about the real owners of dubious found objects after all. However, the resistance to name the name may precisely serve the elusive subject's will. The paternal male subject of enjoyment is far from being guilty in the criminological sense, but the very *presumption* specifically characterizes his identity.

In *Acacia*, the heroine struggles in vain to find her missing adopted son. Once having overcome her resistance to believe that it is her husband who murdered the boy, she finally names the long-repressed name: that of the man of the family. The final opposition between the couple, however, reveals not only that she has misrecognized the husband as the murderer in her paranoiac state but also that it was she who had killed the boy (by pure accident or as an effect of her unconscious will). The flashbacks (of the invisible narrator) reveal that her convenient amnesia led to her false sense of innocence and blind accusation against the husband.

The point that I would like to make through this case of simple misrecognition is that the trauma has taken place without the father's direct involvement and that this exclusion and the ensuing presumption are precisely the way his absent position operates in the game propelled by the uncanny thing in general. As Žižek elaborates, "this [Lacanian] subject does not have to exist effectively: to produce his effects, it is enough for others to presume that he exists."[25] This illusory, *presumed* subject of knowledge is assigned by the analysand to the analyst in the classical Freudian situation. In our cases, the presumed subject of knowledge is also the obscene subject who secretly enjoys the game he devised through his castration fantasy and its mediating plaything. The presumed subject announces in his answer to the questions regarding the symptoms precisely what he is demanded to admit, namely his impotence. The subject is the hysteric position created by the incapacity; this incapacity is substantiated as a thing.

The heroine in *Acacia* presumes the husband to be the core of enjoyment precisely because she thinks that the event materializes *his* fantasy. She is perceptive on the nature of the symptoms to this extent, except that her pinpointing is constituted on the ground where signifiers always slip and every subject has already drifted onto another position in their own "corner game." Her misrecognition opens a fissure in the symbolic, the lack that is far from being outside the language but an effect of the failing system of signification. In presuming that her husband as a signifier is the true player of the game propelled by doubles and misrecognition, the paranoiac mother is at least aware that in the world populated by the signs of the inaccessible mother the absent subject's castration fantasy runs amok in excess.

10

"Tell the Kitchen That There's Too Much *Buchu* in the Dumpling": Reading Park Chan-wook's "Unknowable" *Oldboy*

Kyung Hyun Kim

Oldboy is one of a slew of Korean films recently distributed in the United States (a list that includes *Chunhyang, Memories of Murder, Spring, Summer, Fall, Winter, and Spring, Tae Guk Gi: the Brotherhood of War, Take Care of My Cat, Tell Me Something, Untold Scandal,* and *Way Home* among many others) — but, unlike the others, it has been met with surprisingly negative reviews.[1] *New York Times* critic, Manohla Dargis, acknowledged *Oldboy*'s director Park Chan-wook as "some kind of virtuoso [of cool]," but she also wrote that the film is "symptomatic of a bankrupt, reductive postmodernism: one that promotes a spurious aesthetic relativism (it's all good) and finds its crudest expression in the hermetically sealed world of fan boys"[2] Disappointed by the all-too-apparent nihilism *Oldboy* putatively promotes, Dargis argues that it fails to undertake the kind of tangible philosophical inquiries which Sam Peckinpah and Pier Paolo Pasolini explored in their films during the 1960s and 1970s. Dargis' criticisms and others like hers undoubtedly dampened *Oldboy*'s chances to perform well.[3] Despite the fact that *Oldboy* won numerous awards internationally, including the Grand Prix (second prize) at the Cannes Film Festival in 2004, and despite the cult status it has achieved among young fans of action films, the film managed to generate only mediocre box office receipts in the U.S.

I begin this chapter with Dargis' critique of Park Chan-wook because it indicates a number of vantage points from which *Oldboy* must be considered when discussed in an international context. *Oldboy*, like *Sympathy for Mr. Vengeance (Boksu-neun na-ui geot,* 2002) and other Park Chan-wook films, does not conjure up the kind of humanist themes that Dargis implies to be properly associated with art-house films such as the ones directed by not only Pasolini and Peckinpah, but also Ingmar Bergman, Andrei Tarkovsky, and Krzysztof Kieslowski. Instead of preaching values of tolerance and salvation, Park's protagonists plot revenge by brandishing sharp metal instruments and impatiently waiting for their turn to spill the blood of others. Moreover, the exaggerated male icons featured in Park Chan-wook's films seem to be direct quotations of Japanese *manga* characters or Hong Kong action heroes created by John Woo and Tsui Hark. These contrast with the realism of his predecessors in Korean cinema such as Park Kwang-su or Jang Sun-woo, who, as I have argued elsewhere, have demythologized the masculinity of Korean cinema.[4] While many of Dargis's points are worthy, she fails to point out that Park is not the only filmmaker recognized by Cannes in the recent past who has similarly been uninterested in asking epistemological questions about life. Cannes winners Lars Von Trier, Wong Kar-wei, and Quentin Tarantino have similarly created distance from philosophical or political issues, seeking instead to leave their viewers with an indelibly "cool" impression of violence. Secondly, Dargis' article sidesteps the controversy surrounding filmmakers like Peckinpah, whose intentions and philosophical depth have been continuously questioned by critics. Jettisoning some of the exaggerated claims made by critics such as Stephen Prince, who celebrated Peckinpah's "melancholy framing of violence," Marsha Kinder proposes instead that Peckinpah was the first postwar narrative filmmaker in America who "inflect [ed] the violence with a comic exuberance."[5] Peckinpah choreographed scenes of explicit violence as if they were musical numbers, and was considered a pioneer in American cinema. However, the question of whether or not the violence used in his films truly inspires philosophical questions or simply feeds an orgasmic viewing experience of the kind that has spawned the films of Quentin Tarantino or Park Chan-wook is a serious one. My contention is that Peckinpah and Park Chan-wook are, for better or for worse, similar as filmmakers, not categorically different.

In the three films of Park Chan-wook's "revenge" trilogy, *Sympathy for Mr. Vengeance* (2002), *Oldboy* (2003) and *Lady Vengeance* (2005), one can trace the emergence of "postmodern" attitude that takes up not only the point of view that the grand ideologies (humanism, democracy, socialism, etc.) are faltering, if not entirely dissipated, but also a belief that the image is merely just that: an image. Image here is that which is not an impression of reality, but a perception of matter that approximates the verisimilitudes of both space and time that may not have anything to do with reality. This renders a sense of the "unknowable," which irked many Western critics who have problematized Park's films for having failed to produce social criticism. But is this all that there is to this debate? Are there no history, no significant meaning, and no profound idea behind Park's images? How conveniently indescribable is the "unknowable"?

The aim of this chapter is threefold. First, I will try to identify the ways in which the main tropes of Park Chan-wook's work — including flattened mise-en-scène, the commodified body, the mystification of spatial markers, and the disjointed juxtaposition of images and sound — all aim to explore the potential of cinema in ways that may have vexing epistemological implications. Second, I invoke the Nietzschean *ressentiment* in examining Park Chan-wook's assertion that personal vengeance is a plausible kind of energy in a society where its law and ethics have been virtually ratified by the combined interests of liberal democracy and capitalism. Third, in my conclusion, I will entertain the question whether or not the post-politics or anti-history of Park Chan-wook can yield a political reading when placed in a Korean historical context, just as Peckinpah's work, when contextualized in an American sociopolitical context, was perceived to have cited the violence of Vietnam and the civil rights movement.

Oldboy

Loosely adapted from an eight-volume *manga* (*manhwa* in the Korean pronunciation) mystery novel of the same title,[6] *Oldboy* follows in the footsteps of other Korean films such as *Alien Baseball Team* (*Gongpo-ui oein gudan*, Lee Chang-ho, 1986) and *Terrorist* (Kim Young-bin, 1995) that have adopted the narratives and style of *manhwa* into live-action films. Before Park Chan-wook, the most prominent among the directors who adopted a *manhwa* approach to filmmaking was Lee Myung-se (Yi Myeong-se), whose films during the late 1980s and the 1990s stubbornly departed from the realist trend of the then-New Korean Cinema. Most of Lee's films, such as *Gagman* (1988), *My Love, My Bride* (1990), *First Love* (1993), and *Nowhere to Hide* (1999), have insisted on a cinematic worldview that treats live-action characters as animated ones, thus presenting a distorted vision of the real world. As such, some similarities can be drawn between the works of Lee Myung-se and those of Park Chan-wook. However, it should be noted that Park Chan-wook's cynicism differs radically from Lee's heavily thematized romanticism. Park Chan-wook's films have created an impact so powerful that it has nudged the Korea film industry to look into *manhwa* as its treasure trove for original creative property. *Oldboy* was followed by box office blockbuster films *200-*

Pound Beauty (Kim Yong-hwa, 2006), adapted from a graphic novel by Suzuki Yumiko, and *Tazza: High Rollers* (Choi Dong-hun, 2006), which was originally a *manhwa* series created by Lee Hyun-se.

Oldboy is the second film in Park Chan-wook's "vengeance" trilogy, which has been successful both in the domestic marketplace and on the international film festival circuit.[7] In these films, vengeance is carefully restricted to the realm of the personal, never crossing over into the public domain: it is always aimed at other individuals and almost never against state institutions. This in itself is hardly original. However, in *Oldboy* as in the other two films of the trilogy, *Sympathy for Mr. Vengeance* and *Lady Vengeance* (*Chinjeolhan geumjassi*, 2005), the police play only a perfunctory role. This erasure of authority accomplishes several things. First, it emphasizes the fact that the heroes and villains operate outside the domain of the law. They mercilessly abduct, kill, blackmail, threat, unleash violence, and engage in series of reprisals without ever even implying the existence of a public judicial system of the kind that typically occupies a central position in dramas dealing with individual liberty and freedom. (Examples of this mode can be seen in realist films such as *Chilsu and Mansu* [Park Kwang-su, 1988] or *Peppermint Candy* [*Bakha satang*, Lee Chang-dong, 1999], which foreground the police as sources of corruption or social malaise who meet all acts of transgressions, personal or public, with a violence.

Second, it enables *Oldboy* to suggest a mythical, transhistorical world beyond the mundane realities of a legal system in which figures such as the protagonist Dae-su and the villain Woo-jin freely roam. Philip Weinstein writes about something he calls "beyond knowing," a common symptom of modernist narratives that "tends to insist that no objects out there are disinterestedly knowable, and that any talk of objective mapping and mastery is either mistaken or malicious — an affair of the police" (Weinstein 2005, 253). Although it is difficult to classify Park Chan-wook's films as modernist, they do exploit such Kafkaesque devices by deliberately rejecting "objective mapping and mastery" and consequently aim to dispel the "knowing" sometimes even when the lights are turned on at the theaters. Park unwaveringly refuses to claim the "knowable," despite having been labeled as superficial by several prominent critics.

This *unknowable* attitude can also be seen stylistically in Park's reconstitution of the visual plane, which deliberately rejects realist depth-of-field and instead opts for a flattened mise-en-scène that relies heavily on wide-angle lenses and reduces the distance between the camera and its subjects. These techniques, which deny any density beyond surfaces, once again underscore the relentlessly superficial domain of the unknowable.

Complementing the "unknowable" also is the landscape that remains deleted in films such as *Oldboy*. If the discovery or emergence of landscape, as argued by critic Karatani Kojin,[8] is absolutely vital to the structure of our *modern* perception, is the erasure of landscape essential in shaping a *postmodern* perception? Instead of nature, what gets accentuated in this flattened space are dilapidated concrete cells, meaningless television images, anonymous Internet chats, and chic restaurants and penthouses that condition Korea's postmodern environment.

Also in Park Chan-wook's realm of the *unknowable*, the police are useless. Park's visual invocation of pastiche helps readdress and essentially efface modern history of Korea — one that is marked by tyranny of uniformed men. There is one notable exception to this absence of police in *Oldboy*. At the beginning of the film, the protagonist, Oh Dae-su (Choi Min-sik), appears in a scene that takes place in the police station. Jump cuts centrally figure Dae-su, who is drunk and unruly. He has apparently been brought into the station after having caused some disturbance — in short, he is a public menace. This sequence is shot with a minimum of affect. The realistic lighting and natural acting style differ radically from the saturated colors and highly choreographed action sequences that will later constitute the bulk of the film. Although this police station sequence lasts about two-and-a-half minutes, uniformed policemen rarely appear in the frame. Only their voices are heard, presaging the absence of police throughout the film. Although Dae-su verbally insults the police, going so far as to urinate inside the station, the authorities allow him to leave the station unscathed. The police act as if they were from the 2000s, though this scene is set in 1988. Dae-su's obstreperous acts may be trivial, but as films like Park Kwang-su's *Chilsu and Mansu* (*Chilsu-wa Mansu,* 1988) and Hong Sang-soo's *The Day a Pig Fell into the Well* (*Dwaeji-ga umul-e ppajin nal,* 1996) have proven to audiences time and again, South Korean authorities rarely overlook even the slightest disagreeable incident stirred up by unruly drunkards.[9] Made fifteen and eight years respectively after the release of these other films, *Oldboy* shows the police as having lost their teeth. In this post-authoritarian era, it is not surprising that abuses of power by figures of authority no longer occupy the central concern of the drama.

Dae-su, an ordinary salaryman with a wife and a toddler daughter, is released from the police station only to find himself locked up minutes later in an anonymous cell. No particular reason for his incarceration is cited, and no indication is given as to the duration of his confinement. Days and nights pass, and Dae-su is forced to repeat the same routine every day. Having no one around to talk to, he watches television and masturbates, inhales hypnotic gas that puts him to sleep, eats the fried dumplings (*gunmandu*) fed to him, undergoes rigorous self-training of his body, and digs an escape route through the wall with the tip of a hidden spoon. In other words, he eats, sleeps, masturbates, and labors as if his life inside a prison is a microcosm of a life outside. Before he can escape, however, he is released. Fifteen years have passed since the night of his kidnapping and confinement. Not only is his imprisonment unexplained to him or to us, neither is his release. When he wakes up after a session of hypnosis conducted in his cell, he finds himself on the rooftop of an apartment building.

Fifteen years of solitary isolation have transformed Dae-su, who first appeared as an unruly charlatan at the police station. No longer an ordinary man, he now speaks in a succinct monotone that accords him a god-like transcendental status. Throughout the film, several characters ask, "Why do you speak that way?" His sentences are almost always in present tense, and they lack any modifying clauses — future, conditional, or past. The erasure of the past and future tenses marks Dae-su as a man who is devoid of history, thus achieving for him a status of a-temporality. This mystifies his presence even more as a man who possesses neither temporality nor basic human emotions. The lack of emotions makes Dae-su seem larger-than-life. Furthermore, years of martial arts training while imprisoned has allowed him to achieve a seemingly superhuman agility and strength that he puts to use as a ruthless warrior in search of vengeance. While in captivity, Dae-su had helplessly watched as news reports framed him as the prime suspect in the murder of his wife. Upon his release, he finds out that his orphaned daughter Bora had left for Sweden. With no family to rely on, and no authority figure to appeal to, Dae-su finds himself utterly alone.

The only person he can rely on is his new friend, Mi-do (Kang Hye-jeong). The first place Dae-su visits after he was released from his private cell is a sushi restaurant called *Jijunghae*. He was served by Mi-do, a young woman who has become a sushi chef despite the discriminatory belief that women's hands are too warm to maintain the proper rawness of cold sushi. The two quickly trade lines that mutually invoke a feeling of uncanniness — that is, in Freud's definition, the feeling of "something familiar (homely) that has been repressed and then reappears."[10] Dae-su, who has been given a wallet filled with a sheaf of 100,000 Won bills (US$ 100), quickly orders and consumes an entire octopus, served by Mi-do to him raw and cut. Dae-su loses consciousness when Mi-do reaches out to grab his hand and tell him: "I think I am quite unusual. My hands are very cold." As is later revealed, Mi-do is actually Dae-su's grown-up daughter Bo-ra, who had supposedly been given up for adoption to a Swedish family.

Dae-su overcomes his initial suspicions of Mi-do, who takes him home, and the two of them work as a team to investigate the man behind the arrangement to keep Dae-su in captivity for fifteen years. Feelings grow between the two. Mi-do promises Dae-su that she will serenade him with the 1990 hit "Bogosipeun eolgul" ("Face I Want to See Again") when she is sexually ready for him. This promise — one that is predicated on a future action — ironically restores for Dae-su temporality and historicity — something that he has been denied ever since his release from the cell. Mi-do and Dae-su move closer to the immanent copulation (future action), which ironically enables Dae-su to move closer to the truth behind the reason of his incarceration that knots him to a piece of memory from his high school (past). When Dae-su rescues Mi-do from the thugs threatening to kill her soon thereafter, she sings him her siren song, sending Dae-su into dangerous waters. Unbeknownst to the two of them, they have entered into an incestuous relationship. And only when their incestuous relationship materializes, will Dae-su be given the reason behind his imprisonment.

The only clues with which Dae-su has to work in tracing the origins of the crime unleashed against him are the taste of *gunmandu* (Chinese dumplings) he was fed during the entire period he was locked up and a small piece of chopstick wrapping paper that was accidentally found in one of the dumplings. The paper is printed with the characters for "cheongryong" (blue dragon) — two characters of the restaurant's name. After combing through Seoul, where literally hundreds of Chinese restaurants contain both characters in their names, Dae-su finally locates Jacheongryong (Purple Blue Dragon), the restaurant that matches the taste of the dumplings which he has eaten every day for the last fifteen years.

This in turn leads him to the "business group" that specializes in illegal abductions and detentions. Only a few days elapse before Dae-su is confronted with the film's villain, his high school classmate Woo-jin (Yoo Ji-tae). Both Dae-su and Woo-jin had attended the Evergreen (Sangnok) High School, a Catholic school located in the provinces of Korea. Even after identifying the man responsible for his long imprisonment, Dae-su still fails to understand what could have motivated Woo-jin to commit such heinous crimes against him. After further investigation, Dae-su remembers an event from the past that had completely evaded him during his fifteen-year captivity. This is shown in a flashback in which he remembers a younger version of himself. The young Dae-su is wearing a high school uniform, and is watching a girl riding a bike. It is his last day at Evergreen High School before he transfers to another school in Seoul. Soo-ah (Yun Jin-seo), the pretty female student whom he has been watching, entices young Dae-su's interest even more when they meet briefly on a bench. For no apparent reason other than curiosity, he follows Soo-ah and discovers a dark secret about her: Soo-ah is sexually intimate with her own brother.

"It wasn't my dick that impregnated my sister. It was your tongue," Woo-jin explains when the two finally meet. One of the most intriguing points of *Oldboy* is that linguistic communication almost always falls outside the sphere of rational dialogue. Verbal miscues, infelicitous remarks, and gaps between signifiers and signifieds produce not only miscomprehensions between two individuals, but also help create a world that is "beyond knowable." Was she pregnant or not? Once rumors began spreading that Soo-ah fooled around with her brother and had become pregnant with his child, she committed suicide. After his sister's death, Woo-jin also suffered from heart disease and was forced to replace his heart with an artificial one. What first started as innocuous chatter in high school between Dae-su and his friend about Soo-ah's illicit affair, later resulted in Soo-ah's death and Woo-jin's cardiac arrest. This consequently led Woo-jin to seek revenge against Dae-su, who could not remember any specific wrongdoing that would have earned him fifteen years of incarceration.

A final showdown between the hero, unfairly imprisoned for fifteen years, and his former captor would, in a commercial film, normally favor the victim. But it is Woo-jin who ironically has the last laugh during this confrontation. Once his revenge is complete, Woo-jin descends from his penthouse in an elevator, where he puts a gun to his head and pulls the trigger. Woo-jin's death is a dramatic one, but it could be argued that his heart had already died many years earlier. The only thing that had kept him alive was his desire to seek revenge for his sister. Woo-jin had wanted Dae-su to sleep with his own daughter, as Woo-jin had once slept with his own sister. That mission was accomplished once Dae-su, prostrating himself to protect Mi-do from the knowledge that he is both her lover and her father, voluntarily cuts off his own tongue. Once this happens, Woo-jin has no intention of seeking a further extension of his life. Woo-jin, who resuscitated his life through technological means (an artificial heart), claims his subjectivity through the completion of his revenge, not by foregoing it.

Revenge

As explicated in my book, *The Remasculinization of Korean Cinema*, memory is a crucial site where contestations between individuals and the state take place.[11] The question of whether or not one is capable of remembering the site of one's trauma is directly linked to the question of whether one can achieve a salient form of subjectivity, usually a male one. Many films made during the ten-year period that stretched from the heyday of the *Minjung* Movement in the late 1980s to the inauguration of President Kim Dae-jung in 1998 centered around the demand that official historiography, especially surrounding the Korean War and postwar human rights violations, be revised. The personal remembrances found in many films from this period, such as *Silver Stallion* (*Eunma-neun oji anneunda*, Chang Kil-su, 1991), *A Petal* (*Kkonnip*, Jang Sun-woo, 1995), *A Single Spark* (*Areum daun cheongnyeon Jeon Tae-il*, Park Kwang-su, 1996) and *Spring in My Hometown* (*Areum daun sijeol*, Lee Kwang-mo, 1998), are crucial to this overarching preoccupation with representing alternative histories that work against hegemonic, distorted representations of the state. Given that public history is at stake, these remembrances accompany an objective that reaches far beyond the realm of the individual. For instance, in *A Petal*, the traumatized girl who lost her mother during the 1980 Gwangju massacre must remember what has happened and articulate what she saw on the fateful day when her mother was among those killed by the soldiers. The girl's personal remembrances cannot be disassociated from the public need for a witness who can narrate the truth about Gwangju and contest the official, state-authorized historiography, one which denies any civilian casualties.

The girl from Gwangju is briefly able to remember the day in her hometown where the soldiers ruthlessly opened fire on demonstrators gathered to protest the never-ending military rule, but she quickly relapses into mental disorder. The viewers of *A Petal* in 1995 are offered the truth about Gwangju, but in *Oldboy*, like Park Chan-wook's other vengeance films, remembrance remains in the domain of the personal and never ventures out further. Dae-su's remembrance of himself witnessing the incestuous relationship between Woo-jin and his sister has absolutely no implications beyond a personal matter — its only purpose is to identify the essence of the resentment, the root cause of the revenge that has demanded such a high price of him.

Since the last three films of Park Chan-wook's identify vengeance as the reactive action of resentment, Nietzsche's concept of *ressentiment* (resentment) may serve as a useful reminder of how to better read these works. In *On the Genealogy of Morals*, as well as in other works, Nietzsche uses the concept of resentment to further elucidate the relationship between master and slave, and also between good and evil. The dreadful power of resentment, Gilles Deleuze wrote as he summarized Nietzsche, is that it is "not content to denounce crimes and criminals, it wants sinners, people who are responsible."[12] Deleuze, following Nietzsche, further continues to explain that society ends up acquiring the sense of the evil and good as opposites of each other from the idea of *ressentiment*: "you are evil; I am the opposite of what you are; therefore I am good." This derivation of morality ("slave morality" according to Nietzsche) justifies the spirit of revenge, which is conditioned by a hostile world. In this sense, even destructive energy can potentially become creative, good energy.

All of the main characters in Park Chan-wook's films rely on this Nietzschean (or Old Testament) idea. They continuously assert that vengeance is neither evil nor unethical. Woo-jin tells Dae-su, "Revenge is good for one's health." The invocation of "health" in this statement implies not only physical health, but mental health as well. Woo-jin's acquisition of incredible amounts of wealth, though unexplained in the film, is tacitly understood as the fruit of the drive for revenge he conceived while in high school. Analogously, Geum-ja (Lee Young-ae) in *Lady Vengeance* and Park Dong-jin (Song Kang-ho), the factory owner, in *Sympathy for Mr. Vengeance,* both seek revenge because they are good, not because they are bad. Is revenge according to Park Chan-wook an ethical decision that ironically renders a judiciously responsible subject, not a savage one? Must one seek revenge, rather than forgoing it, to reclaim subjectivity? Are these questions even relevant in Park Chan-wook's entertainment films?

Nietzsche and Deleuze seem to agree that revenge is not antithetical to salvation. Deleuze echoes Nietzsche's idea that no religious value, including Christianity, can be separated from hatred and revenge. He writes, "What would Christian love be without the Judaic power of *ressentiment* which inspires and directs it? Christian love is not the opposite of Judaic *ressentiment* but its consequence, its conclusion and its crowning glory."[13] In the closing sequence of *Sympathy for Mr. Vengeance,* Park Dong-jin shudders and sheds his tears before brandishing his knife in front of his daughter's killer Ryu (Shin Ha-kyun). Park states, "I know you are a good man. So, you understand that I have to kill you, right?" Herein lies the paradox of Park Chan-wook's vengeance trilogy — revenge comes not from hatred, but from love and pity. Park's tears are genuine, and he seems to believe that Ryu had no choice but to abduct his daughter in order to pay for his sister's medical bill before inadvertently killing her. Like the acts of terror (kidnap and demanding of ransom) that in Park's films are sometimes seen to be good and at other times bad, revenge in his films is not always bad, and in fact almost always good, if it is executed with good intentions. Revenge, as such, is both harmful and beneficial, and consequently, in *Oldboy,* the sharp distinction between good and evil crumbles. Derrida once similarly deconstructed Plato's *pharmakon* by showing how this term possesses not a singular but a double meaning of "remedy" and "poison."[14] Park Dong-jin chooses to remain faithful to his feelings of resentment, which thus leads him to react violently against Ryu.

Yet, even though Park Chan-wook's violence is not an act that is categorically severed from salvation and love, one must ask whether a film such as *Sympathy for Mr. Vengeance* is truly Nietzschean. The open acknowledgement that the enemy is good cancels out the possibility of Nietzschean *ressentiment,* since resentment vanishes once the other is re-evaluated to be anything but evil. The question of "what is he seeking justice for" becomes a complicated one. Is Park Chan-wook suggesting that the famous New Testament credo, "love thy enemy," can be just as good when it is reversed into "kill thy brother," a story also found in the Bible (the Old Testament)? What is the point of this if Park does not believe in God? Then, is "kill thy brother" just a playful, if perverse, speech-act and nothing more? Even if an act of violence committed against the "virtuous" accommodates a postmodern sentiment that negates any cogent correlation between the signifier (the subject's violent act) and the signified (the accomplishment of justice against evil), the conclusion Park comes to does not make Nietzschean theory any more relevant. What is the point of giving Park a line telling Ryu that he is good, only if he is to be executed seconds later? The moment a person finds the other to be good, the excitation that arises out of resentment and hostility should cease to take hold of the subject. Once the subject abandons resentment or revenge, he or she, according to Nietzsche, is capable of achieving a sovereign identity based on a superior sense of morality rather than a slave one. Is Park Dong-jin himself then killed for failing to adopt an alternative perspective that is endowed with superman-like power to recognize values beyond good and evil? Are deaths of Ryu and Park, who both fall into the pitfall of mediocrity by trying to be good and avenge the loss of the victims, simply affirmations of Park Chan-wook's cynicism, which deliberately stands to contradict Nietzsche's firm belief that each human being is capable of becoming an "over-man" or a superman? Humans, in other words, rather prefer being pitiful beings by voluntarily choosing not to abandon *ressentiment* — an inferior mentality often associated with slaves.

Body

In the Western philosophical tradition, the body is often figured in opposition to speech and language. Ineffable, impenetrable, and unintelligible, it is the perfect articulation of the *unknowable* discourse. A healthy, virus-free, whole body rarely exists in Park Chan-wook's films, and often the failed heart, the infected liver needing a transplant, or severed body parts constitute the intrusions through which the alliance between the logic of capitalism and the postmodern commercial genre mechanism of thriller becomes naturalized. Bodily pain or dismemberment is such an important characteristic of Park Chan-wook's trilogy that through this recurring motif, his films achieve what I think are an aesthetics, ethics, and politics of the body. In his films, body parts are often dismembered, and human organs such as kidneys or hearts become detached from the human body. They are either sold for profit or replaced with healthier, or artificial substitutes. They are acquired, bartered, relinquished, and redistributed — sometimes legally, but more often outside the law. The body falls far short of sacred in a postmodern capitalist society, where the body's function is configured quite differently than in pre-capitalist ones. A healthy body is a mandatory prerequisite to feeling pleasure and sensations. In nomadic societies, the body was regarded as belonging to the earth; in imperial societies, it belonged to the despot; in the capitalist societies which Park Chan-wook depicts, it belongs to capital. Debunking the mantra of the Confucian society, which posits the familial collective and consequently the nation as being organically linked to individual bodies, the bodies in Park Chan-wook's films are regarded as commodifiable, their organs usually quantifiable in terms of monetary value that can be bought and sold.

Oldboy furthers *Sympathy for Mr. Vengeance*'s thematization of living flesh and organs that metaphorize and make explicit the extreme conditions of late capitalism by attaching price tags to body parts. Park Cheol-ung (Oh Dal-su), the president of the underground business that specializes in private incarcerations, is a minor yet important character in the film. When Dae-su identifies the correct Chinese restaurant and locates Cheol-ung, he tortures him by tying him up and starting to take his teeth out with the aid of a hammer. By the time six teeth are removed from his mouth, Cheol-ung surrenders and provides Dae-su with the leads he wants. The next time Dae-su and Cheol-ung meet, the power dynamics between the two has been reversed. Dae-su has fallen into a trap set by Cheol-ung and is on the verge of having the same number of teeth — six — extracted with a claw hammer. Before Cheol-ung is able to exact his revenge, however, he receives a phone call from Woo-jin asking him to stop in exchange for a briefcase filled with cash. Cheol-ung reluctantly agrees on this exchange and gives up his spirit of revenge for this undisclosed amount of cash. Since the "spirit of revenge" has initially demanded the removal of six teeth, Park Chan-wook sets a price (a briefcase filled with cash) for approximately one-sixth of the entire gallery of teeth.

Cheol-ung accepts this money, and it turns out that he also trades in his right arm in exchange for a building from Woo-jin. Although only a minor character, Cheol-ung's agreements to trade parts of his body for monetary compensation are not insignificant. In recent Korean history, where sacrificial acts such as workers self-immolating themselves or cutting off their own fingers to protest human rights violations or to express nationalist ideologies have become ubiquitous, Cheol-ung's willingness to sacrifice parts of his body for monetary gain deliberately scoffs at and renders profane the sacred and political condition of corporeality. The body of an individual is almost a site of transgression that moves from "serv[ing] to protect the entire community," to use René Girard's description of sacrifice, to a crude repository of private assets where each body part and organ can be exchanged for money in order to help realize the goals of capital gain.[15]

Space

In *realism*, the use of provincial accents clearly marks identity and boundaries that in turn provide a sense of "knowability" and "familiarity." *Modernism* tries to take away that sense of familiarity. For instance, Kafka's novels erase specific national or regional markers, and thus seem deliberately elliptical, anonymous, and atmospheric. The spaces in these non-realist novels become uncanny, unbound by the specificity and particularity of each and every setting.[16] In *postmodern* novels like those of Haruki Murakami or arguably films like *Oldboy* also achieve a similar sense of the unknowable or the uncanny, but these works register a different kind of impact than Kafka's. The fried dumpling and the chopstick wrapper inscribed with the restaurant name "blue dragon" invoke a sense of easy familiarity for many Koreans. However, precisely because of this ubiquity that is trans-Asian (and perhaps even as global as McDonald's or Starbucks), they slip into the anonymity of unfamiliar territory. As such, the search for a restaurant that both matches the exact taste of the dumpling and has a name that includes the characters for "blue dragon" is a complicated one. There is nothing more disconcerting than the effort to find a particular restaurant that matches a ubiquitous and anonymous taste like a Big Mac or a *gunmandu*. Compounded by the sense of global anonymity, the postmodern space constituted in *Oldboy* remains outside a specific locale or time. All of the spatial configurations depicted in this film such as Cheol-ung's private cell enterprise, Dae-su's high school, the cyber chatroom shared by Mi-do and Woo-jin, Mi-do's sushi restaurant, and Woo-jin's penthouse suite located on the top of a high-rise building are framed within post-national, a-historical or *virtual* realms.

Earl Jackson Jr. writes that "[t]he way Oh[O Dae-su] tastes each gyoza, comparing that taste with his specialized knowledge of the gyoza he has eaten for fifteen years, seems a darker parody of the Japanese trope of gourmet nostalgia, exemplified most vividly in popular culture in the film *Tampopo*, on the quest for the perfect ramen."[17] With both globalization and modernization in full swing, Seoul has actively participated in the global, border-crossing culture. Chinese food, particularly *Jajangmyeon* (black bean paste noodles)[18] became the first and only ethnic cuisine to which the general Korean populace had access during the 1960s and the 1970s, but its exoticness was quickly erased, and it became a part of Korean food culture.[19] The use of *gunmandu* (gyoza) in *Oldboy* as the primary evidence that leads Dae-su to his captor is significant not only, as Jackson suggests, because it transforms taste from a high-brow pursuit in the vein of *Tampopo* into a survival skill, but also because it erases the kind of regional identity that is often clearly marked by taste.

"Tell the kitchen that there's too much *buchu* in the dumpling," Dae-su tells the delivery boy from the restaurant that bears the name Purple Blue Dragon and produces dumplings with taste that he had grown accustomed to during his fifteen years in captivity. Excessive use of *buchu*, or thin spring onions, has made it possible for Dae-su to track down the organization which Woo-jin has outsourced to lock him up. But what is the significance of this statement? First, Dae-su's request contains both a complaint and a kind of compliment. He had grown sick of the onion-like vegetable over fifteen years, but if it had not been for the excessive use of *buchu* in the dumpling, Dae-su would never have been able to find the "company" that had held him captive. Even though *gunmandu* has achieved a kind of taste anonymity in Korean food culture, the excessive use of *buchu* in the Purple Blue Dragon's dumplings made them sufficiently unique for Dae-su. Second, the *buchu* statement could be read as cynically reducing one of the most important modern periods of Korean history into a vacuous, insignificant one. Locked up alone in the private jail, this is the only significant memory Dae-su has from the critical years between 1988 and 2003, during which time South Korea became one of the most successful economic and technologically advanced democratic countries in the world. Dae-su does not remember the deaths of numerous demonstrators during rallies held throughout this period of democratization, or the workers fired during the so-called IMF-bailout crisis. What matters most to him is the unforgettable taste of excessive *buchu* that he has had to remember to put his trauma behind him.

The *gunmandu* is one of many references used in the film that also makes space both familiar and unfamiliar. The sushi restaurant where Mi-do works while wearing a kimono, for instance, is called *Jijunghae*, which means the Mediterranean Sea. The high school Dae-su and Woo-jin attended, Evergreen High School, lacks any mention of regional ties in its name, though most high schools, like the one here, are named after their towns or districts. Since all of the high school friends whom Dae-su visits to find out about Woo-jin speak in thick regional accents, the viewer can guess that Evergreen High School is located in the provinces. But where exactly is it located? Do the regional accents offer us any other clues beyond this? *Oldboy* makes the regional accent recognizable, but simultaneously pushes its corresponding spatial identity past the familiar, rendering it anonymous. In so doing, the relationships of the characters in the text to spatial coordinates become largely discombobulated. Our sense of "what is what" has become so disengaged that even when "culinary taste" or "provincial accent" is invoked, it only adds to the mystification. *Oldboy*'s effective underscoring of the sense of "unknowable" makes globalization almost synonymous with anonymity. The abandonment of the "knowable" suggests the end of epistemology, achieving instead a postmodern condition marred by schizophrenia.

Language

There are two modes that Park Chan-wook's vengeance films typically use to disrupt narrative linearity: first, the use of balletic action sequences that become attractions in and of themselves; and, second, the use of performative language. In *Sympathy for Mr. Vengeance*, much of the dialogue that takes place throughout the film is in sign language because the film's protagonist, Ryu, is mute. Park Chan-wook's creative use of subtitles and intertitles, which feature characters other than Ryu speaking verbally while using sign language to Ryu, help the audience to understand the narrative. However, such performative use of bodily gestures and linguistic images complicate the communicative channels of language. The vocal punctuations of sound, the variety of titles, and seeing the movement of bodies and the expressions on faces force us to consider how *Oldboy* may have been influenced by modernist filmmakers like Jean-Luc Godard, who explored the possibility of pure visuality and sound in cinema. In the third and final film of the trilogy, *Lady Vengeance*, the villain is an English teacher who sometimes communicates in English, and the heroine's daughter is an adoptee in Australia who speaks only English. When English is spoken in the film, Park slows down his enunciation so that Korean subtitles can appear word-by-word, choreographed in the exact rhythm and order as the words being spoken so that the audience can witness the process of translation laid bare.

In *Oldboy*, Dae-su makes a dramatic transformation after being locked up for fifteen years. As mentioned earlier, one significant change is signaled through his voice. Not only does he speak in a terse monotone, he also speaks through voiceovers.[20] What makes the voice so unusual is that it detaches itself from the social and the personal, becoming transcendental. If Woo-jin's artificial heart metonymically underscores his heartlessness and ruthlessness, Dae-su matches Woo-jin's inhumanity through the transformation of his voice. Even before Dae-su loses the battle with Woo-jin, and as a consequence, loses his tongue, it is possible to perceive him as a quasi-mute. Michael Chion elaborates that, according to Jacques Lacan, voice — along with the gaze, the penis, the feces, and nothingness — is ranked as *object petit a*, a part object "which may be fetishized and employed to 'thingify difference'."[21] Sexual differences, prohibition, and the law can all be established through the voice. However, Dae-su's *transcendental* voice (sometimes spoken only through voiceover narration) rises beyond the law and everything that is of the social. I argue here that it is through this extraordinary voice, artificially permed hair, and super-athletic body of Dae-su which the audience engages the sensationalized tension between human and non-human. If the origin of modern literature was embedded in the new discovery of landscape and nature, not only have they become irrelevant in *Oldboy*, they have also been ostensibly replaced by this supernatural indestructible being that is positioned between god and human. This anchors a strong sense of the "unutterable" or the "unspeakable," underscoring the film's invocation of the taboo that remains at its heart. Since Dae-su has achieved a non-human voice, it is assumed that a mundane code of ethics, with all of its prohibitions, do not apply to him — that is, until the very end of the film when it is revealed that he has slept with his daughter. It is at this moment that his voice departs from the transcendental and becomes human again — the precise moment that he also decides to cut off his tongue.

In addition, the medium of television emerges a penultimate postmodern instrument through which the relation between subject and space is concretized as dysfunctional. As Dae-su is forbidden from communicating with anyone during his imprisonment, his only access to information is through a television set placed in his cell. Before he is released, Dae-su narrates to the audience that television is capable of being everything from "a clock, a calendar, a school, a home, a church, a friend to a lover." When he states that television is like "a friend," the image on the television in his cell features classic 1931 footage of *Frankenstein*. The corresponding visual image chosen for the linguistic signifier of the "lover" is an image of Min Hae-gyeong, a popular singer from the late 1980s and the early 1990s, singing "Bogosipeun eolgul" ("Face I Want to See Again"). But can an image on television be classified as a real "lover"? Is Min Hae-gyeong, who dances only on the television monitor — untouchable, unable to interact, and therefore unaffective — capable of becoming Dae-su's lover? Being equipped to address every desire and fantasy, but without being able to deliver on any of them, is like simultaneously possessing a perfect dream and one's worst nightmare. This contrasts with more traditional "realist" takes on alienation such as *The Road Taken* (*Seontaek*, Hong Ki-seon, 2003), a Korean film that was released the same year as *Oldboy*. They are both dramas about men unfairly put away in jail. An irreconcilable gap, however, remains between Kim Seon-myeong, the protagonist of *The Road Taken*, and Oh Dae-su: the former is a prisoner convicted by the state for believing in an ideology (Marxism) deemed subversive to the state; the latter is a prisoner put away by a private man for having been a "loud mouth." Despite having been locked away for over thirty-five years, a world record for the longest serving prisoner-of-consciousness, Kim has comrades around him who are equally misfortunate. They have no television or any other electronic devices to keep them entertained, they celebrate birthdays, play games, and plan political actions together. In contrast, Dae-su spends all of his time with his only surrogate friend: the television — not unlike the average person in a postmodern condition who spends far more time communicating with machines than with real human beings. Like the *gunmandu*, Min's dance to the samba beat of the Korean song, "Face that I Want to See Again," underscores an anonymously global pop culture that has lost its genuine regional authenticity while perfectly accommodating the cliché of the television medium.

Postmodernism, which is predicated on the pleasurable use of the difference between the signifier and the signified, is also conditioned in *Oldboy* through the use of voiceover and other creative juxtapositions between image and sound. Gilles Deleuze lauds Jean-Luc Godard's achievements, claiming that Godard is "definitely one of the authors who has thought most about visual-sound relationships."[22] Deleuze continues on to say that "[Godard]'s tendency to reinvest the visual with sound, with the ultimate aim of . . . restoring both to the body from which they have been taken, produces a system of disengagements or micro-cuts in all directions: cuts spread and no longer pass between the sound and the visual, but in the visual, in the sound, and in their multiplied connections."[23] Deleuze insists that the visual and the voice are most often taken from human bodies in film, but as soon as they are processed and textually manipulated through the machine — the camera, sound recording devices and other post-production gadgets — they do not remain natural to the body. What Godard aims at accomplishing is what could be considered the cinematic equivalent to cacophonous sound, but achieved through the potentially disjunctive relationship between sound and image. Park Chan-wook aims for something similar: his soundtracks are designed to transgress beyond the boundary of real and instead to expand the chasm between the human and his vocal signification. He re-appropriates and self-references the unnatural relationship between sound and image that Godard once experimented with in his films, and the one between the real and its representation that narrative cinema had seamlessly sutured together over the years in order to produce admittedly coy comical gags and "cool" effects. But the question remains. Has the contradiction between image and sound or between reality and its representation not already manifested itself to be humorous and playful (for example, in the silent days of cinema)? In other words, isn't this unnaturalness natural to the medium of cinema itself?

"Just Look at the Surface"

"If you want to know all about Andy Warhol," Warhol famously told the press, "just look at the surface of my paintings and films and me, and there I am. There's nothing behind it."[24] As suggested earlier, the emergence of Park Chan-wook in recent years is symptomatic of a Korean cinema that has been ushered into a definite kind of post-remembrance and post-political mode. The gap between the mode of representation and the mode of symbolization from which metaphors and allegories can be figured is reduced in Park's film to the point where only the surface can be perceived. So we can also ask: Does anything exist beyond the surface of Park Chan-wook's films? Or does something lurk behind this deliberately flattened space, something to which we must accede? In Korea, where the film industry developed out of both colonial and anti-colonial interests during the first half of the twentieth century and communist and anti-communist interests during the latter half, one could bluntly say that Korea has made nothing but "social problem" films throughout the last century. Is Park Chan-wook then making a political statement by churning out excessively, rigorously, and relentlessly superficial films that defy politics in a country where politics are discussed on every street corner? One of the best memories to be found in contemporary Korean cinema comes from the last scene in *Sympathy for Mr. Vengeance,* in which the factory owner, Park Dong-jin, whose daughter had been kidnapped, is multiply stabbed by a terrorist organization called the Revolutionary Anarchist Alliance. "Who the hell are you guys?" asks Park Dong-jin of his assailants. Instead of verbally answering, the anarchists peg a prepared note on Park's chest with a knife. If this were a film by Godard, such an abrupt and incoherent insertion of violence would have been welcomed as an allegory of class conflict. However, *Sympathy for Mr. Vengeance*, like Park Chan-wook's other films and unlike Godard's films, is a tightly structured, entertainment film in which every scene is knotted to clear reasoning and causality. Did Park Chan-wook think that he could afford one Godard-ian moment at the end? There are a number of superfluous possible answers to Park Dong-jin's final question. There's the public one (class hostility), the private one (revenge against Ryu's girlfriend who was also an anarchist), none-of-the-above, or all-of-the-above. The final scene refuses to give us an answer. As such, Park is able to maintain the premise that representation (which assigns certain mimetic symbols to reality) is untenable — and therefore, that any kind of agency to be excavated from it is inconceivable. While gasping for his last breath, Park tries desperately to read the note pinned to him. Without the strength to move his body, he can only tilt his head, but the note remains beyond his range of sight. Credits soon roll and no one is spared from the frustration.

11

A Politics of Excess: Violence and Violation in Miike Takashi's *Audition*

Robert Hyland

In recent critical scholarship of Asian cinema and in Asian cinema fandom, much attention has been devoted to the phenomenon colloquially known as Asia Extreme cinema. While most can identify a film which is considered to qualify as "Asia Extreme," little has been done to create a system of genre classification. The general categorization is that if a film originates from Asia and looks extreme, then it must be exemplary of Asia Extreme. Yet, as Carolus Linnaeus argued in the eighteenth century, in order for something to be accurately studied, it must first be classified.

The project of organizing films into the category of Asia Extreme was begun by the British film distribution company, Tartan. The company was established in 1982 and began to release films under its "Asia Extreme" title in 2001. Many titles carrying that label found popularity. These include such films as Nakata Hideo's *Ringu* (1998), Miike Takashi's *Audition* (2000), and Fukusaku Kinji's *Battle Royale* (2000). Tartan heralds the directors Miike, Kim Ki Duk and Park Chan-wook as Asia Extreme's representative directors, and significantly expands its categorization beyond Japan and Korea to include Thailand and Hong Kong.

In this chapter, I argue that extreme cinema uses an extreme aesthetic as a political reaction to the closed, vertically integrated studio systems of Japan, Hong Kong and Korea. Rather than simplistically viewing extreme cinema as a series of gory action and horror films, this chapter argues that extreme cinema is a contemporary radical cinema movement engaging in a political discourse that subverts the conventions and expectations of a cinema audience inured to conservative studio fare. The function of this chapter is twofold: to examine the origins of extreme cinema as a politicized cinema, which uses an extreme aesthetic as a single aspect of its radical politics; and to provide in-depth analysis of Miike Takashi's 2001 film *Audition* as exemplary of that critical stance.

The roots of the *Asia Extreme* movement are directly tied to the independent filmmakers' response to the closed Japanese studio system of the late 1980s and early 1990s. The beginnings of Japanese extreme cinema are found in the early work of Tsukamoto Shinya and "Beat" Kitano Takeshi. Tsukamoto's *Tetsuo: The Iron Man* (1988) and Kitano's *Violent Cop* (1989), both relying on shocking imagery and graphic violence, can be aesthetically and ideologically linked in their being produced outside of the closed, vertically integrated Japanese studio system. Tsukamoto states:

> Foreign acclaim was crucial in allowing me to continue directing because it changed how I was regarded . . . At that time it was very rare for a Japanese film to be shown at a foreign festival, let alone that one would win a prize. So getting that prize resulted in getting appreciation in Japan as well.[1]

Crucial to the film's success was critical acclaim outside of the Japanese studio and distribution systems. Similar operations are evident in the domestic response to the work of Kitano and Nakata Hideo. Nakata states:

> Japanese film studios seemed to be afraid of taking risks in film production. This kind of mentality gradually killed the enthusiasm of the people who worked at the studios. Then, independent filmmakers were spotlighted. They knew how to make good films on low budgets and their enthusiasm never faded.[2]

The independent Japanese filmmakers, who were financing films independently of a stale and cloistered studio system, began making films that were aesthetically and politically reactionary to the conservativism inherent in the studio system.

While local distributors were refusing to handle the product, these independent films had secured international distribution rights and earned the directors enough money to finance future products and future international co-production deals. This enabled the filmmakers to create films of their own devising which reflected their personal tastes. The independent films of Japan, then, were highly charged political films, which probed and questioned the domestic film production company values through their iconographies and ideologies.

The independent film sector of Hong Kong (a film industry which will be treated as distinct from that of Mainland China's, despite the fact that Hong Kong is now politically reintegrated into the Mainland) had a similar response to the increasing competition of Hollywood blockbusters. Kevin Heffernan writes:

> In the lean years leading up to the millennium, Hong Kong movie production plummeted, Hollywood blockbusters showing in gleaming new multiplex theatres were beginning to choke off production funds from regional theatre chains.[3]

This loss of financing resulted in independent producers forging unlikely alliances with other nations' film industries in order to accrue a budget that was capable of competing with the Hollywood production. Heffernan continues:

> Many of the most successful efforts of regional film industries to fight this colonization involved the crafting of self-consciously pan-Asian films in popular genres, with stars, production personnel, and financing coming together from all over Asia in one film or in one distributor's annual release slate. This trend had a huge impact on the way movies were written, cast, financed, shot, and marketed.[4]

Indeed, Danny Pang began to shoot his films in Thailand, exploiting a weaker economy and lowered production costs, while relying on known Asian stars to provide box office fodder. Heffernan argues that the increasingly closed studio system resulted in pan-Asian cross-pollination and co-productions.

> The cross pollination of genres between the national cinemas of Asia and the Pacific Rim, which had always been a key component of popular cinema in the region, began to accelerate at breakneck speed.[5]

Hong Kong cinema began to use known pan-Asian stars in order to market its product to a wider target audience. With the introduction of cross-border filmmaking came an increase in the consumption of foreign product. With greater familiarity of pan-Asian stars came a conspicuous rise in attendance of Asian films produced independently of Hong Kong. With the immense success of Nakata's *Ringu* in Hong Kong, grossing $4 million Hong

Kong dollars at the local box office (Derek Elley, cited in Heffernan 316), the Hong Kong pan-Asian cross-pollination began to subsume elements of the Japanese gothic horror iconography. Films such as *The Eye* (*Gin Gwai,* Danny and Oxide Pang, 2001) and *Inner Senses* (*Yee Do Hung Gaan,* Law, Chi-Leung, 2002) draw heavily upon the Nakata film's atmosphere and mood. It appears that the assimilation of the Japanese independent sector's iconographies was concomitant with the consumption of the Japanese independent filmmakers' ideology of graphic confrontationalism, although it had been initially driven by a desire to cash in on the potential profits of such borrowed iconography.

While South Korea does not suffer the same conservatively restrictive vertically integrated studio system, the country has also had a series of aggressively confrontational films being widely produced and disseminated in the late 1990s. Korean cinema has benefitted from a recent resurgence of liberties following a tightly oppressive censorship regime. Michael Robinson argues:

> While a halting transition to constitutional rule since 1988 has tempered the violent ups and downs of South Korean politics, it is still a society in which cultural production free from the stultifying influence of governmental controls or political passions is a relatively new experience.[6]

Although Korea did not have to endure the directives of a fiscally minded production house, the filmmakers in Korea until the late 1980s were unable to produce films critical or controversial in nature because of a highly restrictive government suffering the effects of an ever-escalating cold war. Robinson reports:

> While South Korea was in name a constitutional republic, Rhee's presidency continued the repressive emergency powers that had evolved during the war years; and he added a National Security Law (NSL) that allowed the police wide latitude to arrest people for their political views.[7]

The restrictions on the film industry began to lessen in the late 1980s as Hollywood began to exert more pressure to change the tight film import laws. This resulted in the indigenous production being faced with the threat of becoming entirely subsumed by their multi-million dollar budget Hollywood counterparts. Darcy Paquet argues:

The local film market which, like that of China, had long enacted strong barriers to foreign imports, had just been forced open. Hollywood studios had established branch offices on Korean soil for the first time, and the spectre of unrestricted competition with the Hollywood majors looked likely to drive Korean cinema into a small corner of the overall market.[8]

While the Korean economy of the late 1980s became increasingly competitive in a global marketplace, so did its film production. Faced with strong competition from Hollywood, the Korean film industry went commercial and with that commercialization came corporate investment. Paquet argues that in the early 1990s the *chaebŏl* or large conglomerate corporations began financing Korean film.

> The *chaebŏl*'s decision to enter the film industry was influenced by several factors, particularly the video market. Three of the largest *chaebŏl* — Samsung, Daewoo and LG — not only manufactured VCRs for domestic and international markets, but also operated video divisions to provide content for this lucrative industry.[9]

Pacquet contends that with the collapse of the Korean economy in 1997, the *chaebŏl* withdrew from the film industry. Their impact upon the way films were produced and financed was lasting and even without the *chaebŏl's* influence Korean cinema continued to be manufactured as a populist commercial cinema. While the *chaebŏl* withdrew their investments, independent venture capitalists who were seizing on the commercial success of Korean cinema, began to finance film production. The venture capital, unlike the money from the *chaebŏl,* was spread across a portfolio of projects which allowed the individual directors greater freedom than when working under the *chaebŏl* system that financed individual films and demanded creative control over the projects in order to assure a good return on their investment. With their newfound freedom a group of young, energetic directors emerged who had mostly come from film school backgrounds and were anxious to express themselves in film. These filmmakers were now free to criticize both contemporary and past Korean society and had the economic means to do so in film. Kim Kyu Hyun argues in his article "Horror as Critique in *Tell Me Something* and *Sympathy for Mr. Vengeance*":

> The potential for Korean horror films to challenge and critique the cultural conventions and ideological strictures imposed by "mainstream" Korean society — especially on women, sexual minorities, economically underprivileged youth and other oppressed groups — are just beginning to draw attention.[10]

Indeed, the Korean extreme films are exemplary in their charting the ideological shifts in recent Korean society, as exemplified in such diverse films as *Sympathy for Mr. Vengeance* (*Boksuneun Naui Geot*, Park Chan-wook 2002), *Memories of Murder* (*Salinui Chueok*, Bong Joon-ho, 2003), *Phone* (*Pon*, Ahn Byeong-ki, 2002) or *Oldboy* (Park Chan-wook, 2003), all of which provide a highly critical stance on the massive corporatization and consumption-based ideologies of contemporary Korean society.

Asia Extreme cinema, therefore, derives from a specific temporal geographical locus that stems from an auteur-driven independent film culture which is directly opposed to the formerly restrictive cinema industries of the Pacific Rim. Genre and aesthetic cross-pollination was a response to closed studio systems, which, coupled with international film festivals bringing financing to the independently produced films enabled the directors to capitalize on their political and aesthetic agendas. This resulted in a series of overtly politicized films which are political through their challenging of mainstream ideologies of aesthetics (violence/sexuality) and also ideologies of economics: not only an aesthetic confrontationalism, but also ideological confrontationalism. Extreme cinema, then, is more than simply extreme in "look" it is also extreme through its overt radical politics.

Miike Takashi, like Nakata, had his beginnings in straight to video cinema which provided him freedom in creativity. Within video cinema he found international success which enabled him to make independent feature films. The film *Audition* (*Odishon*, Miike Takashi, 1999), isn't controversial solely for its graphic aestheticization of female violence, it is also controversial for the polemic usage of that female violence. The film has been argued as a feminist allegory of women's response to patriarchy, although that argument fails to consider the fact that the woman continues to be vilified for her aggressively violent actions. The film, however, while not being a feminist allegory does have a complex and ambivalent relationship to its violent female protagonist's actions.

In his essay "Odition (Audition)" in the anthology *The Cinema of Japan and Korea*, Tom Mes argues that the film has been widely misinterpreted as a feminist statement. Mes suggests that feminists interpret the film as such because the film provides a woman who has been deceived by a man for his sexual pleasure, exacting vengeance. Mes asserts that the film cannot be feminist:

> Asami is not an immaculate, victimised foil. She too has lied to and deceived Aoyama. During her torture, she calls Aoyama a liar and blames him for deceiving her and the women at the audition. She is right, but

self-righteously so. From the moment they met, everything she told Aoyama about herself during their dates was a lie; her feelings for him were true, without doubt, but even they came dressed in lies.[11]

Mes is an excellent critic of Japanese film who has criticized *Audition* in numerous publications both online and in print, and has most recently provided an article for the edited anthology *The Cinema of Japan and Korea*.[12] In his articles, Mes continually analyzes *Audition's* resolution as real rather than allegorical. This is a fundamental misreading of the film which compromises his otherwise excellent analysis of the film's various metaphorical meanings. To read Asami's violence as "real" denies the film's political agenda, and the film at key points defies such a literal reading. Rather than implying that Asami's violence is an attempt to rectify a patriarchal wrongdoing, the film suggests that Asami's "lies" and violence are in fact created by the protagonist Aoyama's imagination in order to assuage his own guilt feelings for deceiving Asami and for letting go of his past love for his long deceased wife.

From this perspective, the ending can be read as positing that Aoyama's physical pain is in fact allegorical of the metaphysical pain of his tormented psychology and his final "paralysis" is caused by his inability to confess the truth of his infidelities to Asami. The film suggests that it is the guilt feelings derived from his own behaviour (as well as patriarchy's abuses) which causes him to project his anxieties upon Asami and consequently construct her as a monstrous other. By doing so, Aoyama assuages the monstrousness inherent in his own deceitful behaviour. The film then can be read as presenting patriarchy as monstrous, but a patriarchy which is unable to face its own monstrosity, and consequently projects that monstrosity upon the innocent woman.

The film can be read as a type of feminist allegory. This is not to say that Miike himself is feminist. Indeed, his films frequently depict graphic mutilations of the female body and are often aggressively misogynistic. Furthermore, regardless of the film's outcome, it continues to visualize (whether as a manifestation of masculine psychological damage or a literalization of the vengeance-driven female psychopath) woman as monstrous.[13] And yet the film is structured around a critique of patriarchal society's attraction/aversion to the monstrous feminine and can be interpreted as a sophisticated analysis of patriarchy's projection upon the female body, the *anima*. Miike's film proposes that the monstrous feminine is in fact entirely a construct of patriarchal society's fears of the female other, compounded and confounded by male anxiety.

The story for *Audition* details a television producer, Aoyama Shigeharu (Ishibashi Ryo), who works for a successful television production company. Feeling in need of a wife, seven years after the death of the mother of his child, Aoyama devises a reality show titled "Tomorrow's Star," in which "tomorrow's star" will be discovered today. In his plan, women will audition for the lead role in a television movie and of all the applicants Aoyama will select one whom he considers an ideal woman. She will then be cast as the first runner-up in the show, leaving her free to date the conniving producer. The show's call for application submissions turns out to be a success and Aoyama selects thirty candidates whom he will audition. While scanning through the applications Aoyama is interrupted by his son. The scene begins with a long shot of Aoyama in his room seated at his desk and looking through the various application profiles. On his desk and prominent within the background is a photograph of his dead wife Ryoko (Matsuda Miyuki). The camera cuts 180° to a low angle reverse shot with the photograph now in the foreground, although with the back of the frame facing the camera. Aoyama, feeling guilty about emotionally deserting his late wife's memory, turns the photo away from himself and directly into the camera's line of vision and so while Aoyama may feel guilty for his actions, he symbolically cannot escape his wife's gaze for it becomes mirrored in the camera's lens.

Aoyama's phone rings and it turns out to be his colleague Yoshikawa (Kunimura Jun). His friend tells Aoyama to be scrupulous in his reading the applications and not to make a judgement based on the accompanying photograph alone. Aoyama hangs up the phone and is immediately interrupted by his son. Once again emphasizing his guilt feelings, Aoyama scrambles to hide from his son what he is doing, where his son informs Aoyama that he too has found a girlfriend. His son leaves and it is at that moment that Aoyama spills his coffee and spies a particular application which he then reads. This is an application from a young woman named Asami (Shiina Eihi), who from this point will capture the imagination of the would-be Lothario. While he reads the application's accompanying cover letter with his wife's image prominent in the foreground, upon the writer's words "Live or die, it's just a thin line between them," the camera cuts to a shot of his late wife sitting up in her deathbed, bathed in blue tones. This is clearly a subjective shot manifesting Aoyama's guilt feelings toward his coming acceptance of his wife's death and his desires to find another love. The camera then cuts to a close-up of the application form, giving weight to Asami's head shot photograph stapled to the application. This is symbolic of Aoyama replacing the image of his wife with that of Asami. Aoyama, then, is first introduced to the mysterious Asami in the context of his guilt feelings toward his ex-wife exemplified by both his subjective memory image of her and his guilty scramble to hide his actions from his son upon his son's unexpected intrusion. Aoyama's guilt will mark his relationship with Asami from the outset.

Aoyama feels minor compunctions about the nature of the audition as a ruse to meet women (he states "I feel like a criminal"). Aoyama's concerns about women are matched by his son who, when asked about his own girlfriend, answers: "She's not exactly what she seems, she's so complex. I'm scared of women." Dauntless, Aoyama phones Asami and they meet for a date. Tom Mes identifies this date as using a subjective shot of Aoyama through Asami's point of view, while not providing a similar subjective shot of Asami from Aoyama's point of view, choosing instead to use a more conventional over-the-shoulder shot. Mes argues that this is a disorientating technique which is used to hint that something is not quite right in the scene (Mes, 182). While it is disquieting, Mes concludes that it is with Asami that we should be worried. This moment is of note because we are, for the first time, asked to identify with someone other than the film's protagonist. Yet in this scene, it is Asami who makes a confession (whether it is an honest confession or not is irrelevant, because for Aoyama and the audience at this point it must be assumed to be the truth) whereas Aoyama, whom the subjective gaze puts under scrutiny, is not confessing that the audition was a ruse in order to meet ladies. It is Aoyama who is objectified by the camera's gaze at this point and it is Aoyama who is continuing a lie while Asami is making a confession. The use of the subjective gaze is not to create identification with Asami but is a filmic strategy to emphasize Aoyama's nervousness at continuing to hide his deceitfulness toward Asami by shooting him in close up and forcing his direct address to the camera. He is literally objectified by the three gazes of cinema — the camera's, Asami's, and the viewer's, and as a result his nervousness is literally placed under scrutiny.

Eventually, the two begin dating in earnest and Aoyama takes Asami on a much more serious second date. The scene begins with Asami walking down the street while her voice is heard on the audio track, stating in a sound bridge, "This may seem brusque, but I was very happy that you called." The camera cuts mid-sentence to a long shot of the two seated at a small café table in a coffee shop cum bar and Asami is finishing the sentence which was started in the previous shot. In a long shot, Aoyama, who is seated frame right, has half a beer in front of him and Asami is seated frame left. Presumably Aoyama had been waiting at the designated meeting point and Asami has just arrived. In a single long take, Aoyama starts the conversation and they exchange pleasantries while a waiter enters the frame to deposit a second beer in front of Asami. At this point the camera begins to cut on the conversation, using a conventional shot reverse shot structure. Aoyama asks Asami about her family, she informs him that her family are doing well, telling him briefly about her father's passion for golf. She ends this portion of dialogue with the statement "my family is very harmonious, an ordinary family." While she talks, the camera is focused on a tight medium shot of her speaking and there are two very subtle, barely perceptible, jump cuts which give the scene a sense of distraction, presumably Aoyama's. The jumps are subtle, but they punctuate Asami's words, thereby questioning the veracity of Asami's prosaic statements of her parents' relatively mundane life. It is at this point that the film begins to undermine its formal realism and begins to move to the realm of allegory. However, this undermining of Asami's statements is then further called into question because when Aoyama begins to speak, and ask Asami where she works, the camera again has a jump cut on *his* statement. The jump cuts do not become a means of probing the truth about the statements made but rather act as a sort of punctuation. The jump cuts emphasize the statements, but do not undermine them; instead they highlight the statements as significant and indeed later when Aoyama is searching for the missing Asami, Aoyama recalls this conversation on two separate occasions.

Aoyama asks Asami if he can visit her workplace and Asami tells him that he can feel free to, but her boss is quite nosy and frequently interferes in her personal life and that it could potentially make her uncomfortable. Aoyama responds that he simply wants to know her better; Asami then states, "I would never lie to you, I swear." The camera then cuts to a close-up of Aoyama looking pained and a reverse shot of Asami, and after that, a long shot of the two seated at the table in which Aoyama begins to make his "confession" about the Tomorrow's Star auditions. Ironically, in this scene Aoyama could conceivably tell Asami the truth about the audition being a system for him to meet women (she has just told him "I would never lie"), but instead he chooses to tell her that the show's sponsors have decided that there are problems with the script and so the show will not be produced. Significantly, this is the first moment in which Aoyama, who has previously preferred to avoid the topic of the television show rather than to misrepresent it, directly lies to Asami. Miike highlights Aoyama's lying to Asami in a very subtle way. The lie begins with a close-up shot of Aoyama, who states "about that movie. . ." This shot is followed by a close-up shot of Asami looking up to him and then a long shot of the two seated at the table. However, the background in the long shot has changed slightly and it is revealed that the two are now seated in an empty room. In a single long take Aoyama tells his entire lie. The image composition is shot from behind a black framed glass wall which effectively bisects the screen image, placing Aoyama in a box and metaphorically separating him from Asami to whom he is lying. The soundtrack, throughout the scene, has been marked by the sound of traffic outside the restaurant. While the soundtrack does not change, the traffic that has previously been visible in the window in the background of the frame now disappears and the window depicts an empty street, contradicting the traffic sounds. The scene continues in an alien space, which disrupts the film's continuity and makes the viewer question what is occurring. As Aoyama's fidelity as a narrator has become undermined, the film's veracity has also been weakened. This highlighting of Aoyama's first lie to Asami is an expressive device that contradicts the film's earlier realism and the film at this point must be seen as allegorical and expressive of Aoyama's thoughts and concerns, rather than as an objective, realist depiction.

Writing of *Fudoh, the New Generation* (*Gokudō Sengokushi: Fudō*, Miike Takashi, 1996), Tom Mes discusses that film's usage of excessive violence and the grotesque. Mes writes:

> The exaggeration in both form and content allows for the creation of a surrealist (in the literal sense of the word) world, which although comparable to the effect achieved in *Shinjuku Triad Society* goes a step further by creating an alternative reality rather than a society that exists side-by-side with our own.[14]

Mes' point is that the film, rather than be read as realist and dismissed as being unbelievable, demands that the viewer read it as allegorical in order to accept the excesses in violence. The form (exaggerated stylization) compliments the narrative (exaggerated violence). The same argument, then, is applicable to *Audition*, in which the realist form compliments the realist subject matter but is only sustainable provided the subject matter maintains its veracity. When Aoyama begins his lie, the film's form must equally change. The film then moves into the realm of allegory.

Aoyama has decided to pursue marriage with Asami and the film cuts to a lone highway with a single car driving on it. It then cuts to a shot from inside a room with the camera focused on the exterior and depicts Asami standing on a balcony. Aoyama, in the room, enters the frame and walks to the doorway. The camera cuts to an objective shot of Aoyama in the doorway looking at Asami and then a point-of-view shot of Asami, who turns and looks directly at the camera (Aoyama). In a few quick shots, Miike has propelled the story several days, informed the viewer that Aoyama wishes to propose to Asami on a weekend getaway, and has placed the viewer into the hotel room where Aoyama will shortly make his proposition.

Asami enters the room, closes the curtains behind her and bathes herself in blue lighting, a color which until this point has been associated with Aoyama's memories of his dead wife Ryoko. He is seated in a chair underneath a lamp which provides him with yellow incandescent lighting that graphically separates the two lovers. She walks over to him and switches off his light, casting him in the same blue tones. She undresses herself and slips into bed, again evoking the images from the prologue of Ryoko in her deathbed. He walks over to the bed and begins to undress, but she stops him, telling him that she wants to show him something. She slowly raises the sheets exposing her legs and informs him that she was burnt as a child. He tells her she is beautiful. She tells him that she wishes him to love her and only her, implicitly asking him to negate the memory of his wife — an image icon that she has come to embody by lying in a bed bathed in blue. Graphically she has replaced Ryoko's image with one of her own. She again asks him to love her and her only. Unable to do so, Aoyama wordlessly gives a slight nod, implying his consent but not actually giving it and climbs on top of her, pressing his lips against hers. She rolls him over and the film again has an abrupt jump cut to Aoyama rolling over in the bed, this time alone. The phone is ringing; a confused and disorientated Aoyama answers the phone. The desk clerk at the other end informs him that his companion has left and asks if he wants to continue his stay at the hotel. At this point, the film's transition from formal realism to expressionism is complete and the film's expressive formal qualities are highly at odds with the earlier realist sequences.

Aoyama, desperate to find Asami, returns to his office. The film cuts to Aoyama's office with the cut occurring in mid-camera movement. In a continuous long take, the camera, tracking down a long corridor in a hand-held shot with dizzying movement, follows Aoyama into his office. The lighting in his office, formerly naturalistic, is now washed with slight tones of blue, a carryover from the prior scene in the hotel room, expressive of his mindset rather than being a realist depiction. Aoyama, in a conversation with his colleague Yoshikawa, explains that Asami has gone missing and asks Yoshikawa for assistance in finding her. The camera, hand held for the duration of the scene and moving continuously, cuts rapidly on the conversation, and thus gives the sequence a frenetic energy that is completely at odds with the realist conventions of the prior scenes.

Aoyama's search for Asami takes him to the ballet school that is mentioned in her resume. There he discovers a mad old man with false legs, playing the piano. Aoyama sees a charcoal brazier with a bundle of rods in the fire, rods which match the burn marks on Asami's legs. The camera then cuts to a subjective shot of Aoyama's imagination in which the child Asami is being burnt by the ballet instructor. He then remembers the restaurant that Asami had told him she worked and discovers that the restaurant is closed. He is informed by a passer-by that the owner of the restaurant had been killed in a brutal murder. When the pieces of the body were put together, the police discovered there were three fingers, a tongue and an ear too many. The film then cuts to another subjective shot of Aoyama's imagination in which he sees the severed body pieces in a pool of blood. Presumably Asami had murdered her former employer.

The film then cuts to a single long take in which the camera, representing what must be Asami's subjective point of view, enters Aoyama's house, attacks his dog and then picks up a bottle of whisky. The camera then returns to the doorway of the house and the lighting changes, signifying the passage of time. Aoyama enters his home, walks into his room and picks up the drugged bottle of whiskey. He pours himself a glass and sits down. The drug begins to take effect and Aoyama rises to his feet. Struggling to right himself, he begins to fall. The camera cuts on Aoyama's fall and the film returns Aoyama to his second date in the café bar with Asami. The lighting has changed to a green tone, and significantly Asami's story about her family has also changed. In this reliving of Asami's telling her family past, she informs Aoyama that she was severely abused as a child, first by her aunt with whom she had been sent to live, and secondly by her stepfather when she was returned to her parents. The scene then cuts to the second restaurant, where their conversation continues. Aoyama expresses his admiration for Asami's ability to transcend her childhood abuse. He tells her that she is his perfect partner, at which point he is interrupted by his dead wife Ryoko, who is seated at the next table. Aoyama is called over by Ryoko who uses the familiar term *anata,* a term that is reserved for wives to call their husbands. This reinforces the idea that he belongs primarily to her rather than to Asami who uses the more formal and distancing third person to address Aoyama. Seated at Ryoko's table is Aoyama's son although as a young child. There is also seated a high school girl. At this point it becomes clear that Aoyama is not remembering his dates with Asami, but rather he is having a drug-induced dream about Asami in an attempt to rationalize from where her violence derives. In his dream, Aoyama walks over to his wife Ryoko in order to introduce Asami. Ryoko then insists that Aoyama not marry Asami. It is significant that Ryoko enters into Aoyama's subconscious imaginings because not only does he fear his replacing his dead wife's memory, his anxiety is also galvanized by the thought of replacing Ryoko with such an unsuitable match as he fears Asami to be.

The dream then cuts to Asami's apartment, where she tells Aoyama that she will do anything for him. She runs to him and begins to undo his trousers, at which point the camera cuts and Asami has been replaced by Aoyama's secretary. She asks him why he only slept with her the one time, and asks if there is something wrong with her. To this question, Aoyama apologizes profusely. The camera then cuts and it is once again Asami; the camera cuts again and now he is being fellated by his son's high school girlfriend who states, "I love to do that." Appalled, Aoyama pushes her away. Clearly, Aoyama projects upon Asami all of the guilt feelings he has for all of his indiscretions with women — his affair with his secretary, his sexual desires for his son's girlfriend, his infidelity to his wife's memory, and his lying to Asami about the auditions. Fleeing the high school girl, Aoyama trips over a mysterious bag that has been seen in Asami's room in prior shots. From inside the bag crawls a man who has had three of his fingers removed, his ear cut off, his tongue cut out and both feet removed. This is presumably the missing talent agent that Asami has earlier lied about, and it is obviously his appendages that have been found at the restaurant crime scene where Asami's boss was murdered.

The dream sequence then cuts to a montage of images; Asami as a young dancer being abused by her instructor, the adult Asami killing her ballet instructor by beheading him with a wire from his piano, Aoyama's partner Yoshikawa suggesting the auditions, his wife Ryoko on her deathbed, a severed finger dropping into formaldehyde, and the head of the ballet instructor falling onto the keyboard. The film then cuts back to the hallucinating Aoyama in his office completing his fall with the drug taking effect. A brief cut back to the severed head falling reinforces the notion that this is indeed Aoyama's dream before cutting back to the drugged Aoyama crashing to the ground. The dream summarizes all of Aoyama's guilt feelings, for betraying his wife's memory, for holding the audition, and for not being truthful to Asami. However, the dream also reinforces Asami's monstrosity by providing imagery (although through Aoyama's imagination) and psychological rationalization for all of the murderous actions that Asami has presumably materialized.

After Aoyama has hit the ground, the film at this point reverts to a realist formal style. This treatment contrasts starkly with the overwhelming use of expressive lighting, color, music and grotesque violent imagery of the dream sequence. The film once again returns to naturalistic incandescent lighting, clear focus, long shots and long takes, and only uses close-up intercuts to reinforce certain images, that forcibly imply Asami's subsequent "real" actions as opposed to the expressionistic depiction of violence in the dream sequence.

Asami enters the room and injects a second paralysing drug into Aoyama's tongue. The film then resorts to a veritable orgy of violence as Asami takes revenge on Aoyama for having lied to her about the auditions and being insincere to her.

Aoyama's son Shigehiko interrupts Asami's violence by unexpectedly coming home and Asami grabs a spray can of mace and attacks the teenager. She begins to make chase but the film at this crisis moment abruptly cuts, and once again returns Aoyama to the hotel room where he had taken Asami in order to propose. On the cut, the film returns Aoyama to the subdued, expressive blue lighting that has come to graphically signify Aoyama's psychological subjectivity through its evocation of his dead wife Ryoko. On the cut Aoyama wakes, panics and checks to discover that he is unharmed.

The film posits that Asami's violence is a dream and the real Asami, sleeping peacefully beside him, also wakes and asks him if everything is okay. He nods to her that he is okay; presumably he has just been having a bad dream. She then tells him that she accepts his proposal for marriage and returns to sleep. The significance of this dream narrative is that Asami's violence is not only a projection on Aoyama's part, but the film's formal system is also returned to a natural order. The film with the insertion of the dream narrative asserts that all of the formal irregularities and expressive tendencies are indicative of Aoyama's sub-consciousness and indeed it is revealed that all of the sequences that involve formal irregularities are expressive of Aoyama's subjectivity. As the horrific narrative content is revealed to be "just a dream" so too are the formal irregularities "just a dream." Paradoxically, throughout this normative sequence, the film is shot in the blue lighting that is expressive of Aoyama's guilt feelings.

Aoyama then gets up, washes his face and returns to the bed he is sharing with the peacefully sleeping Asami. He lies down and the camera focuses on Aoyama's face as he blinks and then closes his eyes. Upon this action, the film then cuts back to Aoyama lying paralyzed in his house with Asami chasing his son. The film returns to the natural incandescent lighting and deep space which through its association with the use of realist formal strategies suggests that unlike the prior dream sequences, the violence is indeed real. Many critics, including Tom Mes, do interpret the violence as literal. But it is important to remember that there are two dream sequences — the drug induced meta-dream which occurs within the violent anxiety dream.

Miike has a canny understanding of film's heteroglossic nature, and confronts and contradicts the audience's expectations. Bakhtin argues that language is heteroglossic and that it is composed of a polyglot of competing voices. Film is similarly heteroglossic, making allusions to prior conventions of filmmaking. Miike, through the course of the film, creates an association between long takes, long shots, use of location sound and minimal use of extra diegetic sound — formal strategies that throughout film history have come to connote the "real" — to present the lived experiences of his protagonist. Miike similarly uses formal strategies that have conventionally been associated with dreaming to express his protagonist's subconscious subjectivity. But by bleeding such formal irregularities into the "real" sequences, Miike is able to blur the boundaries of dream and reality. Indeed, he cheats and places certain formal irregularities into the characters' "lived" experience so that after the excessive formal irregularities of the meta-dream the viewer forgives Miike for using the expressive blue lighting in the waking sequence. The viewer has been so abused by Miike's formal disruptions that s/he ascribes normative qualities to this brief moment and indeed the editing is conventional. This enables Miike in the final scene upon his returning the film to the dream sequence, to cleverly reverse those formal strategies. It is the dream that continues to use realist formal devices but in the service of depicting the fantasy projection of the character's damaged subconsciousness. Miike uses the expressive blue coloring to depict the character's waking environment and remove him from the formal irregularities of the drug-induced meta-dream sequence. But with Aoyama returning to sleep, Miike now constructs the dream world as a verisimilar environment. By constructing the final dream images with realist formal devices, Miike makes the viewer subconsciously question the narrative actions (i.e. Is this a lived experience or is it metaphor?), while the narrative very clearly and explicitly depicts Aoyama dreaming Asami's violence, wake up to realize it was a dream, and then fall back to sleep to return to the dream. The film's subversion of its own formal lexicon posits that the violence is indeed real despite the fact that the viewer explicitly sees Aoyama fall back to sleep. The visual iconography exploits the viewer's belief in the conventional depictions of dream and reality in film, in order to undermine the narrative content.

Returned to his dream, Aoyama watches as Asami chases his son up the stairs, but the teenaged Shigehiko kicks out and sends her falling. She breaks her neck and the film ends with both she and Aoyama becoming paralyzed and facing each other. The two are metaphorically paralyzed by his lies.

The film's principle concern is not with the construction of violence inherent within women. Rather, the film's utilization of both realist and expressive formal styles is in fact Miike's desire to construct Asami's violence as a projection upon women derived from Aoyama's (and patriarchy's) guilt feelings. Gregory Barrett creates the link between the vengeance-seeking woman in Japanese cinema with the *anima*.[15] While the individual presents an outer face or persona to the world, that individual also has an inner face which is turned inward toward the unconscious. The outer face, or the mask that individuals present to society depending on the context, has a dual function: firstly, to allow the individual, regardless of the true nature of his or her inner self to conform to society's expectations; and secondly to hide the inner self from the rest of society.

Jung argues that the *anima* is the inner woman within masculine society, but the depiction of the inner woman is contingent on masculine fear. It is important to remember that the *anima* is a male construction, devised in a patriarchal world complete with its unconscious projections of what it is to be woman. Jung argues "[a]n inherited collective image of woman exists in a man's unconscious, with the help of which he apprehends the nature of woman."[16] Of course, this is no true "nature of woman" but how woman *appears to man.* It is important to see the women in film, not as woman *qua* woman, but woman *qua* unconscious construct. This is particularly true of the *anima* for she represents man's fear of woman or the potential power inherent within women which must be contained and restrained through the reinforcement of hegemony.

Every violent action that Asami performs in the film is perceived through Aoyama and the film in fact constructs Asami as the projected *anima* in very literal ways. The crux of this reading of the film as allegorical of patriarchy's projection of vengeful desires within women upon women is found in the film's drug-induced dream sequence.

In the dream sequence, Aoyama places himself within Asami's apartment, a setting that the viewer up until this point has identified with Asami independently of Aoyama's field of perception. The viewer is fooled into thinking that the images of Asami in her room are an example of dramatic irony, where the viewer knows more than the film's protagonist. Yet Aoyama is able to reconstruct this setting within his own dream with complete fidelity. His dream even conjures the mysterious bag and it is within the dream that its gruesome contents are finally revealed. Closer scrutiny of the films usage of the sequences of Asami at home belie that Asami's apartment is entirely a construct of Aoyama's imaginings and Asami's grotesque nature in fact exists solely in Aoyama's mind.

The first depiction of Asami in her room is shown in the context of Aoyama's guilt feelings toward betraying his wife's memory. The sequence occurs after the two have their first date. Yoshikawa has told Aoyama that Asami had lied about her referees, instilling within Aoyama his first doubts about her. Aoyama sits at his desk and looks over Asami's profile and covering letter with his wife's photograph again prominent in the frame. The film cuts to an image of Asami at home with the burlap sack and then cuts to an image of Aoyama at home asleep, bathed in blue tones. The film then cuts to a close-up of Asami shot with a wide angle lens and showing the sack in the background and then cuts to Aoyama still sleeping but restless in his sleep. The film then cuts to an outdoor location with slight blue tones, depicting a tree in the snow. A woman is standing beside the tree. The film cuts to a close-up of the woman and it is Ryoko, who steps behind the tree. The sequence ends with a shot of Aoyama at home sitting in a chair. The shot construction posits an ambiguity. The image of Ryoko is clearly a memory/dream image from the sleeping Aoyama's subjectivity and sandwiched between those shots are the images of Asami, which must also be seen as subjective shots of Aoyama's imaginings. The baggage, beside Asami, while constructed to represent Asami's mysteriousness, in fact represents Aoyama's insecurities.

The sequence in which the bag first moves, revealing to the viewer that there is something strange about Asami, is similarly constructed in such a way that it can be read as indicative of Aoyama's imagination. After Yoshikawa's dire warning that there is something disquieting about Asami, Aoyama is shown seated at his office desk contemplating phoning Asami. The sequence is punctuated with shots of Asami seated in her room with her baggage. While these shots posit an ambivalence, either being manifest by Aoyama's imagination or being dramatic irony and showing Asami for what she is, on a re-viewing of the film it becomes clear that the shots of Asami at home are a product of Aoyama's imagination.

The first shot of Asami's apartment occurs prior to the introduction of that character. After Aoyama and Yoshikawa decide to host the auditions, Aoyama hears the radio broadcast calling for candidates for the Tomorrow's Star auditions. Aoyama is sitting in his car in the rain. He turns on the radio and some soft music begins to play. A voice comes on announcing that Audrey Hepburn, Julia Roberts and the like were all at one time in life ordinary people. The voice then continues to describe the auditions for a new reality show called "Tomorrow's Heroine," in which the star of tomorrow will be discovered today. While Aoyama is listening to this advertisement, there is a brief cut to a young girl sitting in an apartment similarly hearing the ad. The apartment is the space that the film later comes to define as Asami's. Yet it is not Asami hearing the ad, it is a young girl. This space, then, must be read, not as Asami's physical space, but as Aoyama's fantasy space. Because he has at this point not yet met Asami, Aoyama imagines in the space a young child, one who would potentially dream of becoming "Tomorrow's Heroine". Indeed, that child later becomes the grown Asami, both the film's heroine and Aoyama's. Every scene that occurs in this space is therefore a construct of Aoyama's imaginings. This reading undermines all of Asami's violence, for the images of Asami seated beside the mysterious bag, the images of her murder of the ballet instructor, and the murder of the record producer all occur in Aoyama's various states of imagination. The allegorical reading of the film restores to the film the idea of the dream narrative and of Asami's villainy as Aoyama's projection of the *anima* upon her.

In psychoanalysis, the *anima's* purpose is to provide psychological relief to multiple complexes. Jung states:

> The immediate goal of the analysis of the unconscious, therefore, is to reach a state where the unconscious contents no longer remain unconscious and no longer express themselves indirectly as *animus* and *anima* phenomena; that is to say, a state in which *animus* and *anima* become functions of relationship to the unconscious.[17]

For Jung, the patient who suffers a complex (a hysteric, a person who is possessed by the *anima*, or someone who is burdened by the mask of a persona), can only rid himself or herself of such a complex by recognizing the operations of the unconscious in his or her conscious life. Through analysis, the patient learns to recognize the *anima* as a psychological construction and the complex is dispelled. Resolution for Aoyama, then, lies in his recognizing his conception of Asami to be a projection upon her manifest by his guilt feelings in lying to her. He can only find psychological relief in confessing to her his role in the auditions. The closing minutes of the film involve Aoyama waking. He realizes that Asami's violence is a projection of his imagination, caused by his guilt feelings, toward his wife and of lying to Asami. By this point, Asami has asked him to love her only and he has implied his consent. What is more, he has by this time proposed marriage to her, which she has accepted. Aoyama feels trapped because he has missed his opportunity to confess to Asami his role in the auditions process. He can never tell her the truth for fear of the consequences. He returns to his bed, and closes his eyes as he is returned to the culmination of his fears of Asami discovering his truth and so he has gone back to the image of the *anima* exacting her revenge. The film's ending is a metaphorical paralysis for there can, at this point, never be truth between them.

The final image of the film is of ambivalence. The film's final shot is of the child Asami dancing, an image that is both liberating and terrifying for its evocation of torture. The image of the child is a pure, pre-torture Asami, evoking her pristine nature as well as the torture that is yet to come.

As the Asia Extreme movement has evolved, the mainstream production companies, in order to capitalize on this movement, have begun to finance and produce films that are extreme in look but devoid of the accompanying political agenda. While that may in time allow for a radical politics, the movement is beginning to stagnate. While the Miikes of Asian Extreme continue to shake up the industry with their politicized work, sadly much of what today is labeled as extreme has devolved into simply synonymous with violence.

Notes

Introduction

1. Toby Miller et al., *Global Hollywood 2* (London: British Film Institute, 2005), 120–21.
2. Dave McNary, "Horror's High Hopes," *Daily Variety*, March 18, 2005, 4.
3. Erik Swyngedouw, "Neither Global nor Local: Globalization and the Politics of Scale," in *Spaces of Globalization: Reasserting the Power of the Local* (New York: The Guilford Press, 1997), 142.
4. Aihwa Ong, *Flexible Citizenship: The Cultural Logic of Transnationality* (Durham: Duke University Press, 1999), 4.
5. David Desser, "The Kung Fu Craze: Hong Kong Cinema's First American Reception," in *The Cinema of Hong Kong: History, Arts, Identity*, ed. Poshek Fu and David Desser (Cambridge: Cambridge University Press, 2000), 20.
6. Darcy Paquet, "The Korean Film Industry: 1992 to the Present," in *New Korean Cinema*, ed. Chi-yun Shin and Julian Stringer (New York: New York University Press, 2005), 35.
7. Derek Elley, "Hong Kong," *Variety International Film Guide* 1999, 161.
8. David Chute, "East Goes West," *Variety*, May 10–16, 2004, 7.
9. Paul Willemen, "Action Cinema, Labour Power and the Video Market," in *Hong Kong Connections: Transnational Imagination in Action Cinema*, ed. Meaghan Morris, Siu Leung Li, and Stephen Chan Ching-kiu (Hong Kong: Hong Kong University Press, 2005), 225.
10. David Bordwell, *Figures Traced in Light* (Berkeley: University of California Press, 2005), 233.

11. David Desser, "Hong Kong Film and New Cinephilia," in *Hong Kong Connections*, 216.

12. David Chute, "East Goes West," *Variety*, May 10–16, 2004, 7.

13. Jinhee Choi, "Sentimentality and the Cinema of the Extreme," *Jump Cut* 50 (Spring 2008), http://www.ejumpcut.org/currentissue/sentiment-Extreme/index.html (accessed June 19, 2008).

Chapter 1   J-horror: New Media's Impact on Contemporary Japanese Horror Cinema

1. This chapter's earlier version was published in *Canadian Journal of Film Studies* 16, no. 2 (Fall 2007): 23–48.

2. Lee Bong-Ou, *Nihon eiga wa saikodekiru* [Japanese cinema can revive] (Tokyo: Weitsu, 2003), 8.

3. Geoff King, *American Independent Cinema* (Bloomington and Indianapolis: Indiana University Press, 2005), 8.

4. Ibid., 8–9.

5. Tom Mes and Jasper Sharp, *The Midnight Eye Guide to New Japanese Film* (Berkeley: Stone Bridge Press, 2005), vii. Emphasis is mine.

6. "Profile," *Hideo Nakata Official Page*, the latest update 2005, http://hw001. gate01.com/ hideonakata/ (accessed August 21, 2006).

7. "Shimizu Hiroshi Profile," *Shaiker's Official Page*, the date of publication 2004, http://www.shaiker.co.jp/shimizu_p.html (accessed August 21, 2006).

8. "Trivia for *Marebito*," *International Movie Database* (hereafter IMDb), the latest update 2005, http://www.imdb.com/title/tt0434179/trivia (accessed August 21, 2006).

9. Julia Kristeva, *Power of Horror: An Essay of Abjection*, trans. Leon S. Roudiez (New York: Colombia University Press, 1982).

10. "Trivia for *The Ring*," IMDb, date of publication 2002, http://www.imdb. com/title/tt0298130/trivia (accessed August 21, 2006).

11. Hollywood's version closely follows the conventions of American horror films in this regard; the characters that "get it" often seem to deserve their fate. The sexually promiscuous, the know-it-all, anyone conspicuously upper class, are frequent targets of the monster's rampage. Unlike a lot of J-horror, the films assure us that this is, after all, a moral universe.

12. David Chute, "East Goes West," *Variety*, posted May 9, 2004, http:// www.variety.com/index.asp?layout=cannes2004&content=vstory&articleid =VR1117904412&categoryid=1713&cs=1&query=david+and+chute &display=david+chute (accessed August 21, 2006).

13. It is ironic to sense *The Ring*'s outdatedness regarding the videotape at the center of the dreadful curse in 2002; videotape was still popular at the moment when the original Japanese film was released in 1998, but much

less so in 2002, when the remake came out. Needless to say, the obsoleteness of the tape medium stands out quite awkwardly in *The Ring Two* in 2005.

14. *Pulse's* distribution rights were purchased by Magnolia, and the film was also remade under the same title by Jim Sonzero and released in August 2006. The remake rights for Kurosawa's previous film *Cure* have also been acquired by United Artists.

15. The following information provided by Kurosawa Kiyoshi in an interview with the author in Tokyo, June 2006.

16. Ibid.

17. Ibid.

18. Timothy Corrigan, *A Cinema without Walls: Movies and Culture after Vietnam* (New Brunswick, NJ: Rutgers University Press, 1991), 27.

19. Laura U. Marks, *Touch: Sensuous Theory and Multisensory Media* (Minneapolis: University of Minnesota Press, 2002), 233.

20. Ibid., 158.

21. Kurosawa, interview with the author (see note 14).

22. Ibid. The idea of "reduction" and "addition" is also pointed out by Kurosawa.

23. Shimizu has stated that he would not be directing *Ju-on: The Grudge 3*. Interview with the author in Tokyo, December 2006.

24. Kuroi Kazuo and Hara Masato, "Sokatsuteki taidan: Soredemo anata wa purodyusa ni naruno ka [Summarizing interview: Do you still want to become a producer?]," *Eiga prodyusa no kiso chishiki: Eiga bijinesu no iriguchi kara deguchi made* [A basic guide for the producer: From entrance to exit of the movie business] (Tokyo: Kinema Junposha, 2005), 178.

25. Barbara Klinger, *Beyond the Multiplex: Cinema, New Technologies, and the Home* (Berkeley: University of California Press, 2006), 23.

26. David Bordwell, *Planet Hong Kong: Popular Cinema and the Art of Entertainment* (Cambridge, MA: Harvard University Press, 2000), 82–83.

27. Janet Wasko, *Hollywood in the Information Age: Beyond the Silver Screen* (Austin: University of Texas Press, 1994).

28. "Business Data for *Titanic*," IMDb, the latest update December 2003, http://www.imdb.com/title/tt0120338/business (accessed August 21, 2006).

29. Anne Allison, *Millennial Monsters: Japanese Toys and the Global Imagination* (Berkeley: University of California Press, 2006), 5.

30. William Tsutsui, *Godzilla on My Mind* (New York: Palgrave Macmillan, 2004), 7.

31. Tanaka Jun'ichiro, *Nihon eiga hattatsushi I, katsudo shashin jidai* [The history of Japanese film development I, the age of motion pictures] (Tokyo: Chuo Koronsha, 1975), 117–18.

32. The term *bunka* (culture) came from the German term *kultur*, and the film genre is usually defined as the non-drama or non-news film. It is also known as *kyoiku eiga* (educational film), *kagaku eiga* (science film), and *kiroku eiga* (documentary film). Fujii Jinshi describes *bunka eiga* as a mere representation

or a discursive construction that cannot be fully quantified. See Fujii Jinshi, "Bunka suru eiga: Showa 10 nendai ni okeru bunka eiga no bunseki" [On bunka eiga: Analyzing the discourses of "culture film" in 1935–1945], *Eizogaku* [ICONICS: Japanese Journal of Image Arts and Sciences], 66 (2001): 5–22.

33. Yamamoto Sae, "Yushutsu sareta Nihon no imeji: 1939 nen nyuyoku bankoku hakurankai de joei sareta Nihon eiga" [The export of Japan's image: Japanese films screened at the New York World's Fair, 1939], *Eizogaku* [ICONICS: Japanese Journal of Image and Sciences], 77 (2006): 62–80.

34. Susanne Schermann, *Naruse Mikio: Nichijo no kirameki* [Mikio Naruse: The glitter of everyday life] (Tokyo: Kinema Junposha, 1997), 82.

35. HKFLIX, http://www.hkflix.com/home.asp (accessed August 21, 2007).

36. Hara Masato, *Eiga purodyusa ga kataru hitto no tetsugaku* [Philosophy for making a hit by a film producer] (Tokyo: Nikkei Bipisha, 2004), 193.

37. "Trivia for *The Ring*," IMDb, date of publication 2002, http://www.imdb.com/title/ tt0298130/trivia (accessed August 21, 2006).

38. Shujen Wang, "Recontextualizing Copyright: Piracy, Hollywood, the State, and Globalization," *Cinema Journal* 43.1 (2003): 38.

39. Ibid., 40.

40. "Digital Cinema," *Wikipedia*, date of publication July 2006, http:// en.wikipedia.org/wiki/Digital_cinema (accessed August 21, 2006).

41. Sugaya Minoru and Nakamura Kiyoshi, eds., *Eizo kontentsu sangyo-ron* [Visual content industry studies] (Tokyo: Maruzen, 2002), 207.

42. "T-Joy," *Wikipedia*, http://ja.wikipedia.org/wiki/ T-JOY (accessed January 29, 2009).

43. Peter Hutchings, *The Horror Film* (Essex: Pearson Education Limited, 2004), 1.

44. "Battle Royale," *HKFLIX*, http://www.hkflix.com/xq/asp/filmID.531295/ qx/details.htm (accessed August 21, 2006).

45. Rick Altman, *Film/Genre* (London: British Film Institute, 1999), 194.

46. "*Onibaba*, Criterion Collection (1965)," Amazon.com, www.amazon.com/ gp/product/ B00019JR5Y/sr=1-1/qid=1155234743/ref=pd_bbs_1/104- 0203025-4315974?ie=UTF8&s=dvd and www.imdb.com/title/tt0058430/ (accessed August 21, 2006).

47. Jyotsna Kapur, "The Return of History as Horror: *Onibaba* and the Atomic Bomb," in *Horror International*, ed. Steven Jay Schneider and Tony Williams (Detroit: Wayne State University Press, 2005), 83–97. Adam Lowenstein, *Shocking Representation: Historical Trauma, National Cinema, and the Modern Horror Film* (New York: Columbia University Press, 2005), 83–109.

48. Steven Jay Schneider and Tony Williams, "Introduction," in *Horror International*, ed. Schneider and Williams, 6.

49. Lowenstein, 83.

50. Frederic Jameson, "Third World Literature in the Era of Multinational Capitalism," *Social Text*, no. 15 (Autumn, 1986): 65–88. For criticism of Jameson's approach, see Aijaz Ahmad, *In Theory: Classes, Nations, Literatures* (London and New York: Verso, 1992), 95–122.

51. "Folk tale genre" is cited from "Nihon eiga shokai, *Onibaba'a*" [Introduction of Japanese film, *Onibaba'a*], *Kinema Junpo* 379 (November 1964): 80. "Independent film" is cited from Itoya Hisao, "*Onibaba'a* seisaku no kiroku: Dokuritsu puro, sono genjitsu to daikigyo to no kankei" [The records of *Onibaba'a* film production: Independent production, its situation and relation with major studios], *Kinema Junpo* 387 (March 1965): 23–25.

52. *Kinema Junpo* 380 (December 1964), n.p.

53. The first boom of independent films was 1951–57. The major studios started to exclude those independent filmmakers and their films from the film industry, once they had stabilized their production and distribution system in the late 1950s. Many independent directors gave up filmmaking during this period. Shindo Kaneto was one of the few remaining independent filmmakers. He continued filmmaking by either sending his work to international festivals, as in the case of *The Island* (*Hadaka no shima*, 1960), which was awarded the Grand Prix at the Moscow International Film Festival in 1961, or negotiating with a very limited number of independent movie theaters to screen his films.

54. Interview with Shindo Kaneto, Imai Tadashi, and Daikoku Toyoji, "Imai Tadashi, Shindo Kaneto shinshun taidan: Omo ni eiga sakka no shutaisei wo megutte" [The new year interview, Imai Tadashi and Shindo Kaneto: About filmmaker's subjectivity]," *Kinema Junpo*, 383 (January 1965): 56.

55. Jan Simons, "New Media as Old Media: Cinema," in *The New Media Book*, ed. Dan Harries (London: British Film Institute, 2002), 237.

56. Walter Benjamin, "The Work of Art in the Age of Mechanical Reproduction," in *Illumination*, ed. Hannah Arendt. and trans. Harry Zohn (New York: Harcourt, Brace and World, 1968).

Chapter 2   A Cinema of Girlhood: *Sonyeo* Sensibility and the Decorative Impulse in the Korean Horror Cinema

1. *Korean Cinema Annals*, Korean Motion Picture Promotion Corp. (Seoul: Jibmondang, 1999), 99.

2. Park Ji-yeon, "Yeonghwabeob jejeongeseo je 4cha gaejeongkkajiui yeonghwa jeongchaek (1961–1984)," in *Hanguk yeonghwa jeongchaeksa*, Kim Dong-ho ed., (Seoul: Nanam, 2005), 197–98.

3. Derek Elley, "Identity Search," *Variety*, May 12–18, 1997, 61.

4. Don Groves, "Korean coin back in o'seas pic pursuit," *Variety*, February 28–March 5, 2000, 32.

5. DVD interview included in *Whishing Stairs*.

6. Nam Dong-cheol, "<Yeogo goedam>eseo <Janghwa, Hongryeon>kkaji, Oh Ki-min PDui Yeonghwa Sesang [2]," *Cine 21*, July 4, 2003. http://www.cine21.com/Index/magazine.php?mag_id=197521 (accessed November 25, 2006)

7. "Plex Success Boosts S. Korea Multi Mania," *Variety*, June 29–July 12, 1998, 10.

8. The number of theaters decreased from 507 to 344, while the number of screens rose from 507 to 720.

9. Korean Movie Database http://www.kmdb.or.kr.

10. Derek Elley, *Variety*, August 28, 2005, 62.

11. Korean Film Commission (KOFIC), Korean Cinema Database 1999. http://www.kofic.or.kr.

12. "Top Ten Films of 1999," *Variety*, April 24–30, 2000, 53.

13. Kim So-min, *Hankyeore*, May 20, 2007. http://www.hani.co.kr/arti/culture/movie/210578.html (accessed May 20, 2007).

14. Ibid.

15. Rhona J. Berenstein, *Attack of the Leading Ladies: Gender, Sexuality and Spectatorship in Classic Horror Cinema* (New York: Columbia University Press, 1996), 27. Harry M. Benshoff, *Monsters in the Closet: Homosexuality and the Horror Film* (Manchester: Manchester University Press, 1997).

16. There have been challenges to such an approach. See Carol J. Clover, "Her Body, Himself: Gender in the Slasher Film," *Representations* 20 (1987): 187–228. Excerpts Reprinted in *Horror: The Film Reader*, ed. Mark Jancovich (London: Routledge, 2002), 77–89. In her essay, Clover attempts to explore cross-gender identification in slasher films.

17. Benshoff, *Monsters in the Closet*, 41.

18. Fran Martin, "The China Simulacrum: Genre, Feminism, and Pan-Chinese Cultural Politics in Crouching Tiger, Hidden Dragon," in *Island on the Edge: Taiwan New Cinema and After,* ed. Chris Berry and Feii Lu (Hong Kong: Hong Kong University Press, 2005), 153–54.

19 Nam Dong-cheul, "<Yeogo goedam>eseo <Janghwa, Hongryeon>kkaji, Oh Ki-min PDui Yeonghwa Sesang [1]," *Cine 21,* July 4, 2003. http://www.cine21.com/Index/magazine.php?mag_id=197522 (accessed November 25, 2006).

20. Noël Carroll, *The Philosophy of Horror or Paradoxes of the Heart* (New York and London: Routledge, 1990).

21. Andrew Grossman and Jooran Lee, "*Memento Mori* and Other Ghostly Sexualities," in *New Korean Cinema*, ed. Chi-Yun Shin and Julian Stringer (Edinburgh: Edinburgh University Press, 2005), 183.

22. Benshoff, *Monsters in the Closet*, 38.

23. Noël Carroll, "Film, Emotion, and Genre," in *Passionate Views: Film, Cognition and Emotion*, ed. Carl Plantinga and Greg M. Smith (Baltimore: Johns Hopkins University Press, 1999), 38–39.

24. Mary Ann Doane, *The Desire to Desire: The Woman's Film of the 1940s* (Bloomington: Indiana University Press, 1987).

Chapter 3 *Inner Senses* and the Changing Face of Hong Kong Horror Cinema

1. Derek Elley, "Hong Kong," *Variety International Film Guide,* 1999, 161.
2. David Bordwell, *Planet Hong Kong: Popular Cinema and the Art of Entertainment* (Cambridge: Harvard University Press, 2000), 120–21.
3. Sherman Chau, "Hong Kong's First Completion Bond Specialist Opens," *Screen Daily,* June 19, 2001.
4. For an excellent explanation of the completion bond and its role in feature film production, see the *DV Handbook* website: http://www.dvhandbook. com/index.php?p=21.
5. Sherman Chau, "Hong Kong's First Completion Bond Specialist Opens," *Screen Daily,* June 19, 2001.
6. Patrick Frater, "Hong Kong Legends Light up Filmko's Debut Slate," *Screen Daily,* April 18, 2001.
7. Patrick Frater, "Hong Kong's Filmko Boards Floating Landscape," *Screen Daily,* November 21, 2002.
8. Liz Shackleton, "Hong Kong's eSun Strikes Production Pacts," *Screen Daily,* December 18, 2001.
9. Patrick Frater, "Hong Kong's Filmko Boards Floating Landscape," *Screen Daily,* November 21, 2002.
10. A sustained comparison between the supernatural motifs in *Rouge* and *Inner Senses* can be found in Longtin, "Inner Senses: From Forgetting to Forgive," trans. Jeanie Wong, *Hong Kong Panorama 2001–2002* (Hong Kong: Hong Kong Arts Development Council, 2002), 83.
11. Derek Elley, "Hong Kong," *Variety International Film Guide 2000,* 161.
12. Bono Lee, "The Heart Is a Lonely Hunter: Lo Chi-Leung's *Inner Senses,*" *Hong Kong Panorama 2001–2002* (Hong Kong: Hong Kong Arts Development Council, 2002), 82.
13. Suzuki Koji, *Dark Water,* trans. Glynne Walley (New York: Vertical, Inc., 1996), 28.
14. Ibid., 21.
15. Ibid., 37.
16. Bordwell, *Planet Hong Kong,* 180.
17. Ibid., 122.
18. Ibid., 180.
19. Kristin Thompson, *Storytelling in the New Hollywood: Understanding Classical Narrative Technique* (Cambridge: Harvard University Press, 1999).
20. Liz Shackleton, "Hong Kong's Filmko sells *Inner Senses* to Horizon for Europe." *Screen Daily,* July 10, 2002.

Chapter 4   The Pan-Asian Outlook of *The Eye*

1. Jin Long Pao, "The Pan-Asian Co-Production Sphere: Interview with Director Peter Chan," *Harvard Asia Quarterly* VI, no. 3 (Summer 2002), http://www.asiaquarterly.com/content/view/123/5/.

2. Bliss Cua Lim, "Generic Ghosts: Remaking the New 'Asian Horror Film,'" in *Hong Kong Film, Hollywood and the New Global Cinema: No Film Is an Island*, ed. Gina Marchetti and Tan See Kam (London: Routledge, 2007), 119.

3. Raphaël Millet, *Singapore Cinema* (Singapore: Editions Didier Millet, 2006), 94–95.

4. Tony Rayns, review of *The Eye*, *Sight and Sound* 12, no. 11 (November 2002): 44.

5. On Hong Kong cinema's intertextual bent, see, for example, Patricia Aufderheide, "Made in Hong Kong: Translation and Transmutation," in *Play It Again, Sam: Retakes on Remakes*, ed. Andrew Horton and Stuart Y. McDougal (Berkeley: University of California Press, 1998), 191–99; Esther C. M. Yau, "Introduction: Hong Kong Cinema in a Borderless World," in *At Full Speed: Hong Kong Cinema in a Borderless World*, ed. Esther C. M. Yau (Minneapolis: University of Minnesota Press, 2001), 1–28; and Kwai-Cheung Lo, *Chinese Face/Off: The Transnational Popular Culture of Hong Kong* (Urbana and Chicago: University of Illinois Press, 2006), especially Ch. 7.

6. This trend described in, for example, Lim; and Adam Knee, "The Transnational Whisperings of Contemporary Asian Horror," *Journal of Communication Arts* (Thailand) 25, no. 4 (2007).

7. David Chute, "East Goes West," *Variety*, special supplement on Cannes, May 10, 2004, 7.

8. Lim, "Generic Ghosts," 110. Lo points to a similar conceptualization of "Asian" in Hong Kong by and large: "The word 'Asian' is generally used in Hong Kong to refer only to East Asians, those from China, Japan, and South Korea. People from elsewhere in Asia, such as the brown people from the Indian Subcontinent and Southeast Asia, are often ignored or excluded when the media identify an 'Asian' organization." *Chinese Face/Off*, 109. Interestingly, one of the most useful attempts to describe and theorize a pan-Asian popular culture (by a Singapore scholar) chooses a priori to focus primarily on East Asia, with the addition of Singapore — and yet, references to Southeast Asian nations keep resurfacing throughout his discussion. See Chua Beng Huat, "Conceptualizing an East Asian Popular Culture," *Inter-Asia Cultural Studies* 5, no. 2 (2004): 200–21. Chua makes specific reference to the horror trends discussed in this chapter on p. 208.

9. Lim, "Generic Ghosts," 120.

10. I begin to trace the way a pan-Asian horror discourse has been taken up by some of these other countries in Knee, "Transnational Whisperings."

11. The attitude suggested here is typical of the ways that Hong Kong cinema has envisioned Thailand. See Adam Knee, "Thailand in the Hong Kong Cinematic Imagination," in Marchetti and Tan, esp. 79–81. Relevant in this regard is the fact that the co-producing nation, Singapore, also understands itself as urban and modern, in opposition to the (backward) rural; see Chua, "East Asian Popular Culture," 212–13.

12. To quote producer Peter Chan's own description of his interest in Thai and Korean films (in Pao, "The Pan-Asian Co-Production Sphere"), "I have been very much attracted to the young and energetic films from these two countries, which are not limited by the norms and restrictions we have in Hong Kong. Everything is still relatively fresh for them, and there is no set formula for how to make movies."

13. On the Chinese in Thailand, see, for example, Jonathan Rigg, "Exclusion and Embeddedness: The Chinese in Thailand and Vietnam," in *The Chinese Diaspora: Space, Place, Mobility, and Identity*, ed. Laurence J. C. Ma and Carolyn Cartier (Lanham, MD: Rowman and Littlefield, 2003), 97–115. I am aware of two recent conference presentations on this film which put a particular emphasis on Chinese ethnicity in reading the film's identity politics: Sophia Harvey, "Fractured Visions: Locating the Pan-Asian Gaze in *The Eye*" (paper presented at the annual meeting of the Society for Cinema and Media Studies, March 2–5, 2006); and Arnika Fuhrmann, "The Ghost-Seer: Chinese-Thai History, Female Agency, and the Transnational Uncanny in Danny and Oxide Pang's *The Eye* (2002)" (paper presented at the annual conference of the Canadian Asian Studies Association, November 9–12, 2006).

14. See, for example, the account of Thai cosmology in Niels Mulder, *Inside Thai Society: Interpretations of Everyday Life*, 5th ed. (Amsterdam: The Pepin Press, 1996), 105–6.

15. It is telling as well that the conflagration occurs in stalled traffic, itself emblematizing the speed and technological profusion of modernity in confrontation with the slower pace and narrow street layouts of an older Asia. Mun's earlier definitive discovery of her ability to see dead people also occurs in conjunction with a traffic accident (when she sees the young victim of an accident in Hong Kong being led away by a dark figure) — a fact which in turn further suggests a "haunting" by some of the Hollywood inspirations of the Pang Brothers' film. In *The Sixth Sense*, it is when Cole sees the ghosts of victims of a traffic accident that he is first able to start to convince his mother of his powers, while in *The Mothman Prophesies* (Mark Pellington, released in January 2002), a series of visions that people experience also point toward a major traffic catastrophe (a bridge collapse), presented in a stylized fashion quite similar to that of the final calamity of *The Eye* (released in May 2002).

16. For an account of the events of 1973, 1976, and 1992, see Pasuk Phongpaichit and Chris Baker, *Thailand: Economy and Politics*, 2nd ed. (Oxford: Oxford University Press, 2002), Ch. 9 and 10. The more recent threats to stability to which I allude include rising tensions between Muslims and Buddhists in the south of Thailand during the administration of Prime Minister Thaksin Shinawatra (especially from 2004 onward), and widespread disaffection with the leadership capabilities of the junta which forced Thaksin from office in 2006.

17. Another interesting shift is the substitution of the ghost of a drowned girl in a raincoat for *The Eye*'s Hong Kong-specific ghost of a boy who has committed suicide over a lost report card. Naina is able to use her knowledge of the presence of the missing girl's body in a water tower to prove her supernatural powers to skeptics. Any fan of Asian horror would readily recognize the subplot and its related imagery as indebted to the Japanese horror hit *Dark Water* (*Honogurai Mizu No Soko Kara*, Nakata Hideo, 2002), providing yet another way *Naina* engages a broader Asian horror discourse.

Chapter 5   The Art of Branding: Tartan "Asia Extreme" Films

1. In June 2008, Tartan went into administration after months of speculation about the company's finance. It should be noted though that this chapter was written before the company's demise.

2. See Erika Franklin, "Asia Extreme: It's All in the Name," *Firecracker*, http://www.firecraker-media.com/movie/archive/issue01/interview01_06.shtml.

3. See Tartanvideo.com/ht_asia_extreme.asp?STID=4&C=2&page=1/ (accessed February 10, 2008).

4. The popular sites include kfccinmea.com, hkflix.com, sensasian.com, yesasia.com and asiancult.com.

5. For discussion of cult and art-house film consumption, see Mark Jancovich, Antonio Lazaro Reboll, Julian Stringer and Andrew Wills, eds., *Defining Cult Movies: The Cultural Politics of Oppositional Taste* (Manchester: Manchester University Press, 2003). See also Joan Hawkins, *Cutting Edge: Art-Horror and the Horrific Avant-garde* (Minneapolis: University of Minnesota Press, 2000).

6. Hamish McAlpine, foreword to *The Tartan Guide to Asia Extreme*, by Mark Pilkington (London: Startlux, 2004), iv.

7. Gary Needham, "Japanese Cinema and Orientalism," in *Asian Cinemas: A Reader and Guide*, ed. Dimitris Eleftheriotis and Gary Needham (Edinburgh: Edinburgh University Press, 2006), 11.

8. Edward Said, *Orientalism* (New York: Vintage, 1979), 12, 43.

9. Mike Featherstone, *Undoing Culture: Globalization, Postmodernism and Identity* (London: Sage, 1995), 98–99.

10. Mark Jancovich, introduction to "Part Four: Consuming Fears," in *Horror, The Film Reader*, ed. Mark Jancovich (London and New York: Routledge, 2002), 135.

11. Mark Pilkington, introduction to *The Tartan Guide to Asia Extreme* (London: Startlux, 2004), v.

12. Confident of my analogy, I posed the question to Hamish McAlpine. Disappointingly, McAlpine told me that he actually "pinched" the extreme title from the Channel Four (British TV channel) series as a kind of payback, as Channel Four apparently "stole" the pattern of his Tartan logo! Hamish McAlpine, private conversation with the author, November 12, 2007.

13. Pilkington, *The Tartan Guide to Asia Extreme*, vi.

14. Ryan Mottesheard, "DVD Quick Study: Tartan Takes 'Extreme' Route to Genre Success," *Variety*, September 6, 2005, http://www.variety.com/article/ VR1117928653.htm?categoryid=2063&cs=1 (accessed December 2, 2007). Tartan closed its USA division and sold off its film library shortly before the company went into administration.

15. Tartan's Press and PR Manager, Paul Smith told me that *Battle Royale* was not picked up by any U.S. distributors, possibly because the film is about school kids killing each other, and there have been real shooting incidents at schools in the U.S. Nonetheless, Miramax purchased a remake right to the film. Paul Smith, private interview with the author, January 17, 2007.

16. Paul Smith, interview with the author, January 17, 2007.

17. See Tartanvideo.com/ (accessed February 10, 2008).

18. Tony Rayns, "Sexual Terrorism: The Strange Case of Kim Ki-duk," *Film Comment* 40, no. 6 (November 2004): 51.

19. Rayns, "Sexual Terrorism," 51 and 50. According to Rayns, Kim is "not a master of psychosexual sophistication. Nor, as it happens, is he a great director of actors or an acute analyst of Korean society, politics, or history. In fact, to be frank, the writer-director you can infer from his films comes across as just a teensy bit naive when it comes to sexual politics, social criticism, and religious inklings" (50).

20. Richard Falcon, "*The Isle* (Review)," *Sight and Sound* 11, no. 8 (August 2001): 49.

21. Paracinema refers to a wide range of film genres out of the mainstream, and by Sconce's own description this is "an extremely elastic textual category." In addition to art film, horror, and science fiction films, "paracinema" catalogues "include entries from such seemingly disparate genres" as badfilms, splatterpunk, mondo films, sword-and-sandal epics, Elvis flicks, government hygiene films, Japanese monster movies, beach party musicals, and "just about every other historical manifestation of exploitation cinema from juvenile delinquency documentaries to . . . pornography". See Jeffrey Sconce, "'Trashing' the Academy: Taste, Excess, and an Emerging Politics of Cinematic Style," *Screen* 36, no. 4 (Winter 1995): 372. Joan Hawkins elaborates on the term

"paracinema" and notes its main characteristics as follows. The operative criterion is "affect": the ability of a film to thrill, frighten, gross out, arouse, or otherwise directly engage the spectator's body. It is this emphasis on affect that characterizes paracinema as a low cinematic culture. Paracinema catalogues are dominated by what Clover terms "body genre" films, that which Linda Williams notes, "privilege sensational." See Hawkins, *Cutting Edge: Art-Horror and the Horrific Avant-garde*, 4.

22. See http://classic-horror.com/reviews/isle.shtml/ (accessed February 10, 2008).
23. Roger Ebert, "*The Isle* (Review)," *Chicago Sun-Times*, January 31, 2003, http://rogerebert.suntimes.com/apps/pbcs.dll/article?AID=/20030131/REVIEWS/301310302/1023 (accessed September 19, 2007).
24. See http://classic-horror.com/reviews/audition.shtml/ [accessed February 10, 2008].
25. Mark Schilling, "*Audition*: Mid-Life Crisis Meets Lethal Psychosis," *The Japan Times*, March 14, 2000, http://search.japantimes.co.jp/cgi-bin/ff20000314a1.html (accessed September 19, 2007).
26. Gary Morris, "Gore Galore: Takashi Miike's *Audition*," *Bright Light Film Journal* 34 (2001), http://www.brightlightsfilm.com/34/audition.html/ (accessed February 10, 2008).
27. Peter Bradshaw, "*Oldboy* (Review)," *Guardian Unlimited*, October 15, 2004, http://film.guardian.co.uk/News_Story/Critic_Review/Guardian_Film_of_the_week/0,,1327302,00.html (accessed August 10, 2007).
28. Harry Knowles, *Ain't It Cool* News, December 9, 2003, http://www.aintitcool.com/display.cgi?id=16640 (accessed August 10, 2007).
29. Michael Atkinson, "Die Hard with a Vengeance: Best Served Cold, Park Chanwook's Brutal Revenge Feast Comes with a Side of Live Octopus," *Village Voice*, March 22, 2005, http://www.villagevoice.com/film/0512,atkinson1,62315,20.html (accessed September 19, 2007).
30. Carina Chocano, "*Oldboy*: From Korea Comes a Dream of Deadly Drama," *The Los Angeles Times*, March 25, 2005, http://www.calendarlive.com/movies/chocano/cl-et-oldboy25mar25,0,3031987.story (accessed August 10, 2007).
31. Grady Hendrix, "Vengeance Is Theirs," *Sight and Sound* 16, no. 2 (February 2006): 18.
32. Manohla Dargis, "The Violence (and the Seafood) Is More Than Raw," *The New York Times*, March 25, 2005, http://movies.nytimes.com/2005/03/25/movies/25boy.html (accessed August 10, 2007).
33. The AAJA Media Watch group complained that the review "reduces an entire people to a backward, 'different' lot that's meant to be mocked." See the Internet site: http://www.aaja.org/news/mediawatch/050408_reed/ (accessed February 10, 2008).

34. On April 16, 2007, Cho Seung-Hui, who had history of mental and behavioral problems, killed thirty-two people before turning the gun on himself on the Virginia Tech campus. Cho was South Korean but his family had moved to the U.S. when he was eight. He was a senior English major at Virginia Tech.

35. The possible link was spotted by the Virginia Tech professor Paul Harris, who then alerted the authorities.

36. For example, Gerald Kaufman urged filmmakers to exercise self-censorship on the *Telegraph* website, while filmmaker Bob Cesca described the connection as "the most ridiculous hypothesis yet" writing for the *Huffington Post*. In defending the film, Grady Hendrix at Slate proclaims "*Oldboy* bears no more responsibility for the Virginia Tech shootings than *American Idol*." See the IFC Blog for a roundup of the responses as well as from Tartan Films that issued an official statement that includes the following passages: "We are extremely proud of Chan-wook Park, Tartan movie *Oldboy* and the critical praise it has received. To be associated in any way with the tragic events that occurred at Virginia Tech is extremely disturbing and distressing." http://ifcblog.ifctv.com/ifc_blog/2007/04/oldboy_joy.html/ (accessed February 10, 2008).

37. Julian Stringer, "Putting Korean Cinema in Its Place: Genre Classifications and the Contexts of Reception," in *New Korean Cinema*, ed. Chi-Yun Shin and Julian Stringer (Edinburgh: Edinburgh University Press, 2005), 96.

38. Needham, "Japanese Cinema and Orientalism," 9.

39. Hendrix, "Vengeance Is Theirs," 18.

40. Atkinson, "Die Hard with a Vengeance," *Village Voice*.

41. British distributor Third Window has rights for all of Lee Chang-dong films, apart from his latest *Secret Sunshine* (*Milyang*, 2007), and they are released on DVD.

42. The impact of Asia Extreme label is also evident in the fate of Kim Ji-woon's debut feature *The Quiet Family* (*Choyonghan kajok*, 1998), whose later films include popular Tartan Asia Extreme titles such as *A Tale of Two Sisters* and *A Bittersweet Life* (*Dalkomhan insaeng*, 2005). *The Quiet Family* contains many of Kim's directorial hallmarks, but remains a relatively obscure film in the U.K., mainly because it was picked up by a Hong Kong-based distribution company Tai Seung, whereas its Japanese remake *The Happiness of the Katakuris* (*Katakuri-ke no kôfuku*, Miike Takashi, 2002) was picked up by Tartan Films and subsequently became much more widely available than the original.

43. See www.Tartanfilmsusa.com/ (accessed February 10, 2008).

44. Bill Roundtree, "2005 in Review: Korean Cinema," comment posted January 2, 2006, http://billroundtree.blogspot.com/2006/01/2005-in-review-korean-cinema/ (accessed May 9, 2008).

45. Mark Jancovich, "Genre and the Audience: Genre Classifications and Cultural Distinctions in the Mediation of *The Silence of the Lambs*," in *Horror: The Film Reader*, ed. Mark Jancovich (London and New York: Routledge, 2002), 153.

46. James Naremore, "American Film Noir: The History of an Idea," *Film Quarterly* 49, no. 2 (1995–6): 14.

47. Rick Altman, *Film/Genre* (London: British Film Institute, 1999), 54.

48. See Altman, *Film/Genre*, 54–68.

49. Interestingly, Optimum released more art-house features such as Japanese film *All about Lily Chou Chou* (*Riri Shushu no subete*, Iwai Sunji, 2001) and Chinese title *Balzac and the Little Chinese Seamstress* (*Xiao cai feng*, Dai Sijie, 2002) through their "Optimum World" division rather than Optimum Asia.

50. Film distributors are not alone in trying to reap profits from the success of the Extreme label. Book publishers have joined in and produced titles such as Patrick Galloway's *Asian Shock: Horror and Dark Cinema from Japan, Korea, Hong Kong and Thailand* (Berkeley, CA: Stone Bridge Press, 2006) and D. Chris's *Outlaw Masters of Japanese Films* (London: I. B. Tauris, 2005). In fact, Galloway's *Asian Shock* echoes the Tartan promotional phrase on its back cover: "Asian Extreme cinema is hot, and this book celebrates all its gory glory."

Chapter 6   The Mummy Complex: Kurosawa Kiyoshi's *Loft* and J-horror

1. Kurosawa Kiyoshi, "*Loft* Kurosawa Kiyoshi kantoku intabyu," [An interview with Kurosawa Kiyoshi, the director of *Loft*], *Kansai dotto komu*, http://www.kansai.com/cinema/interview/060907_interview4.html (accessed January 28, 2007).

2. I share this thematic definition of J-horror with Mitsuyo Wada-Marciano. See her "J-Horror: New Media's Impact on Contemporary Japanese Horror Cinema" in this volume.

3. See the chapter on Kurosawa in Tom Mes and Jasper Sharp, *The Midnight Eye Guide to New Japanese Film* (Berkeley: Stone Bridge, 2005), 92.

4. Jerry White, *The Films of Kyoshi Kurosawa: Master of Fear* (Berkeley: Stone Bridge, 2007). Addressing a non-academic, horror fan readership, White's book occasionally offers excellent close analysis of a number of sequences from Kurosawa's oeuvre, including some of his earlier, less known V-Cinema (made-for-video feature) works such as the *Suit Your Self or Shoot It* (*Katte ni shiyagare*) series (1995–96).

5. The timing of the release of Kurosawa's latest film *Tokyo Sonata* (2008), a winner of the 2008 Cannes Jury Prize, did not allow me to integrate a

reading of the film into this chapter. *Tokyo Sonata* brilliantly deconstructs the framework this chapter establishes, particularly in terms of space, gender, and family.

6. The most comprehensible filmography of the director can be found in Kurosawa Kiyoshi, *Kurosawa Kiyoshi no eigajutsu* [Kurosawa Kiyoshi's film art] (Tokyo: Shinchosha, 2006), 278–302. The filmography, complied by Odera Shinsuke and authorized by Kurosawa, lists fifty-seven titles, including 8 mm shorts and TV episodes, of Kurosawa's directorial work at the time of publication in July 2006.

7. Akira Mizuta Lippit's brilliant reading of *Cure* is an exception. See his *Atomic Light (Shadow Optics)* (Minneapolis: University of Minnesota Press, 2005), 143–57.

8. For example, a recent collection, *Japanese Horror Cinema,* ed. Jay McRoy (Edinburgh: Edinburgh University Press, 2005), covers a wide variety of films, including Yoshida Yoshishige's densely arty *Onimaru* (1988), an adaptation of *Wuthering Heights* set in medieval Japan.

9. By calling J-horror a movement that emphasizes psychology and atmosphere rather than gore, this chapter puts aside another important name, Miike Takashi. Miike belongs to the same generation (born in 1960), and works within the same sphere in the industry. He is admired by Kurosawa and Takahashi, but does take a different approach to graphic violence.

10. My approach to J-horror as a movement is informed by Thomas LaMarre's critique of the Gainax discourse on the contemporary otaku culture. The Gainax discourse, as LaMarre constructs, comprises animations produced in Okada Toshio's Gainax studios, such as those by Anno Hideaki, Okada's writings on anime and its fandom, Murakami Takashi's Super Flat, and Azuma Hiroki's theory of postmodernism. These artists and theorists, through collaborations and cross-references, form a discourse on anime fandom and aesthetics within a broader framework of postmodernism. See Thomas LaMarre, "Otaku Movement," in *Japan after Japan: Social and Cultural Life from the Recessionary 1990s to the Present,* ed. Tomiko Yoda and Harry Harootunian (Durham: Duke University Press, 2006), 358–94. However, I do not think the fascinatingly *postmodern* possibility which the Gainax discourse at times presents — the possibility of producing the porous and non-hierarchical horizon where work and play, production, distribution, reception, and the points of view are no longer fixed — can be applicable to J-horror for a number of reasons. In particular, I consider the J-horror discourse to have emphatically *modern* concerns.

11. *Premonition* (Tsuruta Norio, 2004), *Infection* (Ochiai Masayuki, 2004), and *Reincarnation* (Shimizu Takashi, 2005) have come out from this label. For more information on the label's production and distribution strategies, see Toho's webpage, http://www.toho.co.jp/movienews/0403/13jhorror_st. html (accessed April 9, 2008).

12. Shimizu Takashi (born in 1972) is an exception.
13. Kurosawa Kiyoshi, *Kurosawa Kiyoshi no eigajutsu*, 263.
14. Sigmund Freud, "The 'Uncanny,'" in *The Standard Edition of the Complete Psychological Works of Sigmund Freud*, vol. XVII, 217–56.
15. Robin Wood, "Introduction," in *American Nightmare: Essays on the Horror Film*, ed. Robin Wood and Richard Lippe (Toronto: Festival of Festivals, 1979), 17.
16. There are a number of monstrous families, bonded through criminal acts, blood, or incest, as the evil in the work of Kurosawa, who is a great admirer of the American horror of the 1970s.
17. Sawaragi Noi, "Eiga de aru dake de jubun kowai," [Being a film is scary enough] *Bungakukai* [Literary World], Oct. 2006, 160–61.
18. André Bazin, *What Is Cinema?* vol. 1, trans. Hugh Gray (Berkeley: University of California Press, 1967), 9.
19. Kurosawa, *Kurosawa Kiyoshi no eigajutsu*, 146.
20. I thank Aaron Gerow for sharing his insights in discontinuity and information about the filming of *Loft* with me.
21. Matt Hills, "Ringing the Changes: Cult Distinctions and Cultural Differences in US Fans' Readings of Japanese Horror Cinema," in *Japanese Horror Cinema*, ed. Jay McRoy (Edinburgh: Edinburgh University Press, 2005), 167.
22. The set design of *White Noise*'s climax that places numerous TV monitors in the torture chamber in a run-down building apparently comes from *The Serpent's Path*.
23. Tom Gunning, "Heard over the Phone: *The Lonely Villa* and the de Lorde Tradition of the Terrors of Technology," *Screen* 32, no. 2 (Summer 1991): 184–96.
24. Eric White writes on *Ringu*: "The film thus associates ubiquitous technological mediation — that is, the cameras, television sets, videocassette recorders, telephones and other such hardware foregrounded throughout the film — with the intrusion of 'posthuman' otherness into contemporary cultural life. As the imagery at the beginning of the film suggests . . . the unpredictable mutability of the ocean, a traditional metaphor for threatening alterity, can also be understood to figure a cultural upheaval brought about by the simulacral proliferation of information in a media-saturated social sphere." Eric White, "Case Study: Nakata Hideo's *Ringu* and *Ringu 2*," in *Japanese Horror Cinema*, ed. Jay McRoy (Edinburgh: Edinburgh University Press, 2005), 41.
25. Noël Carroll, *The Philosophy of Horror, or Paradoxes of the Heart* (New York: Routledge, 1990), 99–118.
26. Kurosawa says: "Most people think that certain cause motivates people's action. In my case, the flow is reversed. I feel I'd make up a cause later, if necessary. . . . My story starts with some action that interests me. Does a cause motivate people in real life? Probably. Yet, in my case, the cause comes later. I've told myself it's no good, but the order remains reversed to this day." Kurosawa, *Kurosawa Kiyoshi no eiga jutsu*, 82.

27. Wada-Marciano offers an alternative explanation in a compelling way, ascribing the non-linear narrative structure of J-horror films, particularly *Ju-on*, to their intimate connections with other media forms, such as serialized TV programs and the DVD chapter format (see Wada-Marciano, this volume).

28. Konaka Chiaki, *Hora eiga no miryoku: fandamentaru hora sengen* [The fascination of horror films: A manifesto of fundamental horror], paperback ed. (Tokyo: Iwanami Shoten, 2003), 99.

29. Kurosawa, *Kurosawa Kiyoshi no eigajutsu*, 267.

30. For the concept of textualization of "new media" in horror, see Robert Spadoni, *Uncanny Bodies: The Coming of Sound Film and the Origins of the Horror Genre* (Berkeley: University of California Press, 2007). In his analysis of classical Hollywood horror films in the early sound period, Spadoni describes how the initial cognitive shock that the synchronized voice gave to the naïve viewer was *texualized* into this genre as a motif of a ventriloquist, for instance.

31. Another origin is generally located in *Psychic Vision: Jaganrei* (Ishii Teruyoshi, 1988), a pioneering media horror which Konaka Chiaki wrote (credited as *kosei*, "construction"). This made-for-video film about the publicity campaign for a young singer exploits the narrational frame of found footage like *Cannibal Holocaust* (Ruggeo Deotaro, 1980) and *The Blair Witch Project*, and showcases terrors generated by media and technology. *Psychic Vision: Jaganrei* slowly garnered cult followings from amateur and professional horror fans, including Kurosawa and Takahashi. In a way, the J-horror discourse was born when Takahashi wrote a rave review of this obscure film in *Cahiers du cinéma japon*, which led to correspondence and collaboration between the two screenwriters. Takahashi's 1991 review is reprinted in Takahashi Hiroshi, *Eiga no ma* [The demon of the cinema] (Tokyo: Seidosha, 2004), 14–16. For Konaka's career, see his *Hora eiga no miryoku*, 50–92, and his website, http://www.konaka.com (accessed March 2, 2007).

32. Takahashi Hiroshi, *Eiga no ma*, 27.

33. Takahashi, 27–28.

34. White sees them as three facets of one woman (White, 200–1).

35. A number of Japanese critics raved about this shot. For example, see Hasumi Shigehiko's comment in his interview with Kurosawa, "Nijuisseiki wa Kurosawa o minakereba wakaranai" [Without watching Kurosawa, you will never understand the 21st century], *Bungakkai* [Literary World], Oct. 2006, 128. I consider this shot to be referring to the mirror shots in Nakata's film with the same actress Nakatani Miki, *Chaos* (1999). The mirror shots crystallize the sadomasochistic sexual economy between the kidnapper (Hagiwara Masato) and his client (Nakatani) *à la Vertigo* (Hitchcock, 1958).

36. Kurosawa, *Kurosawa Kiyoshi no eiga jutsu*, 269; Kurosawa, "*Loft* Kurosawa Kiyoshi kantoku intabyû."

37. Kinoshita Chika, "Sen'yusha tatch no kukan" [The space of appropriators], *Yuriika* [Eureka] 35 no. 10 (Special issue on Kurosawa Kiyoshi, July 2003): 188–99.

38. For a foundational critique of this dichotomy, see Teresa de Lauretis, *Alice Doesn't* (Bloomington: Indiana University Press, 1984), 103–57.

39. Carol Clover persuasively presents the economic and cultural gap, or uneven development between city and country, as a framework when discussing *I Spit on Your Grave*. See Carol J. Clover, *Men, Women, and Chain Saws: Gender in the Modern Horror Film* (Princeton: Princeton University Press, 1992), 124–37.

40. Kurosawa, *Kurosawa Kiyoshi no eigajutsu*, 269.

41. Tzvetan Todorov, *The Fantastic: A Structural Approach to a Literary Genre*, trans. Richard Howard (Ithaca: Cornell University Press, 1975), 25.

42. Linda Williams, "When the Woman Looks," in *Re-Vision: Essays in Feminist Film Criticism*, ed. Mary Ann Doane, Patricia Mellencamp, and Linda Williams (Los Angeles: The American Film Institute, 1984), 83–97.

43. From the perspective of gender and space, Kurosawa's latest horror *Retribution*, featuring a female ghost (Hazuki Riona) firmly localized in the ruin of the prewar asylum in the Tokyo Bay Area, does not pursue this direction, for all interesting experimentations of representing a ghost.

44. Kurosawa Kiyoshi and Shinozaki Makoto, *Kurosawa Kiyoshi no kyofu no eigashi* [Kurosawa Kiyoshi's film history of terror] (Tokyo: Seidosha, 2003), 186.

45. For a succinct account of the prewar "Return to Japan" and its historical context, see Tetsuo Najita and H. D. Harootunian, "Japan's Revolt against the West," in *Modern Japanese Thought*, ed. Bob Tadashi Wakabayashi (New York: Cambridge University Press, 1998), 207–72.

46. Asada Akira, "J kaiki no yukue" [The future of the return to J], *Voice*, March 2003, available at http://www.kojinkaratani.com/criticalspace/old/special/asada/voice0003.html.

47. Tomiko Yoda, "A Roadmap to Millennial Japan," in *Japan after Japan: Social and Cultural Life from the Recessionary 1990s to the Present*, ed. Harry Harootunian and Tomiko Yoda (Durham: Duke University Press, 2006), 47.

Chapter 7   The Good, the Bad, and the South Korean: Violence, Morality, and the South Korean Extreme Film

1. Whitman shot and killed fourteen people and wounded more than thirty others during a shooting spree at the University of Texas at Austin on August 1, 1966. More than thirty years later Klebold and Harris killed thirteen people and wounded several others at Columbine High School in Jefferson County, Colorado. These individuals were white males, as have

been the majority of individuals who commit mass murders and so-called "spree killings." (See Holley; Kelleher; Newman, Fox, Harding, Mehta, and Roth for discussions of similar cases, as well as public and professional reactions to them.) Cho and Gang Lu, a Chinese national Ph.D. student at the University of Iowa, who shot and killed five people in Van Doren Hall on the school's Iowa City campus, represent two notable exceptions to this rule. Although Cho and Lu had little in common with one another, the "Asian connection" between the two was evidently perceived as so great that the release of a film based loosely on the Iowa event, *Dark Matter* (Chen Shi-zheng, U.S.A. 2007) was indefinitely delayed for fear that it would upset those who lost family and friends at Virginia Tech. According to Lawrence Van Gelder in an article on the topic (*New York Times,* February 18, 2008), producers, evidently undeterred by non-Asian Steven Kazmierczak's attack just two days earlier at Northern Illinois University, announced plans to release the film on April 11, 2008. The film was eventually released as planned in several major cities across the US, and received generally positive reviews.

2. Adrian Hong (*The Washington Post,* April 20, 2007) succinctly discusses the issues of blame and responsibility in the context of national identity. Mike Nizza (*The New York Times,* April 19, 2007); Stewart MacLean (*The Mirror,* April 20, 2007); and Jake Coyle (*The Washington Times Daily,* April 20, 2007), all detail the anti-Korean backlash that these "theories" provoked. Ironically, after disseminating, and thus lending credence to such accusations, news sources were forced to admit that there was no evidence to suggest that Cho had ever seen Park's film.

3. Jean Laplanche and J. B. Pontalis, *The Language of Psycho-Analysis,* trans. Donald Nicholson-Smith (New York: Norton, 1973), 351.

4. Oleysa Govorun, Kathleen Fuegen, and B. Keith Payne, "Stereotypes Focus Defensive Projection," *Personality and Social Psychology Bulletin* 32:06 (June 2006): 781–93.

5. Peter Suedfeld, "Reverberations of the Holocaust Fifty Years Later: Psychology's Contributions to Understanding Persecution and Genocide," *Canadian Psychology* 41:01 (Feb 2000): 1–9.

6. Rex Reed, "Bobby Short, King of Pop," *New York Observer,* March 28, 2005, 20.

7. See, for example, works by directors such as Catherine Breillat, João Pedro Rodrigues, Gaspar Noé, Virginie Despentes, and François Ozon. The use of the term "extreme" to describe a significant wave of recent features from countries throughout Asia is attributed to Hamish McAlpine, head of U.K.-based Tartan Entertainment. McAlpine reportedly came up with the term after watching two Japanese thrillers, *Audition* (Takashi Miike, Japan 1999) and *Battle Royale* (Kinji Fukasaku, Japan 2000). This use of a single, transnational category to accommodate such a wide variety of films with very little in

common is decidedly problematic, given that to group these diverse texts from different nations under one single heading perpetuates a prevalent and highly Orientalist worldview (as illustrated by Reed's comments above) that categorizes all of Asia or "the Orient" as somehow culturally homogeneous, significant only insofar as that it is different from — indeed, the binary opposite of — the U.S.

8. Raymond Bellour, "Symbolic Blockage," [1975] (trans. Mary Quaintance) in *The Analysis of Film*, ed. Constance Penley (Bloomington: Indiana University Press, 2000), 81.

9. Linda Williams, "Melodrama Revised," in *Refiguring American Film Genres: History and Theory*, ed. Nick Browne (Berkeley: University of California Press, 1998), 42.

10. Linda Williams, *Playing the Race Card: Melodramas of Black and White from Uncle Tom to O. J. Simpson* (Princeton: Princeton University Press, 2002), 50.

11. Williams, *Playing the Race Card*, 12.

12. Williams, *Playing the Race Card*, 28.

13. Williams, *Playing the Race Card*, 50.

14. Kyung Hyun Kim, *The Remasculinization of Korean Cinema* (Durham: Duke University Press, 2004), 28.

15. Kim, *The Remasculinization of Korean Cinema*, 9.

16. Kim, *The Remasculinization of Korean Cinema*, 10.

17. Kim (2004) discusses the crisis of masculinity in the post-IMF era using the 1999 feature, *Happy End* (Jeong Ji-woo). However, it is Cynthia Childs, in her essay, "Jung Ji-woo's *Happy End*: Modernity, Masculinity, and Murder," who most clearly maps out the relation of Jung's film to the post-IMF Americanization of South Korean culture.

18. Charles Armstrong, *The Koreas* (London: Routledge, 2007), 32.

19. Jeeyoung Shin characterizes the *segyehwa* strategy thus: "This economically oriented globalization was not simply designed to enhance the Korean economy's international competitiveness by encouraging Korean companies to operate on a global level. Regarding increasing demands for market liberalization, it was also meant to improve Korean firms' competitiveness with foreign corporations in the domestic market."

20. Kim, *The Remasculinization of Korean Cinema*, 271.

21. Seung-ho Joo, "U.S.-R.O.K. Relations: The Political Diplomatic Dimension," in *The United States and the Korean Peninsula in the Twenty-first Century*, ed. Tae-hwan Kwak and Seung-ho Joo (Burlington, VT: Ashgate, 2006), 53.

22. For other analyses of South Korea's views on American military occupation, see Bruce Cumings, *Korea's Place in the Sun* (New York: Norton, 2005) and Selig S. Harrison, *Korean Endgame: A Strategy for Reunification and U.S. Disengagement* (Princeton: Princeton University Press, 1998).

23. Paul Willemen, "Detouring through Korean Cinema," *Inter-Asia Cultural Studies* 3:2 (2002): 169.

24. Elayne Rapping, "Globalization," in *The Critical Dictionary of Film and Television Theory*, ed. Roberta Pearson and Philip Simpson (New York: Routledge, 2001), 200 (italics in original).
25. Armstrong, *The Koreas,* 4.
26. C. Fred Alford, *Think No Evil: Korean Values in the Age of Globalization* (Ithaca: Cornell University Press, 1999), 2.
27. Alford, *Think No Evil*, 145.
28. Roy Richard Grinker, *Korea and Its Futures: Unification and the Unfinished War* (New York: St. Martin's Press, 1998), 78.
29. American Psychiatric Association, *Diagnostic and Statistical Manual of Mental Disorders: DSM-IV-TR* (Washington, DC: American Psychiatric Association, 2000), 900.
30. Alford, *Think No Evil*, 80.
31. Nancy Abelman, *Echoes of the Past, Epics of Dissent: A South Korean Social Movement* (Berkeley: University of California Press, 1996), 37.
32. Grinker, *Korea and Its Futures*, 80.
33. Although some Korean critics have voiced skepticism regarding the use of *han*, especially by non-Koreans, in the present manner, the author feels that, given the formative role played by the melodramatic mode in both U.S. and South Korean cinema, and given the affinities that exist between conversion hysteria in the West and *han* in the East, that the comparative methodology used in this work is valid. It is not the assumption of the author or any of the authors whom he cites that *han* emerges exclusively from the experience of modernization or globalization, but rather that the concept of *han* can, like hysteria in the work of Nowell-Smith, provide a productive metaphor for representing and understanding the unconscious workings of South Korean media texts. Jongju Kim explores the possible connections between Korean conceptions of *han* and various Western psychoanalytical approaches in his "Psychoanalytic Approaches to Han and its Correlation with the Neo-Confucian four-seven thesis," while Aaron Han Joon Magnan-Park examines the important cultural roles played by the related concepts of *han, jeong*, and *hwabyeong* in his forthcoming study, "South Korea's Cinema of *Jeong* Consciousness."
34. Geoffrey Nowell-Smith, "Minnelli and Melodrama," in *Home Is Where the Heart Is*, ed. Christine Gledhill (London: British Film Institute, 1987), 73.
35. Christine Gledhill, "Dialogue on *Stella Dallas* and Feminist Film Theory," *Cinema Journal* 25:04 (Summer 1986), 45.
36. Although some of these works are viewed as "extreme" in Asia as well — for example, the films of Kim Ki-duk have never garnered the kind of popularity in South Korea that they have at international film festivals around the world — the term "extreme" is unquestionably Western in origin. The term was coined by the president of Great Britain's Tartan Entertainment to describe a collection of Asian films he was to eventually market as a kind

of new sub-genre in Europe and the U.S. Furthermore, although, as mentioned above, a moral ambiguity similar to the one that marks these works manifests itself in films by European directors, these films are, in general, not marginalized in the same way as the Korean films, nor are they used as a means by which to make broad identity-based judgments of individuals from the countries in question. In other words, neither the reception of these works as "extreme" nor the moral ambiguity that identifies these works as such is significant in and of itself. Rather, it is the reaction to moral ambiguity of these works, their subsequent characterization of them as "extreme" or dangerous, and the eventual misuse of these texts as the basis for leveling unfounded criticism that is at stake in this reading.

37. I borrow the phrase "passionate submission" from the work of Kim So-young, who uses it to describe events in films in which dualistic oppositions (the traditional versus the modern) are destroyed in the interest of finding "new ways of thinking about Korean cinema and Korean modernity — or, I would venture to say, cinema in Korean and modernity in Korea." Kim So-young, "Modernity in Suspense: The Logic of Fetishism in Korean Cinema," *Traces* I (2000): 301–17.

38. The film's original Korean title, *Dalkomhan Insaeng*, actually translates as "sweet life" (as does the title of Fellini's film). The reference to Fellini and notably to several other works clearly illustrates the film's debt to Hollywood, Europe, and Japan. Here I would like to point out that media related to both Kim's film and Park's *Oldboy* use references to Hollywood (and other) motion pictures in ways that point toward a project of contextualization, albeit in different ways.

The DVD release of Kim's *A Bittersweet Life* features chapters named after specific films. The titles of these chapters (and the content of the films to which they refer) sum up the material that each chapter contains. The films referenced on the DVD are: *La Dolce Vita* (Federico Fellini, Italy 1960); *Trop belle pour toi* (Bertrand Blier, France 1989); *True Romance* (Tony Scott, U.S.A. 1993) [Film written by Quentin Tarantino]; *Irréversible* (Gaspar Noé, France 1993); *Battles without Honor and Humanity* (*Jingi naki tatakai*, Kinji Fukasaku, Japan 1973); and *Way of the Gun* (Christopher McQuarrie, U.S.A. 2002). The titles both appear to comment (ironically in some cases) on the content of specific chapters, while at the same time unmistakably situate the work within a framework of influences from modern world cinema.

Likewise, all of the tracks on the original soundtrack for Park's film (with the exception of an excerpt from Vivaldi's *The Four Seasons*) bear the titles of feature films, most of them Hollywood pictures, and the majority of those, Hollywood classics from the studio era. The films referenced are as follows: *Look Who's Talking* (Amy Heckerling, U.S.A. 1989); *Somewhere in the Night* (Joseph Mankiewicz, U.S.A. 1946); *The Count of Monte Cristo* (adapted to the screen numerous times, from the silent era to the present); *Jailhouse Rock* (Richard Thorpe, U.S.A. 1957); *In a Lonely Place* (Nicholas Ray, U.S.A. 1950); *It's Alive!* (Larry Cohen, U.S.A. 1974); *The Searchers* (John Ford, U.S.A. 1956); *Look Back in Anger* (Tony Richardson, U.K. 1958); *Room at the Top* (Jack Clayton, U.K. 1959); *Cries and Whispers* (*Viskningar och rop*, Ingmar Bergman, Sweden 1972); *Out of Sight* (Steven Soderbergh, U.S.A. 1998); *For Whom the Bell Tolls* (Sam Wood, U.S.A. 1943); *Out of the Past* (Jacques Tourneur, U.S.A. 1947); *A bout de souffle* (Jean-Luc Godard, France 1960); *Dressed to Kill* (Brian DePalma, U.S.A. 1980); *Frantic★* (Roman Polanski, U.S.A. 1988); *L'ascenseur pour l'echafaud★* (Louis Malle, France 1958); *Cul de Sac* (Roman Polanski, France 1966); *Kiss Me Deadly* (Robert Aldrich, U.S.A. 1955); *Point Blank* (John Boorman, U.S.A. 1967); *Farewell, My Lovely★* (Dick Richards, U.S.A. 1975); *Murder, My Sweet★* (Edward Dmytrik, U.S.A. 1944); *The Big Sleep* (Howard Hawks, U.S.A. 1955); and *The Last Waltz* (Martin Scorsese, U.S.A. 1978).

★ = In both of these cases (i.e., *Frantic* and *Farewell, My Lovely*) the titles used on the DVD might refer to either of two distinct titles. I have included both here because they seem equally well suited to the themes of the film, although the latter adaptation of *Farewell, My Lovely*, and notably, the only one of the two films to be released under that title, matches the trajectory set forth in Park's film.

39. Jinhee Choi has noted other significant elements of this film that reflect its commentary on South Korea's tenuous position in a new global society, citing the presence of Russian arms dealers and Southeast Asian hitmen as signifiers of a different kind of "globalization" (perhaps "internationalization" might be a more appropriate term here) presently affecting Korea.

40. See Otto Rank (1914), *The Double: A Psychoanalytic Study*, trans. Harry Tucker, Jr. (London: Karnac-Maresfield, 1998).

41. I thank Bryn Scheurich for this observation.

Chapter 8   Magic, Medicine, Cannibalism: The China Demon in Hong Kong Horror

1. Stephen Teo, "Ghost, Cadavers, Demons and Other Hybrids," in *Hong Kong Cinema: The Extra Dimensions* (London: BFI Publishing, 1997) and Cheng Yu, "Under a Spell," in *Phantoms of the Hong Kong Cinema: The 13th Hong Kong International Film Festival* (Hong Kong: Urban Council, 1989).

2. Stephen Teo, "The Tongue," in *Phantoms of the Hong Kong Cinema: The 13th Hong Kong International Film Festival* (Hong Kong: Urban Council, 1989), 45.

3. Yu Mo Wan, "Hong Kong Horror Cinema," in *Phantoms of the Hong Kong Cinema: The 13th Hong Kong International Film Festival* (Hong Kong: Urban Council, 1989), 77.

4. Poshek Fu and David Desser, eds., *The Cinema of Hong Kong: History, Arts, Identity* (New York: Cambridge University Press, 2000); Esther Yau, ed., *At Full Speed: Hong Kong Cinema in a Borderless World* (Minneapolis: University of Minnesota Press, 2001); Yingchi Chu, *Hong Kong Cinema: Colonizer, Motherland and Self* (London and New York: RoutledgeCurzon, 2003). For Chinese sources, please see Zhang Meijun and Zhu Yaowei, eds., *Between Home and World: A Reader in Hong Kong Cinema* (Hong Kong: Oxford University Press, 2004).

5. Rey Chow, "Between Colonizers: Hong Kong's Postcolonial Self-Writing in the 1990's," in *Ethics after Idealism: Theory-Culture-Ethnicity-Reading* (Bloomington: Indiana University Press, 1998), 157.

6. Ackbar Abbas, "The Last Emporium: Verse and Cultural Space," *positions: east asia cultural critique* 1.1 (1993): 4.

7. Tony Williams, "Space, Place and Spectacle: The Crisis Cinema of John Woo," in *The Cinema of Hong Kong: History, Arts, Identity*, ed. Poshek Fu and David Desser (New York: Cambridge University press, 2000), 150.

8. Yau Ka Fei, "Cinema 3: Towards a 'Minor Hong Kong Cinema,'" *Cultural Studies* 15.3 (2001): 552.

9. Kung Ho-fung, "Preliminary Study of Northbound Colonialism: Reading Leung Fung Yee from the Gap-ism of Hong Kong," in *Cultural Imagination and Ideology*, ed. Stephen Chan (Hong Kong: Oxford University Press, 1995, Chinese), 200; Law Wing-sang, "Northbound Colonialism: A Politics of Post-PC Hong Kong," *positions: east asia cultural critique* 8.1 (2000): 201–33.

10. Wendy Gan, "The Representation of Mainland Chinese Woman in *Durian Durian*," in *Fruit Chan's Durian Durian* (Hong Kong: Hong Kong University Press, 2005), 47.

11. Cynthia Freeland, "Feminist Frameworks for Horror Films," in *Film Theory and Criticism*, ed. Leo Braudy and Marshall Cohen (Oxford: Oxford University Press, 2004), 745.

12. Darrell William Davis and Emilie Yueh-yu Yeh, "Pan-Asian Cinema: Finance, Marketing, Distribution," in *East Asian Screen Industries* (London: British Film Institute, 2008), 93–97.

13. Darrell William Davis and Emilie Yueh-yu Yeh, "Genre/Nation: Cultural Commerce and Signature Narratives," in *East Asian Screen Industries* (London: British Film Institute, 2008), 119–26.

14. For the current state of Applause Pictures, see Emilie Yueh-yu Yeh, "China and Pan-Asian Cinema: A Critical Appraisal," in *Re-Orienting Global Communication: Indian and Chinese Media Beyond Borders*, ed. Michael Curtin and Hemant Shah (Urbana-Champaign: University of Illinois Press, 2008), 238–66.

15. Barbara Creed, "Horror and the Monstrous-Feminine," in *Feminist Film Theory: A Reader*, ed. Sue Thornham (New York: New York University Press, 1999), 253.

16. Julia Kristeva, *Powers of Horror: An Essay on Abjection* (Oxford: Columbia University Press, 1982), 4.

17. Wimal Dissanayake, "The Class Imaginary in Fruit Chan's Films," *Jump Cut: A Review of Contemporary Media.* 49 (2007), http://www.ejumpcut. org/currentissue/Dumplings/text.html.

18. Freud Sigmund, "Three Essays on the Theory of Sexuality," in *The Standard Editions of the Complete Psychological Works of Sigmund Freud, Vol. XVII*, trans. James Strachey (London: Hogarth, 1964), 198.

19. Caleb Crain, "Lovers of Human Flesh: Homosexuality and Cannibalism in Melville's Novels," *American Literature* 66.1 (1994): 36.

20. Melanie Klein, "A Contribution to the Psychogenesis of Manic-Depressive States," in *The Selected Melanie Klein*, ed. Juliet Mitchell (New York: Free Press, 1987), 116.

21. Abbas, *positions*, 4.

22. Judith Jordan, "The Relational Self: A Model of Women's Development in Daughter and Mothering," in *Female Subjectivity Reanalysed*, ed. Jhanneke Van Mens-Verhulst and Karlein Schreurs (London: Routledge, 1993), 138.

23. Freeland, *Film Theory and Criticism*, 745.

Chapter 9 That Unobscure Object of Desire and Horror: On Some Uncanny Things in Recent Korean Horror Films

1. These are direct translations of the Korean titles. They were introduced outside Korea as *No Manners* (*Pumhaeng Zero*, Jo Geun-shik, 2002), *Public Enemy* (*Gonggongui Jeog*, Kang Woo-suk, 2002), *Sympathy for Mr. Vengeance* (*Boksuneun Naui Geot*, Park Chan-wook, 2002), *A Bittersweet Life* (*Dalkomhan Insaeng*, Kim Ji-woon, 2005), *The Scarlet Letter* (*Juhong Geulshi*, Byun Hyuk, 2004), *A Dirty Carnival* (*Biyeolhan Geori*, Yoo Ha, 2006), and *The Red Shoes* respectively.

2. Kim Yong-gyun, *The Red Shoes* (Showbox Entertainment, 2005).

3. Slavoj Žižek, *The Sublime Object of Ideology* (London and New York: Verso, 1989), 59.

4. For a comprehensive historical overview on monsters, see Beate Ochsner, "Monster: More Than a Word . . . From Portent to Anomaly, the Extraordinary Career of Monsters," *Monsters and Philosophy*, ed. Charles T. Wolfe (London: College Publications, 2005), 231–79.

5. In the past, there had been a number of Godzilla-like monsters for children before *The Host* (*Gwoemul*, Bong Joon-ho, 2006) and *Dragon Wars: D-War* (Shim Hyung-rae, 2007) followed the thread.

6. The typically harmless and noble prototype *teo-gwisin*, a spiritual master of a site, has translated itself into a number of recent horror stories, not without drastic transformation. Such films as *Unborn But Forgotten* (*Hayanbang*, Lim

Chang-jae, 2002), *Whispering Corridors III: Whispering Stairs* (*Yeogo Goedam 3: Yeowoo gyedan, Yun Jae-yeon,* 2003), *Dead Friend* (*Ryeong,* Kim Tae-kyeong, 2004), and *Red Eye* (Kim Dong-bin, 2005) feature specific places where trauma and death are relived. The sites barely render themselves as harmful threats; they host virgin ghosts to carry the actual effects upon the living.

7. Adding a hint of the coming-of-age film, flashbacks, the most important and popular device in these films, reveal the growing pains that everyone in and outside the screen should know about to understand the contents of the horror. The flashbacks, however, hardly represent the heroine's recollection necessarily; most often, they only belong to the invisible, anonymous, omniscient narrator. The obtrusive detective that propels the plot in *film noir* is replaced by a ghostly vision that penetrates private memories.

8. See Jacques Lacan, *The Seminar of Jacques Lacan Book I: Freud's Papers on Technique 1953–1954,* ed. Jacques-Alain Miller, trans. John Forrester (New York and London: W. W. Norton and Company, 1991).

9. See Lacan, *The Seminar of Jacques Lacan Book VII: The Ethics of Psychoanalysis, 1959–1960,* ed. Jacques-Alain Miller, trans. Dennis Porter (New York: Norton, 1992).

10. See Lacan, "The Signification of the Phallus," in *Écrits: A Selection,* trans. Alan Sheridan (New York and London: W. W. Norton and Company, 1977), 281–91.

11. Carol J. Clover, "Her Body, Himself: Gender in the Slasher Film," in *Horror, the Film Reader,* ed. Mark Jancovich (Abingdon and New York: Routledge, 2002), 77–89.

12. Harry M. Benshoff, "The Monster and the Homosexual," in *Horror: The Film Reader,* 91–104.

13. Žižek, "Hitchcockian Sinthoms," in *Everything You Always Wanted to Know about Lacan (But Were Afraid to Ask Hitchcock),* ed. Slavoj Žižek (London and New York: Verso, 1992), 125–28.

14. Ibid., 126.

15. Sigmund Freud, "The Uncanny," in *The Standard Edition of the Complete Works of Sigmund Freud, Volume 17,* ed. James Strachey et al. (London: The Hogart Press and the Institute of Psychoanalysis, 1953–74), 217–56.

16. See Nicholas Royle, *The Uncanny: An Introduction* (New York: Routledge, 2003).

17. Nakata Hideo, *Ring* (*Ringu,* Kadokawa Shoten Publishing Co. and Omega Project, 1998).

18. See Lacan, "The Purloined Letter," *Yale French Studies,* Volume 48 (New Haven: Yale University Press, 1972), 61–62.

19. Mladen Dolar, "Hitchcock's Objects," in *Everything You Always Wanted to Know about Lacan (But Were Afraid to Ask Hitchcock),* 31–46.

20. Žižek, "Alfred Hitchcock, or, The Form and Its Historical Mediation," in *Everything You Always Wanted to Know about Lacan (But Were Afraid to Ask*

Hitchcock), 6. It is perhaps useful to make a note of the irony, with which Žižek refuses to give this materially based, concrete object a fixed name whereas he readily categorizes the empty signifier with a determinately concrete name.

21. Ibid., 8.
22. Pam Cook, "Duplicity in *Mildred Pierce*," in *Women in Film Noir*, ed. E. Ann Kaplan (London: British Film Institute, 1998), 79.
23. Seo Hyun-suk, "To Catch a Whale: A Brief History of Lost Fathers, Idiots, and Gangsters in Korean Cinema," in *The Film Journal*, Issue 2 (2002), http://www.thefilmjournal.com.
24. Žižek, *The Sublime Object of Ideology*, 175.
25. Ibid., 187.

Chapter 10 "Tell the Kitchen That There's Too Much *Buchu* in the Dumpling": Reading Park Chan-wook's "Unknowable" *Oldboy*

1. *New York Times* and *LA Weekly*, both enormously important publications for any independent films opening in the U.S., printed harsh reviews of *Oldboy*.
2. Manohla Dargis, "The Violence (and the Seafood) Is More than Raw," *New York Times*, (March 25, 2005): B14.
3. *Oldboy* failed to reach the US$1 million gross mark, which is usually held as a benchmark of moderate success for limited release films. It eventually recorded $707,391, which is not a bad figure for a Korean film, but certainly well below the U.S. box office record ($2.38 million) set by a Korean film: *Spring, Summer, Fall, Winter and Spring*.
4. Kyung Hyun Kim, *The Remasculinization of Korean Cinema* (Durham, NC: Duke University Press, 2004).
5. Marsha Kinder, "Violence American Style: The Narrative Orchestration of Violent Attractions," *Violence and American Cinema*, edited by J. David Slocum (New York and London: Routledge, 2001), 67.
6. The Japanese *manga* version, first published in 1998, was written by Tsuchiya Garon and illustrated by Minegishi Nobuaki.
7. Both *Oldboy* and *Lady Vengeance* were bona fide blockbuster hit films while *Sympathy for Mr. Vengeance* was not as successful in the box office.
8. See particularly the chapter, "The Discovery of Landscape," in Karatani Kojin's *Origins of Modern Japanese Literature*, trans. Brett de Bary (Durham, NC: Duke University Press, 1994), 11–44.
9. In *Chilsu and Mansu* (Park Kwang-su, 1988), drunkard Mansu's bar brawl lands him at a police station where he is detained overnight for additional questioning. A small misdemeanor that should have only led to a small fine

escalates into a far more punitive action because Mansu, as it is revealed, has a father who is in jail as a long-term political prisoner. *The Day a Pig Fell into the Well* (Hong Sang-soo, 1996) also includes a scene in which its protagonist Hyo-seop is sentenced in court to a three-day detention for instigating a fight with a restaurant worker at a Korean barbeque spot.

10. Sigmund Freud, "The Uncanny," in *The Uncanny*, trans. David McClintock (London: Penguin Books, 2001), 152.

11. See particularly Chapters 3 and 4 in *The Remasculinization of Korean Cinema*: "'Is This How the War Is Remembered?': Violent Sex and the Korean War in *Silver Stallion, Spring in My Hometown*," and "*The Taebaek Mountains* and Post-trauma and Historical Remembrance in *A Single Spark* and *A Petal*."

12. Gilles Deleuze, *Nietzsche and Philosophy*, trans. Hugh Tomlinson (New York: Columbia University Press, 1962), 119.

13. Ibid., 122.

14. Jacques Derrida, "Plato's Pharmacy," *Dissemination*, trans. Barbara Johnson (Chicago: University of Chicago Press, 1981), 61–84.

15. René Girard, *Violence and the Sacred*, trans. Patrick Gregory (Baltimore: Johns Hopkins University Press 1977), 8.

16. On "Kafkan uncanny," see Weinstein (2005), 101–6.

17. Earl Jackson Jr., "Borrowing Trouble: Interasian Adaptations and the Dislocutive Fantasy." Paper presented at "Film Aesthetics in East Asian Countries and Transculture" panel, Asia/Cinema/Network: Industry, Culture and Technology Conference, Pusan International Film Festival (Pusan, Korea, October 12, 2005).

18. Young-Kyun Kim, "Jajangmyeon and Junggukjip," *Korea Journal* 45.2 (Summer 2005): 60–88.

19. In *Sympathy for Mr. Vengeance*, protagonist Ryu's girlfriend, Cha Yeong-mi (played by Bae Doona), orders a bowl of *jajangmyeon*. After placing her order over the phone, she mistakenly thinks that her intruder, Park Dong-jin, is a Chinese delivery man. Instead of getting her *jajangmyeon*, she receives electric torture.

20. Park Chan-wook began experimenting with voiceover narration in *Oldboy*. In *Lady Vengeance*, he employed a 60-year-old female narrator with long experiences in radio and television narration, whose voice nostalgically reminded the viewers of radio dramas or popular television documentary programs such as *Ingan sidae* (*Human Life*) from the 1970s and the 1980s.

21. Michael Chion, *The Voice in Cinema*, trans. Claudia Gorbman (New York: Columbia University Press, 1999), 1.

22. Gilles Deleuze, *Cinema 2: the Time-Image*, trans. Hugh Tomlinson and Robert Galeta, (Minneapolis: University of Minnesota Press, 1989), 249.

23. Ibid., 249.

24. Entry on "Andy Warhol," *Wikipedia.org* (February 26, 2008).

Chapter 11 A Politics of Excess: Violence and Violation in Miike Takashi's *Audition*

1. Shinya Tsukamoto as quoted in Tom Mes and Jasper Sharp, *The Midnight Eye Guide to New Japanese Film* (Berkeley, CA: Stone Bridge Press, 2005), 147.
2. Hideo Nakata in Mes, Tom and Jasper Sharp. *The Midnight Eye Guide to New Japanese Film*, xi.
3. Kevin Heffernan, "Inner Senses and the Changing Face of Hong Kong Horror Cinema," Conference Proceedings. *National, Transnational, and International: Chinese Cinema and Asian Cinema in the Context of Globalization. Centennial Celebration of Chinese Cinema.* Beijing/Shanghai, June 6–10, 2005, 314.
4. Ibid.
5. Ibid.
6. Michael Robinson, "Contemporary Cultural Production in South Korea: Vanishing Meta-Narratives of Nation," *New Korean Cinema*, ed. Chi-Yun Shi and Julian Stringer (Edinburgh: Edinburgh University Press, 2005), 15.
7. Ibid.
8. Darcy Paquet, "The Korean Film Industry: 1992 to the Present," *New Korean Cinema*, 37.
9. Ibid.
10. Kyu Hyun Kim. "Horror as Critique in *Tell Me Something* and *Sympathy for Mr. Vengeance*," *New Korean Cinema*, 107.
11. Tom Mes, "Odishon (Audition)" *The Cinema of Japan and Korea* (London: Wallflower Press, 2004), 202.
12. Some of Mes' publications on *Audition* can be found in *Agitator, The Cinema of Takashi Miike, The Midnight Eye Guide to New Japanese Film*, and on the online journal of Japanese cinema *Midnight Eye*.
13. Barbara Creed, in her work *The Monstrous Feminine: Film, Feminism, Psychoanalysis* uses the term "monstrous feminine," to describe such projected instances of the *anima*.
14. Tom Mes, *Agitator: The Cinema of Takashi Miike* (London: Fab Press, 2003), 96.
15. Gregory Barrett, *Archetypes in Japanese Film: The Sociopolitical and Religious Significance of the Principal Heroes and Heroines* (London and Toronto: Associated University Press, 1989), 104.
16. Ibid.
17. C. G. Jung, *Selected Writings*, ed. Anthony Storr (London: Fontana Paperbacks, 1983) 122.

Bibliography

Abbas, Ackbar. "The Last Emporium: Verse and Cultural Space." *Positions: East Asia Cultural Critique* 1.1 (1993): 1–23.

Abelmann, Nancy. *Echoes of the Past, Epics of Dissent: A South Korean Social Movement*. Berkeley: University of California Press, 1996.

Ahmad, Aijaz. *In Theory: Classes, Nations, Literatures*. London and New York: Verso, 1992.

Akira, Asada. "J kaiki no yukue" [The future of the return to J]. *Voice*, March 2003. http://www.kojinkaratani.com/criticalspace/old/special/asada/voice0003.html (accessed May 3, 2008).

Alford, C. Fred. *Think No Evil: Korean Values in the Age of Globalization*. Ithaca, NY: Cornell University Press, 1999.

Allison, Anne. *Millennial Monsters: Japanese Toys and the Global Imagination*. Berkeley: University of California Press, 2006.

Altman, Rick. *Film/Genre*. London: BFI Publishing, 1999.

American Psychiatric Association. *Diagnostic and Statistical Manual of Mental Disorders DSM-IV-TR*. 4th edition. Washington, DC: American Psychiatric Association, 2000.

Armstrong, Charles K. *The Koreas*. London: Routledge, 2007.

Atkinson, Michael. "Die Hard with a Vengeance: Best Served Cold, Park Chanwook's Brutal Revenge Feast Comes with a Side of Live Octopus." *Village Voice* (March 15, 2005). http://www.villagevoice.com/film/0512,atkinson1,62315,20.html (accessed August 10, 2007).

Aufderheide, Patricia. "Made in Hong Kong: Translation and Transmutation." In *Play It Again, Sam: Retakes on Remakes*, edited by Andrew Horton and Stuart Y. McDougal. Berkeley: University of California Press, 1998. 191–99.

Barrett Gregory. *Archetypes in Japanese Film: The Sociopolitical and Religious Significance of the Principal Heroes and Heroines*. London and Toronto: Associated University Press, 1989.

Bazin, André. *What Is Cinema?* Vol. 1, translated by Hugh Gray. Berkeley: University of California Press, 1967.

Bellour, Raymond. "Symbolic Blockage (on *North by Northwest*)." In *The Analysis of Film*, edited by Constance Penley, translated by Mary Quaintance. Bloomington: Indiana University Press, 1975. 77–192.

———. "Un jour, la castration." *L'arc* 71 (1978): 9–23.

Benjamin, Walter. "The Work of Art in the Age of Mechanical Reproduction." In *Illumination*, edited by Hannah Arendt, translated by Harry Zohn. New York: Harcourt, Brace and World, 1968. 217–51.

Benshoff, Harry M. *Monsters in the Closet: Homosexuality and the Horror Film*. Manchester: Manchester University Press, 1997.

———. "The Monster and the Homosexual." In *Horror: The Film Reader*, edited by Mark Jancovich. London and New York: Routledge, 2002. 91–104.

Berenstein, Rhona J. *Attack of the Leading Ladies: Gender, Sexuality and Spectatorship in Classic Horror Cinema*. New York: Columbia University Press, 1996.

Bordwell, David. *Figures Traced in Light: On Cinematic Staging*. Berkeley: University of California Press, 2005.

———. *Planet Hong Kong: Popular Cinema and the Art of Entertainment*. Cambridge, MA: Harvard University Press, 2000.

Bradshaw, Peter. "*Oldboy* (Review)." *Guardian Unlimited* (October 15, 2004). http://film.guardian.co.uk/News_Story/Critic_Review/Guardian_Film_of_the_week/0,,1327302,00.html (accessed August 10, 2007).

Carroll, Noël. "Film, Emotion, and Genre." In *Passionate Views: Film, Cognition and Emotion*, edited by Carl Plantinga and Greg M. Smith. Baltimore: Johns Hopkins University Press, 1999. 21–47.

———. *The Philosophy of Horror or Paradoxes of the Heart*. New York: Routledge, 1990.

Childs, Cynthia. "Jung Ji-woo's *Happy End*: Modernity, Masculinity, and Murder." *Asian Cinema* 16.2 (Fall/Winter 2005): 210–20.

Chion, Michael. *The Voice in Cinema*. Translated by Claudia Gorbman. New York: Columbia University Press, 1999.

Chocano, Carina. "*Oldboy*: From Korea Comes a Dream of Deadly Drama." *The Los Angeles Times* (March 25, 2005). http://www.calendarlive.com/movies/chocano/cl-et-oldboy25mar25,0,3031987.story (accessed August 10, 2007).

Choi, Jinhee. "Sentimentality and the Cinema of the Extreme." *Jump Cut* 50 (Spring 2008). http://www.ejumpcut.org/currentissue/sentiment-Extreme/index.html (accessed June 19, 2008).

Chow, Ray. "Between Colonizers: Hong Kong's Postcolonial Self-Writing in the 1990's." In *Ethics After Idealism: Theory-Culture-Ethnicity-Reading*. Bloomington: Indiana University Press, 1998. 149–67.

Chua, Beng Huat. "Conceptualizing an East Asian Popular Culture." *Inter-Asia Cultural Studies* 5.2 (2004): 200–21.

Chute, David. "East Goes West." *Variety* (special supplement on Cannes, May 10, 2004): 7.

Clover, Carol J. "Her Body, Himself: Gender in the Slasher Film." *Representations* 20 (1987): 187–228. Excerpts reprinted in *Horror: The Film Reader*, edited by Mark Jancovich. London and New York: Routledge, 2002. 77–89.

———. *Men, Women, and Chain Saws: Gender in the Modern Horror Film*. Princeton: Princeton University Press, 1992.

Cook, Pam. "Duplicity in *Mildred Pierce*." In *Women in Film Noir*, edited by E. Ann Kaplan. London: British Film Institute, 1998. 68–82.

Corrigan, Timothy. *A Cinema without Walls: Movies and Culture after Vietnam*. New Brunswick, NJ: Rutgers University Press, 1991.

Coyle, Jake. "Cho Video Linked to Korean Movie." *Washington Times Daily* (April 20, 2007): A16.

Crain, Caleb. "Lovers of Human Flesh: Homosexuality and Cannibalism in Melville's Novels." *American Literature* 66.1 (1994): 25–33.

Creed, Barbara. *The Monstrous-Feminine: Film, Feminism, Psychoanalysis*. London: Routledge, 1993.

Cumings, Bruce. *Korea's Place in the Sun*. New York: Norton, 2005.

Dargis, Manohla. "The Violence (and the Seafood) Is More Than Raw." *New York Times* March 25, 2005: 14.

Davis, Darrell William, and Emilie Yueh-yu Yeh. "Pan-Asian Cinema: Finance, Marketing, Distribution." In *East Asian Screen Industries*. London: British Film Institute, 2008. 85–111.

De Lauretis, Teresa. *Alice Doesn't: Feminism, Semiotics, Cinema*. Bloomington: Indiana University Press, 1984.

Deleuze, Gilles. *Cinema 2: The Time-Image*. Translated by Hugh Tomlinson and Robert Galeta. Minneapolis: University of Minnesota Press, 1989.

———. *Nietzsche and Philosophy*. Translated by Hugh Tomlinson. New York: Columbia University Press, 1962.

Derrida, Jacques. "Plato's Pharmacy." In *Dissemination*, translated by Barbara Johnson. Chicago: University of Chicago Press, 1981. 61–84.

Desser, David. "Hong Kong Film and New Cinephilia." In *Hong Kong Connections: Transnational Imagination in Action Cinema*, edited by Meaghan Morris, Siu Leung Li, and Stephen Chan Ching-kiu. Hong Kong: Hong Kong University Press, 2005. 205–222.

———. "The Kung Fu Craze: Hong Kong Cinema's First American Reception." In *The Cinema of Hong Kong: History, Arts, Identity*, edited by Poshek Fu and David Desser. Cambridge: Cambridge University Press, 2000. 19–43.

Dissanayake, Wimal. "The Class Imaginary in Fruit Chan's Films." *Jump Cut: A Review of Contemporary Media* 49 (2007). http://www.ejumpcut.org/archive/jc49.2007/FruitChan-class/index.html (accessed September 17, 2008).

Doane, Mary Ann. *The Desire to Desire: The Woman's Film of the 1940s*. Bloomington: Indiana University Press, 1987.

Dolar, Mladen. "Hitchcock's Objects." In *Everything You Always Wanted to Know about Lacan (But Were Afraid to Ask Hitchcock)*, edited by Slavoj Žižek. London and New York: Verso, 1992. 31–46.

Falcon, Richard. "*The Isle* (Review)." *Sight and Sound* 11.8 (August 2001): 48–49.

Featherstone, Mike. *Undoing Culture: Globalization, Postmodernism and Identity*. London: Sage, 1995.

Freeland, Cynthia. "Feminist Frameworks for Horror Films." In *Film Theory and Criticism*, edited by Braudy Leo and Cohen Marshall. Oxford: Oxford University Press, 2004. 742–63.

Freud, Sigmund. "The Uncanny." In *The Standard Edition of the Complete Psychological Works of Sigmund Freud*. Vol. 17, translated and edited by James Strachey. London: Hogarth Press, 1974. 217–56. (Reprinted in *The Uncanny*. Translated by David Mclintock. London: Penguin Books, 2001.)

Fuhrmann, Arnika. "The Ghost-Seer: Chinese-Thai History, Female Agency, and the Transnational Uncanny in Danny and Oxide Pang's *The Eye* (2002)." Paper presented at the annual conference of the Canadian Asian Studies Association, November 9–12, 2006.

Fujii, Jinshi. "Bunka suru eiga: Showa 10 nendai ni okeru bunka eiga no bunseki" [On bunka eiga: Analyzing the discourses of "culture film" in 1935–1945]. *Eizogaku* [ICONICS: Japanese Journal of Image Arts and Sciences] 66 (2001): 5–22.

Girard, René. *Violence and the Sacred*. Translated by Patrick Gregory. Baltimore: Johns Hopkins University Press. 1977.

Gledhill, Christine. "Dialogue on *Stella Dallas* and Feminist Film Theory." *Cinema Journal* 25.4 (Summer 1986): 44–48.

Govorun, Oleysa, Kathleen Fuegen, and B. Keith Payne. "Stereotypes Focus Defensive Projection." *Personality and Social Psychology Bulletin* 32.6 (June 2006): 781–93.

Grinker, Roy Richard. *Korea and Its Futures: Unification and the Unfinished War*. New York: St. Martin's Press, 1998.

Grossman, Andrew, and Jooran Lee. "*Memento Mori* and Other Ghostly Sexualities." In *New Korean Cinema*, edited by Chi-Yun Shin and Julian Stringer. Edinburgh: Edinburgh University Press, 2005. 180–92.

Gunning, Tom. "Heard over the Phone: *The Lonely Villa* and the de Lorde Tradition of the Terrors of Technology." *Screen* 32.2 (Summer 1991): 184–96.

Hara, Masato. *Eiga purodyusa ga kataru hitto no tetsugaku* [Philosophy for making a hit by a film producer]. Tokyo: Nikkeibipisha, 2004.

Harrison, Selig S. *Korean Endgame: A Strategy for Reunification and U. S. Disengagement*. Princeton: Princeton University Press, 2004.

Harvey, Sophia. "Fractured Visions: Locating the Pan-Asian Gaze in *The Eye*." Paper presented at the annual meeting of the Society for Cinema and Media Studies, March 2–5, 2006.

Hasumi, Shigehiko, and Kurosawa Kiyoshi. "Nijuisseiki wa Kurosawa o minakereba wakaranai" [Without watching Kurosawa, you will never understand the 21st century]. *Bungakkai* (October 2006): 106–32.

Hawkins, Joan. *Cutting Edge: Art-Horror and the Horrific Avant-garde.* Minneapolis: University of Minnesota Press, 2000.

Heffernan, Kevin. "Inner Senses and the Changing Face of Hong Kong Horror Cinema." Conference Proceedings. *National, Transnational, and International: Chinese Cinema and Asian Cinema in the Context of Globalization. Centennial Celebration of Chinese Cinema.* Beijing/Shanghai, June 6–10, 2005.

Hendrix, Grady. "Vengeance Is Theirs." *Sight and Sound* 16.2 (February 2006): 18–21.

Hills, Matt. "Ringing the Changes: Cult Distinctions and Cultural Differences in US Fans' Readings of Japanese Horror Cinema." In *Japanese Horror Cinema*, edited by Jay McRoy. Edinburgh: Edinburgh University Press, 2005. 161–74.

Hutchings, Peter. *The Horror Film.* Essex: Pearson Education Limited, 2004.

Itoya, Hisao. "*Onibaba'a* seisaku no kiroku: Dokuritsu puro, sono genjitsu to daikigyo to no kankei" [The records of *Onibaba'a* film production: Independent production, its situation and relation with major studios]. *Kinema Junpo* 387 (March 1965): 23–25.

Jackson, Earl, Jr. "Borrowing Trouble: Interasian Adaptations and the Dislocutive Fantasy." Paper presented at the "Film Aesthetics in East Asian Countries and Transculture" panel, *Asia/Cinema/Network: Industry, Culture and Technology* Conference, Pusan International Film Festival Korea, October 12, 2005.

Jameson, Frederic. "Third World Literature in the Era of Multinational Capitalism." *Social Text* no. 15 (Autumn, 1986): 65–88.

Jancovich, Mark, ed. *Horror, The Film Reader.* London and New York: Routledge, 2002.

Jentsch, Ernst. "On the Psychology of the Uncanny," translated by Roy Sellars. *Angelaki* 2.1 (1995): 7–16.

Joo, Seung-ho. "U. S.-ROK Relations: The Political-Diplomatic Dimension." In *The United States and the Korean Peninsula in the Twenty-first Century*, edited by Tae-hwan Kwak and Seung-ho Joo. Burlington, VT: Ashgate, 2006. 39–60.

Jung, C. G. *Aion. Collected Works.* Vol. 9, Part 2, translated by R. F. C. Hull. London: Routledge, 1969.

———. *Selected Writings*, edited by Anthony Storr. London: Fontana Paperbacks, 1983.

Kapur, Jyotsna. "The Return of History as Horror: *Onibaba* and the Atomic Bomb." In *Horror International*, edited by Steven Jay Schneider and Tony Williams. Detroit: Wayne State University Press, 2005. 83–97.

Kelleher, Michael D. *Flash Point: The American Mass Murderer.* New York: Praeger, 1997.

Kim, Jongju. "Psychoanalytic Approaches to Han and Its Correlation with the Neo-Confucian Four-seven Thesis." (Undated, unpublished manuscript)

Kim, Kyu Hyun. "Horror as Critique in *Tell Me Something* and *Sympathy for Mr. Vengeance.*" In *New Korean Cinema*, edited by Chi-Yun Shi and Julian Stringer. 106–16.

———. *The Remasculinization of Korean Cinema*. Durham, NC: Duke University Press, 2004.

Kim, So-young. "Modernity in Suspense: The Logic of Fetishism in Korean Cinema." *Traces* I (2001): 301–17.

Kim, Young-Kyun, "Jajangmyeon and Junggukjip." *Korea Journal* 45.2 (Summer 2005): 60–88.

Kinder, Marsha. "Violence American Style: The Narrative Orchestration of Violent Attractions." In *Violence and American Cinema*, edited by J. David Slocum. New York and London: Routledge, 2001. 63–102.

King, Geoff. *American Independent Cinema*. Bloomington and Indianapolis: Indiana University Press, 2005.

Kinoshita, Chika. "Sen'yusha tatch no kukan" [The space of appropriators]. *Yuriika* 35.10 (Special Issue on Kurosawa Kiyoshi, July 2003): 188–99.

Klein, Melanie. "A Contribution to the Psychogenesis of Manic-Depressive States." In *The Selected Melanie Klein*, edited by Juliet Mitchell. New York: Free Press, 1987. 116–45.

Klinger, Barbara. *Beyond the Multiplex: Cinema, New Technologies, and the Home.* Berkeley: University of California Press, 2006.

Knee, Adam. "Thailand in the Hong Kong Cinematic Imagination." In *Hong Kong Film, Hollywood and the New Global Cinema*, edited by Gina Marchetti and Tan See Kam. London and New York: Routledge, 2007. 77–90.

———. "The Transnational Whisperings of Contemporary Asian Horror." *Journal of Communication Arts* (Thailand) 25.4 (2007).

Kojin, Karatani. *Origins of Modern Japanese Literature*, translated and edited by Brett de Bary. Durham, NC: Duke University Press, 1994.

Konaka, Chiaki. *Hora eiga no miryoku: fandamentaru hora sengen* [The fascination of horror films: A manifesto of fundamental horror]. Paperback ed. Tokyo: Iwanami Shoten, 2003.

Kristeva, Julia. *Power of Horror: An Essay of Abjection*. Translated by Leon S. Roudiez. New York: Colombia University Press, 1982.

Kuroi, Kazuo, and Hara Masato. "Sokatsuteki taidan: Soredemo anata wa purodyusa ni naruno ka" [Summarizing interview: Do you still want to become a producer?]. In *Eiga prodyusa no kiso chishiki: Eiga bijinesu no iriguchi kara deguchi made* [A basic guide for the producer: From entrance to exit of the movie business]. Tokyo: Kinema Junposha, 2005. 178–88.

Kurosawa, Kiyoshi. *Kurosawa Kiyoshi no eigajutsu* [Kurosawa Kiyoshi's film art]. Tokyo: Shinchosha, 2006.

———. "*Loft* Kurosawa Kiyoshi kantoku intabyu" [An interview with Kurosawa Kiyoshi, the director of *Loft*]. *Kansai dotto komu*. http://www.kansai.com/cinema/interview/060907_interview4.html (accessed May 3, 2008).

Kurosawa, Kiyoshi, and Shinozaki Makoto. *Kurosawa Kiyoshi no kyofu no eigashi* [Kurosawa Kiyoshi's film history of terror]. Tokyo: Seidosha, 2003.

Lacan, Jacques. "The Purloined Letter." *Yale French Studies* Volume 48 (1972): 61–62.

———. *The Seminar of Jacques Lacan Book I: Freud's Papers on Technique, 1953–1954*, edited by Jacques-Alain Miller, translated by John Forrester. New York and London: W. W. Norton and Company, 1991.

———. *The Seminar of Jacques Lacan Book VII: The Ethics of Psychoanalysis, 1959–1960*, edited by Jacques-Alain Miller, translated by Dennis Porter. New York: Norton, 1992.

———. "The Signification of the Phallus." In *Écrits: A Selection*, translated by Alan Sheridan. New York and London: W. W. Norton and Company, 1977. 281–91.

LaMarre, Thomas. "*Otaku* Movement." In *Japan after Japan: Social and Cultural Life from the Recessionary 1990s to the Present*, edited by Tomiko Yoda and Harry Harootunian. Durham: Duke University Press, 2006. 358–94.

Laplanche, Jean, and J. B. Pontalis. *The Language of Psycho-Analysis*, translated by Donald Nicholson-Smith. New York: Norton, 1973.

Lee, Bong-Ou. *Nihon eiga wa saiko dekiru* [Japanese cinema can revive]. Tokyo: Weitsu, 2003.

Lim, Bliss Cua. "Generic Ghosts: Remaking the New 'Asian Horror Film.' " In *Hong Kong Film*, edited by Gina Marchetti and Tan See Kam. 109–25.

Lippit, Akira Mizuta. *Atomic Light (Shadow Optics)*. Minneapolis: University of Minnesota Press, 2005.

Lo, Kwai-Cheung. *Chinese Face/Off: The Transnational Popular Culture of Hong Kong*. Urbana and Chicago: University of Illinois Press, 2006.

Lowenstein, Adam. *Shocking Representation: Historical Trauma, National Cinema, and the Modern Horror Film*. New York: Columbia University Press, 2005.

Magnan-Park, Aaron. "*Han* (Everlasting Woe) in the Land of *Daehanminguk* (The Republic of Korea): A Critique of Korean Cinema and National Essence." (Unpublished manuscript)

Marchetti, Gina, and Tan See Kam, ed. *Hong Kong Film: Hollywood and the New Global Cinema: No Film Is an Island*. London: Routledge, 2007.

Marks, Laura U. *Touch: Sensuous Theory and Multisensory Media*. Minneapolis: University of Minnesota Press, 2002.

Martin, Fran. "The China Simulacrum: Genre, Feminism, and Pan-Chinese Cultural Politics in *Crouching Tiger, Hidden Dragon*." In *Island on the Edge: Taiwan New Cinema and After*, edited by Chris Berry and Feii Lu. Hong Kong: Hong Kong University Press, 2005. 149–59.

Mes, Tom. *Agitator: The Cinema of Takashi Miike*. London: Fab Press, 2003.

———. "Odishon (Audition)." *The Cinema of Japan and Korea*. London: Wallflower Press, 2004. 199–204.

Mes, Tom, and Jasper Sharp. *The Midnight Eye Guide to New Japanese Film*. Berkeley: Stone Bridge Press, 2005.

Miller, Barbara L. *Postmodernism: Artistic Ploy or Cultural Response?* PhD dissertation, University of Rochester, 1993.

Miller, Toby, Nitin Govil, John McMurria, Richard Maxwell, and Ting Wang. *Global Hollywood 2.* London: BFI Publishing, 2005.

Millet, Raphaël. *Singapore Cinema.* Singapore: Editions Didier Millet, 2006.

Morris, Gary. "Gore Galore: Takashi Miike's *Audition*." *Bright Light Film Journal* 34 (2001). http://www.brightlightsfilm.com/34/audition.html/ (accessed February 10, 2008).

Mulder, Niels. *Inside Thai Society: Interpretations of Everyday Life.* 5th ed. Amsterdam: The Pepin Press, 1996.

Najita, Tetsuo, and H. D. Harootunian. "Japan's Revolt against the West." In *Modern Japanese Thought*, edited by Bob Tadashi Wakabayashi. New York: Cambridge University Press, 1998. 207–72.

Naremore, James. "American Film Noir: The History of an Idea." *Film Quarterly* 49.2 (1995–6): 12–27.

Needham, Gary. "Japanese Cinema and Orientalism." In *Asian Cinemas: A Reader and Guide*, edited by Dimitris Eleftheriotis and Gary Needham. Edinburgh: Edinburgh University Press, 2006. 8–16.

Newman, Katherine S., Cybelle Fox, David J. Harding, Jal Mehta, and Wendy Roth. *Rampage: The Social Roots of School Shootings.* New York: Basic Books, 2004.

Noi, Sawaragi. "Eiga de aru dake de jubun kowai" [Being a film is scary enough]. *Bungakuka* [Literary World] (October 2006): 160–61.

Nowell-Smith, Geoffrey. "Minnelli and Melodrama." In *Home Is Where the Heart Is: Studies in the Melodrama and the Women's Film*, edited by Christine Gledhill. London: British Film Institute (1977) 1987. 70–74.

Ong, Aihwa. *Flexible Citizenship: The Cultural Logic of Transnationality.* Durham: Duke University Press, 1999.

Pao, Jin Long. "The Pan-Asian Co-Production Sphere: Interview with Director Peter Chan." *Harvard Asia Quarterly* VI, no. 3 (Summer 2002). http://www.asiaquarterly.com/content/view/123/5/ (accessed February 14, 2007).

Paquet, Darcy. "The Korean Film Industry: 1992 to the Present." In *New Korean Cinema*, edited by Chi-Yun Shi and Julian Stringer. 32–50.

Pasuk, Phongpaichit, and Chris Baker. *Thailand: Economy and Politics.* 2nd ed. Oxford: Oxford University Press, 2002.

Pilkington, Mark. *The Tartan Guide to Asia Extreme.* London: Startlux, 2004.

Rank, Otto. *The Double: A Psychoanalytic Study* (1914), translated by Harry Tucker, Jr. London: Karnac-Maresfield, 1998.

Rapping, Elayne. "Globalization." In *The Critical Dictionary of Film and Television Theory*, edited by Roberta Pearson and Philip Simpson. New York: Routledge, 2001. 200–4.

Rayns, Tony. "Review of *The Eye*." *Sight and Sound* 12.11 (November 2002): 43–44.

————. "Sexual Terrorism: The Strange Case of Kim Ki-duk." *Film Comment* 40.6 (November 2004): 50–52.

Reed, Rex. "Bobby Short, King of Pop." *New York Observer* (March 28, 2005): 20.

Rigg, Jonathan. "Exclusion and Embeddedness: The Chinese in Thailand and Vietnam." In *The Chinese Diaspora: Space, Place, Mobility, and Identity*, edited by Laurence J. C. Ma and Carolyn Cartier. Lanham, MD: Rowman and Littlefield, 2003. 97–115.

Robinson, Michael. "Contemporary Cultural Production in South Korea: Vanishing Meta-Narratives of Nation." In *New Korean Cinema*, edited by Chi-Yun Shin and Julian Stringer. 15–31.

Said, Edward. *Orientalism*. New York: Vintage, 1979.

Sawaragi, Noi. "Eiga de aru dake de jubun kowai." *Bungakukai* (October 2006): 160–61.

Schermann, Susanne. *Naruse Mikio: Nichijo no kirameki* [Mikio Naruse: The glitter of everyday life]. Tokyo: Kinema Junposha, 1997.

Schneider, Steven Jay, and Tony Williams. "Introduction." In *Horror International*, edited by Steven Jay Schneider and Tony Williams. Detroit: Wayne State University Press, 2005. 1–12.

Sconce, Jeffrey. "'Trashing' the Academy: Taste, Excess, and an Emerging Politics of Cinematic Style." *Screen* 36.4 (1995): 371–93.

Seo, Hyun-suk, "To Catch a Whale: A Brief History of Lost Fathers, Idiots, and Gangsters in Korean Cinema," *Film Journal* Issue 2 (2002). http://www.thefilmjournal.com (accessed February 5, 2009).

Shin, Chi-Yun, and Julian Stringer, ed. *New Korean Cinema*. Edinburgh: Edinburgh University Press, 2005.

Shin, Jeeyoung. "Globalization and New Korean Cinema." In *New Korean Cinema*, edited by Chi-Yun Shin and Julian Stringer. 51–62.

Shindo, Kaneto, Imai Tadashi, and Daikoku Toyoji. "Imai Tadashi, Shindo Kaneto shinshun taidan: omo ni eiga sakka no shutaisei wo megutte" [The new year interview, Imai Tadashi and Shindo Kaneto: About filmmaker's subjectivity]. *Kinema Junpo* 383 (January 1965): 56.

Simons, Jan. "New Media as Old Media: Cinema." In *The New Media Book*, edited by Dan Harries. London: The British Film Institute, 2002. 231–41.

Spadoni, Robert. *Uncanny Bodies: The Coming of Sound Film and the Origins of the Horror Genre*. Berkeley: University of California Press, 2007.

Stringer, Julian. "Introduction" In *New Korean Cinema*, edited by Chi-Yun Shin and Julian Stringer. 1–12.

————. "Putting Korean Cinema in Its Place: Genre Classifications and the Contexts of Reception." In *New Korean Cinema*, edited by Chi-Yun Shin and Julian Stringer. 95–105.

Suedfeld, Peter. "Reverberations of the Holocaust Fifty Years Later: Psychology's Contributions to Understanding Persecution and Genocide." *Canadian Psychology/Psychologie Canadienne* 41.1 (February 2000): 1–9.

Sugaya, Minoru, and Nakamura Kiyoshi, ed. *Eizo kontentsu sangyo-ron* [Visual content industry studies]. Tokyo: Maruzen, 2002.

Swyngedouw, Erik. "Neither Global nor Local: 'Globalization' and the Politics of Scale." In *Spaces of Globalization: Reasserting the Power of the Local,* edited by Kevin R. Cox. New York: The Guilford Press, 1997. 137–66.

Takahashi, Hiroshi. *Eiga no ma.* [The demon of the cinema]. Tokyo: Seidosha, 2004.

Tanaka Jun'ichiro. *Nihon eiga hattatsushi I, katsudo shashin jidai* [The history of Japanese film development I, the age of motion pictures]. Tokyo: Chuo Koronsha, 1975.

Teo, Stephen. "The Tongue." In *Phantoms of the Hong Kong Cinema: The 13th Hong Kong International Film Festival.* Hong Kong: Urban Council, 1989. 41–45.

Thompson, Kristin. *Storytelling in the New Hollywood: Understanding Classical Narrative Technique.* Cambridge: Harvard University Press, 1999.

Todorov, Tzvetan. *The Fantastic: A Structural Approach to a Literary Genre,* translated by Richard Howard. Ithaca, NY: Cornell University Press, 1975.

Totaro, Donato. "Sono Otoko, Kyobo ni Tsuki. Violent Cop." *In the Cinema of Japan and Korea,* edited by Justin Bowyer. London: Wallflower Press, 2004. 129–36.

Tsutsui, William. *Godzilla on My Mind.* New York: Palgrave Macmillan, 2004.

Wada-Marciano, Mitsuyo. "J-Horror: New Media's Impact on Contemporary Japanese Horror Cinema." *Canadian Journal of Film Studies* 16.2 (Fall/Automne 2007): 23–48.

Wang, Shujen. "Recontextualizing Copyright: Piracy, Hollywood, the State, and Globalization." *Cinema Journal* 43.1 (2003): 25–43.

Wasko, Janet. *Hollywood in the Information Age: Beyond the Silver Screen.* Austin: University of Texas Press, 1994.

Weinstein, Philip. *Unknowing: The Work of Modernist Fiction.* Ithaca and London, Cornell University Press, 2005.

White, Eric. "Case Study: Nakata Hideo's *Ringu* and *Ringu 2.*" In *Japanese Horror Cinema,* edited by Jay McRoy. Edinburgh: Edinburgh University Press, 2005. 38–50.

White, Jerry. *The Films of Kyoshi Kurosawa: Master of Fear.* Berkeley: Stone Bridge, 2007.

Willemen, Paul. "Action Cinema, Labour Power and the Video Market." In *Hong Kong Connections: Transnational Imagination in Action Cinema,* edited by Meaghan Morris, Siu Leung Li and Stephen Chan Ching-kiu. Hong Kong: Hong Kong University Press, 2005. 223–47.

———. "Detouring Through Korean Cinema." *Inter-Asia Cultural Studies* 3.2 (2002): 167–86.

Williams, Linda. "Melodrama Revised." In *Refiguring American Film Genres: History and Theory,* edited by Nick Browne. Berkeley, CA: University of California Press, 1998. 42–88.

————. *Playing the Race Card: Melodramas of Black and White from Uncle Tom to O. J. Simpson*. Princeton: Princeton University Press, 2002.

————. "When the Woman Looks." In *Re-Vision: Essays in Feminist Film Criticism*, edited by Mary Ann Doane, Patricia Mellencamp, and Linda Williams. Los Angeles: The American Film Institute, 1984. 83–97.

Williams, Tony. "Space, Place and Spectacle: The Crisis Cinema of John Woo." In *The Cinema of Hong Kong: History, Arts, Identity*, edited by Fu Poshek and Desser David. New York: Cambridge University Press, 2000. 137–57.

Wood, Robin. "Introduction." In *American Nightmare: Essays on the Horror Film*, edited by Robin Wood and Richard Lippe. Toronto: Festival of Festivals, 1979. 195–220.

Yamamoto, Sae. "Yushutsu sareta Nihon no imeji: 1939 nen nyuyoku bankoku hakurankai de joei sareta Nihon eiga" [The export of Japan's image: Japanese films screened at the New York World's Fair, 1939]. *Eizogaku* [ICONICS: Japanese Journal of Image and Sciences] 77 (2006): 62–80.

Yang, Young-Kyun. "*Jajangmyeon* and *Junggukjip*." *Korea Journal* 45.2 (Summer 2005): 66–88.

Yau, Esther C. M. "Introduction: Hong Kong Cinema in a Borderless World." In *At Full Speed: Hong Kong Cinema in a Borderless World*, edited by Esther C. M. Yau. Minneapolis: University of Minnesota Press, 2001. 1–28.

Yoda, Tomiko. "A Roadmap to Millennial Japan." In *Japan after Japan: Social and Cultural Life from the Recessionary 1990s to the Present*, edited by Harry Harootunian and Tomiko Yoda. Durham: Duke University Press, 2006. 16–53.

Žižek, Slavoj. "Hitchcockian Sinthoms." In *Everything You Always Wanted to Know about Lacan (But Were Afraid to Ask Hitchcock)*, 1992. 125–28.

————. "Introduction: Alfred Hitchcock, or, The Form and Its Historical Mediation." In *Everything You Always Wanted to Know about Lacan (But Were Afraid to Ask Hitchcock)*. London and New York: Verso, 1992. 1–12.

————. *The Sublime Object of Ideology*. London and New York: Verso, 1989.

Index